Dolls in Trees

Dedication

To every person with a story—everybody

Also by Patty Huston-Holm
(hustonpat@gmail.com)

Shattered: True Story of an American Teenager
Kid in the House
Inviting a Giraffe to Tea (English & Spanish)
Inviting a Giraffe to Tea: Color me Different
Inviting a Giraffe to Tea: Teacher–Parent Guide

Contents

Elsewhere

Appendix

* = Author's choice of top 12

Acknowledgments

Four people in my life told me I couldn't or shouldn't write. Two were former associates—one who wanted to impress an attractive coworker and another who said I asked too many questions. The other two were jealous. Years later, I know all this and regret wasting time in tears and losing sleep over naysayers while intermittently waking up with strategies for how to please them or push them over a cliff.

Strange as it may seem, these four are my first acknowledgments. I may have allowed them to rob me of some joy, but I am stronger and wiser for it as I nurture young aspiring writers as I once was. I try to help and not harm.

My own positive mentoring came early. With encouragement from teachers and seasoned editors, I boldly started my published writing career at age 12—first with a fiction piece in a long-gone magazine called *Read* and closely thereafter for a weekly newspaper in Buckeye Lake, Ohio. After that sixth grade teacher (the late Mrs. Oldham) and an editor of what is now a paper mostly filled with advertisements, I was fortunate to be guided by kind, professional reporters (Mary Hargrove, Diana Blowers, among them) and editors (the late Janet Long, Bruce Humphrey, Bob Wunderlin, among them) at the *Newark* (Ohio) *Advocate.*

High school teachers, David Lehman, Bill Mann and Joe Dyser, literally (pun intended) saved my life (no exaggeration) with their guidance of what all three said was my gift, allowing me platforms to use it in a time of low self-esteem. At The Ohio State University, I acknowledge Prof. Diana Stover Tillinghast (undergraduate) and then Prof. Sharon West (graduate school). They were kind but stern teachers from whom I learned a lot.

My long-time friend and journalism colleague, Alan Johnson, has been a godsend in this project, nudging me when I needed it, and backing off when I needed that. The best part is prayer as we both do that. I thank God that we circled back to our early spiritual upbringing, growing from young, crazy party animals to believers in Jesus Christ. Among several Uganda journalism colleagues who kept me going is Douglas Olum—half my age and politically polarized. When I felt ready to quit, he nudged me ahead.

I appreciate my parents, both deceased, for having one more baby despite their poverty and for reading my early stuff while boasting about it to their friends.

I thank my husband, Mike Holm, who allows me to be the best of myself, which sometimes means solitary writing way into the night and early morning hours with insufficient time and energy for him. My life partner, also an editor for some of this book content, gets me like no other.

My design team, Gennai Sawvel and Josh Frink, are amazing, along with Joshua Kabitanya, the cover designer. Gennai also helped with editing.

More than 100 names are connected somehow to the *Dolls in Trees* stories. Except for a few anonymous ones, they are found in these pages. I am grateful to all the men, women, critters and places enabling my word lens into my life and theirs. All serve as a reminder that we don't slow down enough to observe and to listen.

Friends and family in the USA and Uganda are invaluable encouragers, complementing my story-telling abilities and indicating excitement for me to finish. For them and all, I'm finally there.

I plan to keep using my craft to tell stories, but for a book, you have to stop somewhere, so I did.

Foreword

By Mary Hargrove

Turn each page, and examine your heart. Patty Huston-Holm's series of stories elicit a range of emotions as she captures smiles, tears and life lessons that those of the people she meets rarely reveal.

When I first met Patty Huston-Holm—then Pat Huston—we were rookie reporters at *The Newark Advocate* in Ohio. She would later become an editor, podcast host, teacher and a mentor in Uganda to a 10-member East African student team.

I was an investigative reporter for 32 years. I eventually served as President and Chair of the national, non-profit board of Investigative Reporters and Editors and was inducted into the Oklahoma Journalism Hall of Fame.

The most difficult part of reporting involves building trust with sources—getting a stranger to offer a glimpse into their heart.

"Most people don't take the time to deeply listen to each other," Patty explains. "I'm starting to write about a 52-year-old woman confined to a wheelchair because of a diving accident when she was 20. While most of my interviews are ordinary people doing extraordinary things, this woman is an extraordinary person trying to do very ordinary, everyday things."

Her more than 100 stories in *Dolls in Trees* convey how we cope when facing a fractured world.

Jimmy, a boyhood friend, recalls the chilling words, "Layton, you're going to Nam" when the recent high school graduate was drafted during the Vietnam War in the 1970s. He opens up with Patty, detailing the fear, the life-and-death moments and the loss of a friend killed in action—only to be spit upon and denigrated when he returned from the controversial war.

Patty shares her own first-person experiences, including a poignant letter she wrote following the death of her beloved Labrador Retriever, Eddie.

"You laid by my side when I was sick, soothed my worry with your nudge and lick, savored my scent. You loved me. Correction. You adored me."

The perspective is unique. The struggles of everyday people that help us to better understand ourselves and the world... and maybe think about telling our own stories.

Dolls in Trees

Introduction

The first lie I remember telling was when I was about age five. I might have the age wrong, but the lie is clear.

I told my parents that I hurt myself climbing on our backyard swing set when the truth is I was hurting "down there" from an adolescent boy who violated my body. Usually, it was only touching that I didn't know enough to mind. But at least one day—maybe the only day—it was rape, which was a word I didn't know then. But I did know it was wrong enough to lie about it and that lying was wrong.

I lied anyway.

Maybe my parents believed my lie. Maybe they didn't. They sent me to bed without the powdered-sugar doughnut that I always got at the end of the day. It was a sugary, messy confection that I never wanted again.

I don't remember any blood. I don't remember the pain. I simply remember the lie.

Researchers—scholars often drawing conclusions with no actual experience on a topic, relying on what their subjects tell them or data they gather—say that children can remember from as early as age one. They also say that when something happens before age six that it will be most traumatic for a lifetime but a forgotten memory as adults.

I thought I had forgotten. But then people who were older and there at the time reminded me in my adult years, so I remembered. I recalled the tiny, wooden shed and the light coming in the gaps of the poorly constructed walls. I remembered, too, something seldom addressed when it comes to child sexual abuse—that a child needing attention relishes whatever form that attentiveness may take.

My parents were good parents. My mother dutifully cared for my father's aging and ill mother in our tiny Midwestern Ohio house while Dad worked all day. He was exhausted from work and the travel there and back. Mom was tired from caring for an aging woman and two young girls just 15 months apart. At night, we bathed in a kitchen sink because there was no bathroom. In the day and as Mom cleaned, cooked and attended to my grandmother—my father's mother—mostly sleeping in a bed in the middle of the shag-carpeted main room, she allowed us to roam in what she thought was a safe but poor neighborhood beyond our smelly, two-hole latrine.

Mom was grateful for a teenage boy who removed some of the burden of watching two preschool girls.

In my 60s, Mom admitted that she didn't know what the boy was doing until it was too late. In her final years before dying in June of 2021, Mom shared what she knew. A boy named "Danny" that she thinks ended up dying in Vietnam. Mom said she had bad things happen to her, too.

With my parents and sister, Penny, in a First Community Church "Family of the Year" photo, I am a smiling seven-year-old. I am smiling as a teenager wearing a "Miss Lakewood" sash over a bathing suit and in pictures with my high school cheer-leading squad.

Except in this writing now and in the fading memories of a few friends and one sensitive teacher, my childhood violation along with a teen suicide attempt and young-adult reckless behavior are buried among smiles, a stellar resume and career with plaques.

We can hide from our past, fold under it, or build from it. Telling is a way to build. This telling is but one slice.

In our current era of quick sound bites and abbreviated phone text messages, we can and should listen, understand and share our deeper stories. As no two people have the same frame of reference, stories might vary.

Admittedly, while relishing in the delightful, inspirational and tragic stories of others and using my gifts of curiosity and writing to share those, I'm not a fan of telling mine, especially this sliver.

As I sit cross-legged and type into my laptop in the silent and dark early morning hours on a day in my seventh decade of living, I know this reveal will cause discomfort for some as it does for me.

I may regret it.

Or I might regret not telling it.

Uganda

AFRICA

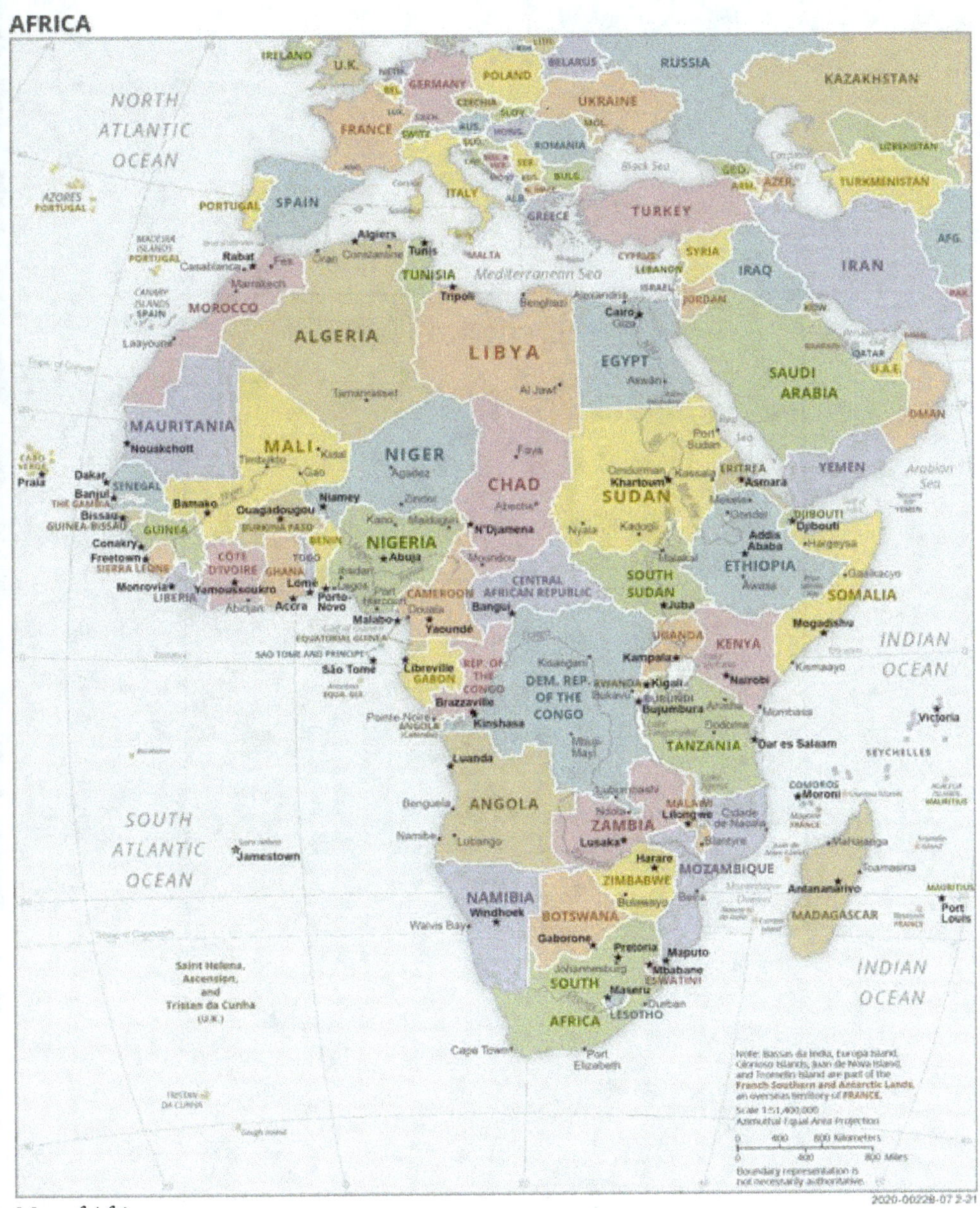

NORTH ATLANTIC OCEAN
SOUTH ATLANTIC OCEAN
INDIAN OCEAN
Mediterranean Sea
Black Sea
Red Sea
Arabian Sea
IRELAND
U.K.
FRANCE
PORTUGAL
SPAIN
ITALY
GERMANY
POLAND
BELARUS
UKRAINE
RUSSIA
KAZAKHSTAN
UZBEKISTAN
TURKMENISTAN
ROMANIA
GREECE
TURKEY
CYPRUS
SYRIA
LEBANON
ISRAEL
JORDAN
IRAQ
IRAN
AFG.
QATAR
U.A.E.
OMAN
YEMEN
SAUDI ARABIA
GEO.
ARM.
AZER.
AZORES PORTUGAL
MADEIRA ISLANDS PORTUGAL
CANARY ISLANDS SPAIN
Algiers
Rabat
Casablanca
Marrakech
Fes
Oran
Constantine
Tunis
MALTA
TUNISIA
Tripoli
Benghazi
Alexandria
Cairo
Giza
Aswân
MOROCCO
Laayoune
ALGERIA
LIBYA
EGYPT
Tamanrasset
Al Jawf
Faya
CABO VERDE
Praia
Dakar
SENEGAL
Banjul
THE GAMBIA
Bissau
GUINEA-BISSAU
Conakry
Freetown
SIERRA LEONE
Monrovia
LIBERIA
Yamoussoukro
Abidjan
CÔTE D'IVOIRE
GHANA
Accra
Lomé
TOGO
BENIN
Porto-Novo
Abuja
NIGERIA
Lagos
Ibadan
Port Harcourt
MAURITANIA
Nouakchott
MALI
Tombouctou
Kidal
Gao
NIGER
Niamey
Agadez
Zinder
BURKINA FASO
Ouagadougou
Bamako
GUINEA
Kano
Maiduguri
CHAD
N'Djamena
Abéché
SUDAN
Khartoum
Omdurman
Kassala
Nyala
Kadogli
El Obeid
Malakal
ERITREA
Asmara
DJIBOUTI
Djibouti
Hargeysa
ETHIOPIA
Addis Ababa
Awasa
Galkacyo
SOMALIA
Mogadishu
Kismaayo
SOUTH SUDAN
Juba
CENTRAL AFRICAN REPUBLIC
Bangui
CAMEROON
Yaoundé
Douala
Malabo
EQUATORIAL GUINEA
SÃO TOMÉ AND PRÍNCIPE
São Tomé
GABON
Libreville
REP. OF THE CONGO
Brazzaville
Pointe-Noire
DEM. REP. OF THE CONGO
Kinshasa
Kisangani
Bukavu
RWANDA
Kigali
BURUNDI
Bujumbura
UGANDA
Kampala
KENYA
Nairobi
Mombasa
TANZANIA
Dodoma
Dar es Salaam
Victoria
SEYCHELLES
COMOROS
Moroni
Mombasa
Luanda
Benguela
ANGOLA
Lubango
Namibe
Lubumbashi
ZAMBIA
Lusaka
MALAWI
Lilongwe
Blantyre
MOZAMBIQUE
Beira
MADAGASCAR
Antananarivo
Toamasina
Mahajanga
MAURITIUS
Port Louis
NAMIBIA
Windhoek
Walvis Bay
BOTSWANA
Gaborone
ZIMBABWE
Harare
Bulawayo
SOUTH AFRICA
Pretoria
Johannesburg
Cape Town
Port Elizabeth
Durban
Maputo
MAPUTO
ESWATINI
Mbabane
LESOTHO
Maseru
Saint Helena
Jamestown
Saint Helena, Ascension, and Tristan da Cunha (U.K.)
Scale 1:51,400,000
Azimuthal Equal Area Projection
0   400   800 Kilometers
0   400   800 Miles
Boundary representation is not necessarily authoritative.

Map of Uganda

Art

A dead crab on the beach would be repulsive or ignored by most. But for William Kayumba, it was an inspiration. He processed the image, along with that of a nearby rock, into rugged texture and brown color to design and produce a pitcher.

On a late October day and from his office in the art building section of Uganda Christian University's (UCU) Tech Park, he turned his computer screen around to show a photo of his handiwork. Like an artist, which he is, he talked about how the brown color weaves uniquely around the handle and about the one-of-a-kind texture in the pitcher's white ceramic.

Artists see art within the people, places and things around them. Art students, like those in the UCU undergraduate Arts with Education program, learn those insights and applications. As head of the art department, Professor William is one of their teachers.

"Look at her ear," Prof. William nodded as he motioned for one of his students to turn sideways to make a point about sculpting ears from clay. "See that her ear looks different from yours and everybody else's. Every human hand, every eye is different. Even your own left eye is not the same as your right one."

Abilities to create uniqueness for visual, educational and emotional impact as well as functionality translate into employment and sustainability. On this particular October day, students manipulated clay for hands, fingers, ears and faces while sharing how they might use this skill in future jobs. One student wants to be a teacher. One student aspires to be a fabric designer or interior designer. Another talks about owning a hotel and designing the rooms and placing artwork throughout. A third wants to be a teacher.

"One of my students designed her own wedding dress," the 58-year-old professor noted. "UCU student work is all over the place in Uganda and not just the pieces in Tech Park."

Other examples include a white elephant and fish at a beach gate in Jinja, a cement tribal figure in Wakiso, anniversary celebration pieces at the Martyrs Shrine in Kampala and a metal couple dancing when the wind blows in a central location of Gulu. Functional pieces are just as prevalent—from beverage mugs to tables and chairs.

One of Prof. William's visions is to open a UCU student art studio in Mukono.

Uganda government education leadership recently recognized the value of art through legislation that, starting in September 2018, requires visual and performance art to be provided in secondary schools. This comes on the heels of an assessment of arts education report from the Uganda National Commission of the United Nations Educational, Scientific and Cultural Organization. The report concluded that there is a need to "establish ways in which the arts can interface with other educational and development aspects in Uganda."

Prof. William started teaching art at UCU in 1998—a year after the university opened. His artistic path started at age 10, when he drew a church in the dirt that was quickly destroyed by a car that drove over it. He continued drawing everything from plants and animals to people and was in demand during primary and secondary school to create charts and graphs for teachers. Sculpting came later. His skills were honed at Makerere University, where he attained a Fine Arts degree.

A gap in his UCU teaching occurred when he was injured in a car accident in 2008. With a slight limp, he travels to his 113 students and around the campus using a cane.

"A job in the arts can support a family or help support a family," he said. "Clay is in our soil. We need to think of art not just as something nice to know, but a need to know."

In the meantime, he urges all UCU staff and students to take a walk over to Tech Park and see the three dozen pieces—crosses, fists, human figures, bicycles and more—displayed around the art buildings there.

(2016, Uganda)

Bad Behavior*

Barefooted and frightened, I ran, feeling the wet, early evening grass between my toes. The space was small, requiring me—us—to sprint in circles. I was smaller. He grabbed my shoulders and took me down. Squirming proved futile, so I endured his hands on my arms and his messy mouth, mostly missing mine but getting enough for him to rise victoriously. Dazed, I sat up and wiped his saliva off with the back of my hand. Mom, Dad and two neighbors were laughing.

I was four. Buster, the victor, was five. People say you don't remember at that young age, but you do.

I recall the laughter the most, and that only my sister, slightly older, was not laughing but staring horrified like me and at me. And I recall how we little girls realized that we, too, should giggle because the people we trusted were doing it that evening in the small plot of land behind our tiny Buckeye Lake, Ohio, home in the 1950s. So, we did.

Fast-forward to a weekday fall morning in 2018, to the White Horse Inn in Kabale, Uganda, Africa. Seated alone just inside the dining area among mostly Ugandans, I was in clear earshot of a group of Americans taking their hearty breakfast on the open-air veranda. There were four men, late 20's to mid 30's, mostly physically fit except for an overweight guy wearing a backwards baseball cap.

They laughed. Not the kind of laughter that engages everyone, but the kind that shuts some people out or down. I have come to know this as "good old boy" merriment that is rarely challenged and often joined in by men and women.

These were Americans behaving badly.

With flashbacks to that early childhood time and other times when I felt belittled or misunderstood, I put my breakfast plate of pineapple, beans and potatoes to the side and pulled out my laptop. I listened, and I typed.

I typed as they made fun of the birds. They mocked and labeled "annoying" the looks and sounds of the majestic black bird walking on the Inn's hillside that was his home. Uganda has more than 1,000 species of birds, including the shiny, ebony-colored, long-legged crane. I doubt they are aware that the raised leg of a crane is a symbol of forward movement for this East African country.

Many beautiful feathered creatures can be found at Lake Bunyonyi, a deep body of water named for the word "bird" and a 20-minute, dirt road drive from where we sat.

While eagerly eating sausages, they ridiculed local pig farmers. They derided them as illiterate and dirty. Pork is second to beef in meat production in Uganda. When you are poor, pigs are a good investment because their litters are large, and they are ready for market in less than six months.

As he sipped his tea, one of the men ridiculed the "horrible" and "Oh my God" painting that a Ugandan artist had gifted him the day before.

Uganda is teeming with amazing artists. While Ugandan musician-turned-politician Bobi Wine (Robert Kyagulanyi) is the globally best-known performing artist, there are others like Comedian Anne Kansiime, who opened a Bunyonyi resort a year earlier. Dancers are incredibly fit and talented. So was the painter I had met during a child sacrifice awareness event a year ago and who lives near my apartment and sells me his original paintings every year.

The derogation continued.

The chubby American was the ringleader, enjoying how his stories elicited more laughter and elevated his status in the group. In his baggy, cream-colored shirt and green khakis, he flip-flopped past me to remove the large hot water container from the buffet table. As a Ugandan server protested and explained that other guests also needed hot water for their tea, he arrogantly brushed her off and flip flopped back to his table with the canister.

The server's eyes and pain matched mine. My compassion and personal angst grew to anger as the men's topic turned to women amidst recorded, background music from a female vocalist. Ironically, the song included the words "Please say you love me, too…"

Love was not part of this conversation.

"I remember one trip to Reno," the American boasted. "You see a man's true colors at a strip club. I mean (name omitted purposely) was getting a blowjob downstairs. (Heee… Heee) It was 3 a.m., and we were rounding everybody up. This Asian girl was dancing alone. I told her my name was Daniel (intentional omission of last name). She couldn't even pronounce my name. (Heee…Heee) I was really drunk and felt sorry for her, so I spoke to her."

Eating area of White Horse Inn, Kabale

Heee... Heee.

Sex workers worldwide, especially in Third World countries, do it for the money and not the pleasure. Nobody enjoys exploitation. Men who engage in sex tourism while claiming themselves to be doing good work counteract the efforts of well-meaning, caring people and organizations that try to provide women with knowledge and skills for more meaningful, healthier and less degrading work.

"Are there strip clubs in Kabale? You know a place where girls take their clothes off and we can look at them naked?" the overweight American asked a Ugandan driver who approached the table. "Of course, you must have them as this is a border town (near Rwanda). You might call it performing arts. In America, we call it the fine arts district."

Heee, Heee, Haw, Haw.

During my first trip to Uganda in 2009, I met a well-spoken, well-dressed woman in a literacy training that my friend Sue and I did. At the end of our teaching, the woman admitted she was a prostitute trying to better herself. In a small room in Mukono, Uganda, she humbly gave me a wine glass—the only possession she had—as a gift in appreciation. It's in an honored place in my home.

The good ole boys continued.

"We like to have a good time for birthdays, bachelor's parties with sisters on the other side of the river," the American explained to his clearly uncomfortable driver. Standing above those who hired him and observing them eat, the driver had his hands on the back of a chair as he shifted from one foot to the other.

Human trafficking negatively impacts 800,000 humans, mostly women, around the globe each year.

"You would enjoy it, Joe—even just watching," the driver's American boss said.. "You can get a lot for $5. We would like to see some banging and drinking of your black labels before we leave."

Heee, Hee. Haw, Haw.

I closed my laptop to greet my two Uganda Christian University interns—wonderful, intelligent young women with great promise who have supported my work and whose salaries were sponsored by generous American friends, Claudia and Bob. I was grateful for what their ears did not hear.

Sadness enveloped me as I realized the change that still needs to occur. I am aware of injustices to women in Uganda but also the increasing numbers of respectable men. I was reminded that my own country, too, has incredible men but is not devoid of gender inequities. Slobbery little boys who were encouraged to overpower little girls can grow up to be men doing the same to women.

To Buster, my childhood predator wherever you are, I hope you learned to behave better as you grew.

(Without knowing I was party to their conversation, the four men later told me that they were from California and Colorado, contracted to shoot a video at a midwifery hospital. Two are married.)

(2018, Uganda)

Best Place

In the 5:30 a.m. darkness from a canvas chair and with about a dozen jackson hartebeest quietly eating vegetation while enduring my flashlight scan to assure they aren't more dangerous prey, this—Kidepo National Park in Uganda's uppermost right corner—is one of the quietest of places I've been in the world.

It is the best place I've ever laid my head.

As the unseen fowl cooing signifies dawn, there is something natively comforting about waking up where the deer-like jacksons, giraffes, elephants, hyraxes, jackals, patas monkeys and, yes, even lions, reside.

Giraffes rarely sleep or even curl their long legs to sit. Perhaps they don't need to as they calmly eat acacia leaves and rarely run.

Elephants—like the herd of more than 30 we observed moving on the savanna two days ago—sleep three to seven hours a day, standing up or laying down under a tree. Manyimanyi Gilbert, our Uganda Wildlife Authority guide, says they sleep happier and better after consuming tamarind from the Kikalian African "sausage tree." After Gilbert pulled one of the foot-long fruits down and forced it open with his assault rifle, we licked it…just not enough to get an elephant drunk.

The much smaller, rabbit/rat-like rock hyraxes scamper and sleep on, of course, rocks. Ironically, this smallest of African wildlife is much like the world's largest land animal. Like elephants, these furry creatures have tusks among their teeth and nails on their toes.

Wildlife at Kidepo National Park

Jackals, who I saw for the first time this trip and who wistfully reminded me of dogs from home, sleep in crevices in rocks and dens made by other animals.

The patas monkeys, quieter than most, sleep around. With the black-haired babies that turn golden with white faces and legs as they get older, they lay their heads cushioned among their bodies wherever they feel like it. Lions do that, too. Our guide, Tonny Kato, said two of the jungle queens were sleeping in the nearby parking lot recently.

As the sun begins to emerge, the jacksons show me their white behinds, swaying like those of the Karamoja ladies I see moving up the mountain with water and firewood on their heads. Almost like a tightly composed song or choreographed dance, the patas move in and pose for photos.

Humans zipping tents clear their throats, move in and out and secure where they sleep from deadly scorpions.

Luke 9:58 (NIV) tells us "Foxes have dens and birds have nests, but the Son of Man has no place to lay his head."

Not so in Kidepo.

(2020, Uganda)

Bidibidi

At 8:55 a.m. on a Saturday in October, we left the fairly modern Northern Uganda village of Arua. By modern, I mean there is electricity at least half of every 24 hours and sidewalks in a portion of the business district. By "we," I mean a driver named Tony from Mukono, a pastor named Geoffrey from Arua, a French–American named Patti and me.

In a van packed mostly with books and teddy bears, we headed for Bidibidi, a refugee settlement believed to be the largest in the world and located at the border of South Sudan.

On fairly good roads, we passed Kjomoro, Koyi, Oluffe, Marach, Oleba, Yoyo, Kuru and other places I can't pronounce. We saw the normal amount of houses with straw roofs. Likewise, eucalyptus trees, goats and cows with single humps on their brown or white backs and women carrying twigs and colorful plastic plates filled with food on their heads, were not out of the ordinary. A young boy walked a black and white pig to market. An open truck carrying five colorfully dressed women and a baby passed, throwing the usual dose of Ugandan dust for us all to share.

About 90 minutes into our two-hour drive and approaching the village of Yumbe, the landscape changed. The signposts emblazoned with charity organization names and the more balanced ratio of white-skinned and black-skinned people were an indicator that the camp, or settlement as the workers prefer that it be called, was nearby. The mostly United Nations-dominated signs advertised assistance for farmers, the disabled, and so on. On bicycles and bodabodas (motorcycles), inside shops, along dirt roads and peering out of car windows was a cultural melting pot unlike the majority dark-skinned people in the rest of Uganda.

So why was I there?

A friend, Diane Ross, asked me to go. Well, it wasn't quite that easy. Diane, a professor at Otterbein University in Ohio, is a tireless worker in northern Uganda and, like me, has a heart for the voiceless. She met a woman, Faidah Dede Obombasa, working with refugee girls in the settlement. When at Bidibidi together, Diane and Faidah had the girls write or draw their stories. Diane carried the pieces of paper back to the United States.

"Patty, I need to meet with you," Diane said. "We need to do something with these."

So we met. Over wine and salads at the Olive Garden Restaurant in Reynoldsburg, Ohio, we read and touched the papers from the girls in another continent. The accounts of witnessing murder, rape, carrying a murderer's baby—in short, hopelessness—were heart wrenching.

That was June of 2017. I was just back from three months work in Uganda. I was tired. And, unlike my days as a journalist when I thirsted for the bizarre and when my Christianity was weaker, I was trying to discern whether God wanted me to go to this refugee location for Him.

I continued to discern in July and over dinner in Columbus, Ohio, with a priest from Uganda. I did not want to be labeled another "tourist attraction" visitor to the settlement.

"If you can, you should help tell these stories," Father Phillip said. "You should go."

So there we were, driving on rugged, dirt roads and past housing emblazoned with blue "UN" lettering on white plastic. We passed the homes of regular villagers and tall grasses. There are no fences around this settlement, which stretches for miles and includes five zones and numerous villages.

The girls we saw were living in Bidibidi's Zone 2. At first, and in a tent with about 100 girls, we sang and danced. They kicked off pink, black and brown shoes and sat cross-legged, smiling. Just like normal girls. Then the stories started to flow, or didn't, as they spoke, sometimes choking on tears and retreating to sit silently in the back.

I took the hand of one girl, 16-year-old Esther, and walked to a rock where we sat and talked alone. She shared how her father had died in the war between Sudan and South Sudan and her mother remarried. The mom lives nearby, but the new husband doesn't want the daughter of another man around, and her mother abides by those wishes. That is as much as Esther wants to talk about it, at least at the moment.

In today's world, bombarded with tragedy, it's easy to learn about suffering and then forget, moving on with our daily lives and turning a blind eye. Doing nothing. It's even easier if there is no name or face for the tragedy.

Better than nothing, I tell this story.

(Uganda, 2017)

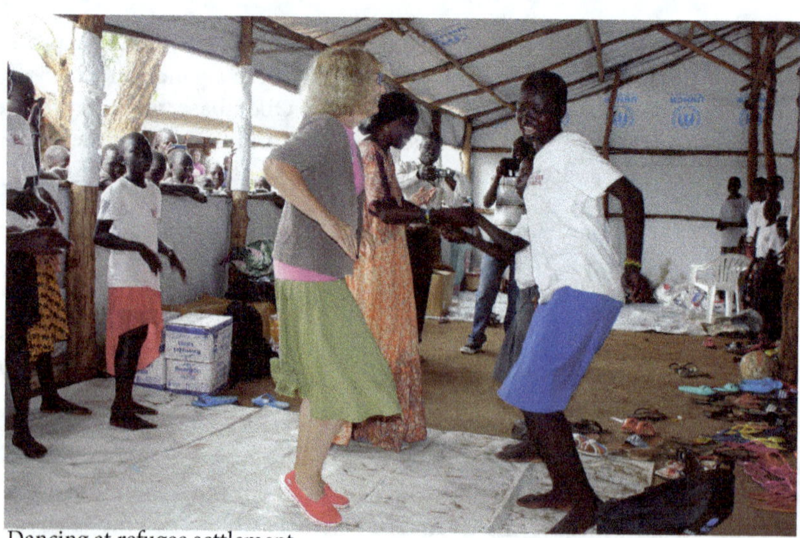
Dancing at refugee settlement

Chicken

The first thing I saw when coming into the apartment where I would live for the next 34 days was the splotch of red on the black and white skirt of the woman whose space I would occupy. The splotch—three splotches of differing sizes actually—on Catherine Ranger's skirt was from when she slaughtered the chicken we would have for dinner the next night.

"I didn't have my knee on him strong enough," she said.

Thus, after severing the neck, the body of a rooster continued moving around with blood splattering and to the amusement of a few neighbor children and women and three male observers peaking through the bushes surrounding a nearby fence.

This was the second such personal slaughtering by Catherine, a late-60s, former USA-fundraiser with a law degree celebrating a year as a missionary in Mukono, Uganda. Before the personal killing, she was an observer of the demise of one other chicken and one duck given to her live over the last 12 months.

Subsequently, she figured "if I eat it, I should own it." Kill it.

An expert cook, she fixed the bird with rice, wine vinegar and pork fat for our Sunday night dinner. Together with her husband, Richard, who remarked that he didn't know he had "married a village girl" and Immaculate, a mother-of-four learning to be a seamstress, we ate the meat while engaged in the moral debate of deliberately ending the life of an animal.

Chickens, we concluded, are not as high up as mammals or as low down as fish. Yet, all feel pain. Chickens are even known to shed a tear.

Tear or not, Catherine didn't want to eat her slaughtered rooster's head or legs like Dorothy, a Ugandan who showed up to retrieve the less desirable body parts for her next-day meal. Catherine could not, she said, slaughter a goat.

Me neither.

(2022, Uganda)

Circumcision

It might seem strange that after four months of not seeing my husband and during our only two-day getaway in Uganda that the topic of mutilation is on my mind.

At 8 p.m. Uganda time on a Saturday and as I sit with Mike in a "semi-luxury" hut with no electricity, my thoughts are stimulated by whistles and drumming in the distance. We are in Kapchorwa district, where public male circumcision ceremonies occur.

We did, in fact, meet just last night three young men, ages 17 to 19, who will be cut in six days—Dec. 1. They were excited to finally be recognized as men, they told us. With whistles between their lips and black and white monkey tails in one hand, they ran past us and around the village in pre-celebration.

"Will you be drunk?" I asked the 17-year-old, thinking this might dull the pain.

"No," he quickly replied. "If we drink alcohol, we might get angry and disrespect ourselves."

I didn't ask the young men or our local hiking guide, Roger, if the newly circumcised males still had a license to rape a virgin girl of their choice, as I knew was part of the custom. During a portion of our Sipi Falls hike in a cave, Roger who was once part of this male tribal ritual did say that the practice of female circumcision, also known as genital mutilation, no longer exists. Later, however, a missionary from Louisiana said it still happens to girls in parts of Uganda—the point being that if you destroy a female body part that might help girls find sex enjoyable, the girls won't have sex outside of marriage.

Mutilation, of course, is what most of the Western world does to male babies as soon as they are born.

In the midst of the beautiful plants, waterfalls, people, and coffee plantations in this eastern part of Uganda, and with no judgment on customs here or elsewhere, I'm wishing for no hurt.

Plants hurt each other. Earlier this week as we hiked in the Mabira Rainforest, I became aware of how plants harm one another. Our guide there explained that while tree branches and roots communicate nicely, vines can strangle a tree into a slow death.

Animals hurt each other. Lions eat zebras. Larger monkeys kill smaller ones.

If we can't help somebody, at the very least, let's not hurt.

(2018, Uganda)

Cockroaches

Cockroaches are an important part of the ecosystem.

But try explaining that to my homemade juice supplier, Beatrice, who woke up one morning as the pest was chewing on her lip, or my student intern, Nathan, who has had them munching on his fingernails in the night.

"There are a lot of them," according to Paul, a local guy tending to a garden outside my Uganda Christian University (UCU), Mukono, Uganda, apartment. "They are good for nothing."

So it was without a hint of regret, I killed a female and 16 unborn babies one early morning in February. The four-inch cockroach was playing dead on her back in my Tech Park apartment kitchen. I scooped her from the floor onto the bottom of one of my flip-flops. Yet, before my shoe's rubber sole and what I believed to be an insect corpse reached the wastebasket, she leaped—only to quickly thereafter meet her demise.

I took a post-mortem photograph of a smashed American cockroach along with her sack of more than a dozen eggs at 8:16 a.m.

I surmised it was "American" by comparing the shape and color to pictures on the Internet. While I didn't look at all 3,000 species, I did study the most common. A friend back in Ohio said she found a smaller version recently in a restaurant pot roast.

Yep. This dead girl in UCU's T4 Tech Park apartment on February 19, 2019, was American.

Plus, my cockroach looked similar to what some Ohio State University guy friends used to capture and keep in transparent jars for display at parties in the 1970s.

When exercising around the track at day's end, my friend Elizabeth asked me why I brought them (American cockroaches) here from the States. That's debatable since I don't think we have them in our house back home. The bigger debate about their origin includes the contention by some Americans that they came to our country on dirty ships that transported Africans as slaves in the 1600s. We gave them our name, we say, but we didn't cause them.

Ah, yes, Americans do like to blame.

Everything has some purpose. My patient, environmentalist husband listened as over the phone I extolled my newfound research about the virtues of cockroaches that release nitrogen in their feces that goes into the soil and is used by plants. And birds, which I like, and chickens, which a lot of Ugandans have, feed on the dead ones.

I'm not sure why I, or all of us for that matter, like the looks of certain things—birds and chickens over cockroaches—more than others.

But I do know that I don't want cockroaches on or around me.

And the one I killed would have died within a year on its own anyway.

(2019, Uganda)

Dog Gone

It's a dog's life.

A few months ago and after weeks of hearing a howling dog in the middle of the night, I made the time to investigate the origin of the noise. At 6 p.m. with the sun going down in Uganda, I did the solitary walk up a narrow, dirt path, pushing back tall grass and following the canine's distressed voice. As I entered an open area, I saw him. A medium-haired, tan and relatively young pooch tethered to a tree. Pulling on his four-foot-long chain, he had nearly worn out himself and the grass around a tree. Nearby was his master's nice, neat house.

Try as I might to embed myself in African culture, the differences in treatment of dogs evades me. Likewise, Ugandans look at me as if I am a lunatic when I talk with affection about Eddie, my chocolate Labrador Retriever, laying his head on my lap.

The dog lives in your house? Yes. He has a name? Yes, named after inventor Thomas Edison. Americans have more than one kind of dog? Affirmative. About 350 different breeds.

"All these dogs look the same," my sister, Penny, remarked on her first trip to Uganda in March of 2017. "Same color. Tan. Same size. Skinny." In 2016 and on her first visit, my former college roommate, Maggie Gainer, from California had a similar observation.

Unloved, I might add. The humans surrounding them are mostly afraid of them, hate them or both. Dogs eat their food. They bite their children. They leave stool and urine. They bark.

This fear and disdain make survival rates and life spans dismal. During a recent trip from Mukono to Kampala to a former student's graduation lunch, I saw a bronze-colored, clearly female dog, weaving her way in seeming grace with six teats hanging but no babies in sight. Feeble endurance likewise was ever present with a pack of four I encountered on one shopping trip back up the hill from Mukontown to my university apartment. As I carefully watched my feet to avoid a stumble on loose stones, I nearly missed seeing them huddled together in a nearby, tiny patch of green grass. Too tired to even pant, these "best friends" appeared to be as one except for the huge, bleeding gash on a single forehead, the likely misfortune of not moving fast enough to avoid a bodaboda.

"Don't look," my missionary friend, Mary Chowenhill, said.

Too late. The visual haunts me still.

Neglect of life is somehow easier to handle than outright physical abuse. It hits me in the gut to know that poisoning is commonplace. Culling is the polite term. "Wild dogs" is what the victims are labeled. One night, while lying in bed, I sensed the painful, 15-minute process of a poison death for an annoying, barking feral pack. Their usual howls became agonizing squeals and then silence. Later, I learned that the pet cat of a faculty member died the same night, possibly from partaking of the same deliberate venom.

A *Global Press Journal* article in August of 2016 quotes the existence of 20,000 dogs in Uganda's capital city of Kampala with 8,000 of them roaming the streets. Despite protests from animal rights groups, the Kampala Capital City Authority attempts to reduce the feral population by dropping off chunks of meat ingested with poison. As quietly as they can, their workers make the rounds the next day to pick up carcasses. The killing is justified, officials say, for reasons that include 600 schoolchildren with dog bites in a three-month period in 2016. Neutering, they protest, is too expensive and doesn't solve the problem of ownership for dog feeding and other care.

In a sick kind of way, it seems that the occasional Ugandan accused of dog consumption, or passing it off to sell as goat meat, is on a bit higher ground.

While the mental pictures of Ugandan dogs are vivid, I can't bring myself to take photos lest their abbreviated lives would further pierce themselves into my memory. To deal with my raw emotions, I attempt to put Ugandan dogs in a category discriminately different than those living in the United States with the realization that this is also what we do to people from places we don't reside or have never visited.

Except for right now, I deliberately forget a time or two when I myself wasn't so kind to a mutt. When growing up, two of our dogs were relegated to tethering to the ground and—even in harsh Ohio winters—to the outside elements. Outside our house, they got table scraps, water, some straw in a wooden doghouse and an occasional pat on the head. Another more recent time, when jogging on the track at Uganda Christian University and when two young dogs started nipping at my heels, I found myself being less than kind and kicking them away.

My husband, Mike, says I anthropomorphize dogs, assigning them human qualities. I can't help but love them for their devotion, protection and downright acceptance of every flaw in my bones.

I try to push this fondness on those without such cultural frames of reference with some success—like when a Ugandan female student, Sarah, living with us got to know friend Emily Buck's service companion and a male student, Sailas, from Uganda did an experience with a Columbus, Ohio, organization that trains dogs to help the blind. I share about bomb sniffing dogs and how a former work colleague, Mary Lenning, says she works better with a dog on her lap.

Later, I learned that the distressed dog I found tethered on a too-short leash was brought in by a Ugandan family to help a 12-year-old wanting to be a veterinarian. My solace is that he might bond and adore his first canine, as well as all the others he has in a lifetime, in the way I love mine.

(2017, Uganda)

Dummies

Sort of like how Haley Joel Osment "sees dead people" in *The Sixth Sense* movie, I see dummies.

I'm not talking about stupidity or the rugby fake pass or the last-look mock-up in my print media days of hot type. I'm talking about mannequins that have been around since the 1950s but that I'm seeing more during my recent trip to Uganda.

For some reason, this visit—my 14th—I'm taken with plastic men, women and children.

Most are white. Not really white as my skin isn't, but tan, yellowish, pink. Outside wooden shops among cooked goat and vegetable vendors along dusty roads, the "white" plastic replicas are adorned with used dresses, sweaters, tops and trousers. In shopping malls with higher-end restaurants and ice cream shops, I've seen dummies colored black or silver or gold under new sexitized (yes, that's a word) garments.

En-route to and around Kampala on Tuesday, my long-time driver and friend, Tonny Kato, humored my curiosity with stops for dummy photos, including one with his sister, Nakato Lydia, who has a new shop with a dozen dummies. Some of hers have arms and heads. Others have only torsos.

Lydia says she was new to the dummy business when she selected hers from a large Kampala warehouse. Her cost was 70,000 to 150,000 shillings ($18 to $40 USD), depending on appendages. Websites out of Kampala quote prices double and triple that. One source says the dummies in the United States cost upwards of $900.

No surprise that China is the biggest producer of dummies. But they also are manufactured in Germany, Turkey, France, Greece, Italy, Russia, the United Kingdom, Belgium, Poland, South Korea, Taiwan and the USA. Most are plastic. The ones in Uganda are hollow and often held upright with rocks.

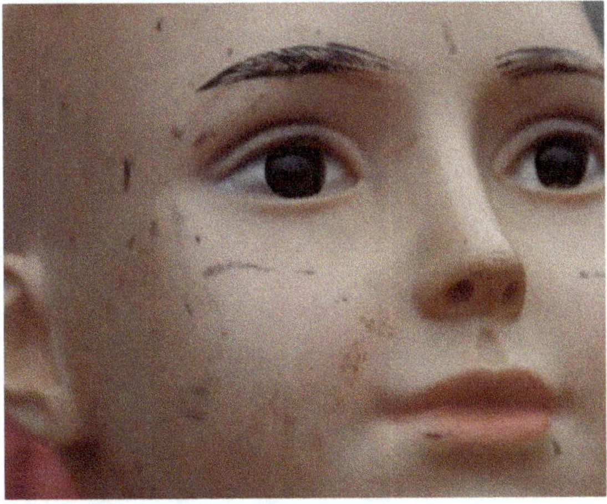

Face of a dummy in a Mukono shop

I've noticed the dummy replica of a white guy with a painted mustache in multiple places over the past several weeks. I saw one of a child with a hole in its forehead but nevertheless soldiering on to sell the clothes it wore. On a rainy Tuesday afternoon, I saw 20 naked females—dummies, that is.

Earlier today, I asked Eriah Lule, a young journalist friend, about the lifespan of a dummy. Between spoons of chocolate and coconut ice cream he shared his guess of one year and his belief that Uganda's sun and dust quickly bring about a dummy's demise.

Eriah and others I asked have no idea why white is so common in a culture where most customers are Black, why the posteriors of the female dummies protrude so much, if clothing sells better when displayed on a dummy, what happens to discarded dummies and why I ask so many questions about a dumb subject.

(2023, Uganda)

Ebola

As I watch muzungu adults and children with a half-dozen red-tailed monkeys, doing "primate-and-me" selfies and teasing with half-peeled bananas snatched within an inch of their fingers, I read an email from my husband in Ohio.

"The Ebola virus," he wrote, "is 300 miles away from Bwindi, Uganda."

That's the area I'm in. For three days, and in the midst of doing southwestern Uganda interviews for stories to help demonstrate that this country has the intellectual ability to lead itself out of poverty, the deadly virus growth has accelerated next door in the Congo.

Out loud, I mention that bats and monkeys are the source of Ebola transmission to humans. Still mesmerized by monkey antics, the muzungus (another name for white people) laugh. Even in the face of facts, the Western world has become insular from Third World vulnerabilities.

Inside the lodge of this beautiful Impenetrable Forest area of Uganda, I hold up my laptop to two doctors—one Ugandan, one American—taking morning coffee and tea.

CNN reports (September 26, 2018) 150 Ebola victims with 60 deaths.

Calmly, they remind me that even though the latest outbreak is in a Lake Albert fish market area visited by Ugandan businessmen, that the rugged roads from there to here would require long transportation time by anyone remotely in touch with the condition. Plus, when Ebola rears its head in the Democratic Republic of Congo, Ugandans, like many living in the ignorant anxiety of a disease, overreact. Whenever someone vomits, they assume the person is going to die.

The American pediatrician smiled at that, and to my question about border control.

"There is none," he said. "If we get one confirmed case here, it's time to get out."

The Ugandan newspaper, *Observer*, quoted four days ago that the World Health Organization has more than 1,750 African Ebola cases under active surveillance. None of these are in Uganda.

I tell you this, friends, not to cause you angst about me and not to deter you from your mission-minded objective to come to this beautiful country. I tell you this so you know that I do due diligence with health and safety here and that Africa is a continent—not a country.

To put things in perspective, when there was a mass shooting in Las Vegas, Nevada, some of my Ugandan friends in a country with fewer guns emailed me, expressing concern about my safety in Ohio, which is 2,000 miles from the tragedy.

(2018, Uganda)

Exercise

Very few people go where I go at 6:45 a.m. on the Uganda Christian University (UCU) campus. But maybe they should.

At most, there are 12 of us—exercise disciples—on and around the UCU track at this hour. When nearly everybody else is sleeping or trying to get through the traffic outside of Mukono-town, we are jogging, stretching and lifting. It is a special time and place for me at UCU. I suspect it is the same for the two guys who run together in sandals, the four Save The Mothers students encouraging each other at the parallel bars, the young woman jogging with earbuds, the male student jumping the concrete steps and even the Vice Chancellor, John Senyonyi, who frequents the track before his busy day.

While Uganda's is a communal culture, these exercise warriors become Americans like me in the sense that we stay in our own "zone" and seldom talk. A wave or a smile is customary. In addition to starting the day by taking care of the bodies God gave us, we are nourishing our minds.

There are Biblical (NIV)scriptures supporting exercise. Among these are 1 Corinthians that alone has verses that address driving and training "my body" (9:27), realizing "your body is a temple of the Holy Spirit" (6:19) and having "every athlete exercise discipline" (9:25). Proverbs addresses the value of strength (24:5) and exerting "arms with vigor" (31:17). In short, says Phillipians 4:13, "I can do all things in Him who strengthens me."

For me, I use this time and movement to think about the people in my life who I cherish or those I should like a little bit more, saying silent prayers for them and me. Oftentimes, I reflect on how I can be a more creative and overall better person. Sometimes, I sing a hymn; nobody is annoyed.

Truth be known, I also really enjoy a good sweat uninhibited by formal attire before the heat of the midday sun. There is something special about doing it to jump-start your day. My roommate from California was initially a bit perplexed by this routine of mine. Wiping the sleep from her eyes as I exited our apartment in my T-shirt, stretch pants and sneakers one morning, she asked me why. Later and on a rare morning when I didn't exercise, she noticed I was irritable most of that day, so she never asked again.

I love the early morning laughter of the hadada ibis (one of Uganda's more than 1,000 bird species) and the beep-beep of insects who sound like a life-support machine in a hospital. I love greeting security guards and other workers as I make my way to the track. I love hearing roosters crow without audible competition, watching the red-tailed monkeys swing from trees and feeling the air without the dust of a multitude of boda boda (small, motorcycle taxis) commotion on the road outside the campus fence as my orange and blue shoes make their way on the red dirt.

One recent morning, I saw a broken piece of white chalk next to the stone where I sat my water bottle; a flattened frog near one soccer goal post; and a few yellow, white and red roses in various stages of decomposition after the previous day's graduation ceremony.

On a different morning and in a break from the normal silence among us, a second-year education student sought advice on how to reduce weight in her abdominal area. Together and as the mist of 7 a.m. arose over the dormitories and trees, we laughed and did sit-ups and planks on the net-ball court concrete and then barre fitness stretches using two wooden school desks gently covered with dew.

Another time, I picked up a yellowed, torn page with the number 188 at the bottom. My right sneaker hit the barely noticeable, dirtied, 6-inch by 5-inch page. The text referenced how people in some countries and in some centuries were punished if they worked during the hours of 3 p.m. Saturday to sunrise on Monday. One violator of the "no labor" hours suffered consequences of seeing blood while grinding his corn. I wondered about the owner of the page, the reason for the blood and what UCU course might require this knowledge and how it got separated from the rest of the book.

The only two morning exercise annoyances, to date, are one time two dogs nipped at my ankles and another when a recent graduate approached me wanting money. In the first instance, a fellow runner chased the stray canines away from me. In the second, my firm "no," chased away further monetary requests.

With hesitation, I write this as I wish not to disturb the solitude of my morning exercise mates and me. Alas, I reasoned, God would want this experience toward an enhanced mind and body to be shared.

Just remember the rules of the club. See you at 7 a.m. tomorrow.

(2016, Uganda)

Food

I'm not a foodie. Give me Stoney Tangawizi over matooke, cassava and rice any day. Plus, some good conversation.

With rain hitting the patio's tin roof, I'm finishing the brown-bottled, ginger-based soda now and remembering the earlier two hours at the home of long-time friend and former work colleague, Frank Obonyo. His wife, Kate, served it to me with cookies while their three children drank orange soda nearby.

As I sipped, Kate shared the backstory of male circumcision ceremonies from her native Mbale area.

My husband, Mike, and I encountered a portion of that "becoming a man" tradition when in the Mt. Elgon area a few years back. But I hadn't heard about the bird and snake part and that only non-Christians do it.

Kate and Frank shared how they met under a mango tree on the Uganda Christian University Campus. They spoke about the generous man who donated a night in a hotel for their honeymoon.

I talked about what was real and what wasn't as depicted in American life by Hollywood movies. I shared a gift of West Virginia coal molded to look like a bear and talked about why coal is not as friendly to the environment as other fuels and that there are places in the USA with no Internet or cell service, including the state of West Virginia.

With that boy-shooting-a-beautiful-African bird experience outside my apartment from a few days ago, we talked about the right and wrong with nature. Uganda has rules against killing wildlife but no teeth to make the regulations stick unless it's the Crested Crane. The Bible has rules but not everybody reads or believes the book. Frank's family only kills what it eats.

Before the rain hit the patio's tin roof, before the downpour stopped the music from a wedding outside the gate, before a text from my sleepy husband back in Ohio, the brown-bottled Stoney Tangawizi was by my side. Coca-cola makes the ginger-based soda in several East African countries, including Uganda. If it were available back in Ohio, I wouldn't like it as much here.

And I would miss the conversation that is my food.

(2022, Uganda)

Food Security

Hungry people dive into trash bins for discarded food picked over by cats, dogs and birds. They climb trees for fruit half-eaten by monkeys. They steal. They drink dirty water. They exhibit anger, hopelessness and desperation.

"You'll do anything for a soda," the Rev. Richard Mulindwa, coordinator of the Uganda Christian University (UCU) Church Relations office, said, adding, "Prayer is important, but if you're hungry, you can't listen, and you can't learn."

The World Health Organization Global Hunger Index ranks Uganda at 41.4%, which means that more than 4 of 10 people living in the country are not able to meet minimum calorie requirements. They are in need of prayer, Mulindwa agrees, but they need more.

"You can't begin a discussion about God when someone is hungry," he said.

Mulindwa's UCU Church Relations job includes teaching other pastors about delivering God's message through technology and understanding land issues and food—the lack of it. Among many biblical reminders of the value of proper nutrition are that Jesus fed the disciples before teaching them and in Matthew 25:35–40 (NIV) that says, in part, "For I was hungry…You gave me something to eat."

For a half dozen years, Mulindwa, now an Anglican priest, has been practicing what he preaches about food. It started with a few visits carrying porridge for empty stomachs followed by an officially established Community-Based Organization (CBO) focused on bringing seeds to help people grow their own food. The CBO, with registration now lapsed, was named Tessa Community Development Initiative. Tessa is borrowed from Kuteesa (meaning "dialogue" in Luganda), which is the name of Mulindwa's first-born son, now age 12.

"I plant alongside them," he said of the visits he continues. "It's amazing to see how a family can be transformed with a little help, love and support."

Feminine hygiene, an increasingly common focus on teaching adolescent girls how to replace the rags and old newspapers they use with reusable pads during their menstrual cycles, is part of the initiative. In African culture, often "blood is taboo" and sex education for boys and girls is nearly non-existent, according to Mulindwa.

"There are seven girls in one location I visit now who are HIV positive and need special diets," he said. "That's food insecurity."

Likewise and sadly, it's food insecurity when girls bargain their bodies for it.

At the same time, the bigger umbrella is what Mulindwa calls "famine hygiene" impacting men, women and children of all ages. Famine can result in starvation, malnutrition, disease and even death.

Mulindwa, an orphan whose parents died when he was 12 and who lived on the streets for sometime when an aging grandmother was unable to support him, has first-hand experience with food deprivation and how he was pulled out of it. At age 17, he was taken in by an Anglican priest who "loved me, fed me, got me back in school." Two priests, in fact, supported Mulindwa in his late teens to early 20s.

"God spared my life," he said. "I was determined to give back."

The positive influence of the two priests, Rev. Capt. Titus Baraka (Director of Words of Hope ministries) and now the Most Reverend Stephen Kaziimba, the Church of Uganda archbishop, are part of Mulindwa journey into theology and formation. Mulindwa's theological path is paved with multiple careers, which is a slow-growing trend among East African pastors who see the added value of non-religious professional experience.

Mulindwa's undergraduate degree in development studies is from Kyambogo University. He has master's degrees in public health and leadership (Faculty of Public Health, Nursing and Midwifery/Save the Mothers) and Master of Divinity (Bishop Tucker School of Divinity and Theology) from UCU. He's finishing his PhD in religious studies from the University of Pretoria, South Africa.

"Relating to people in multiple ways is an important part of bringing someone to Christ," he said. "Churches don't lack theologians; they lack other professionals."

For Mulindwa, his profession in development enabled him to hone his skills in grant writing while seeing further the needs for those funds. His passion for the Save the Mothers program connects to how his mom and sister died from pregnancy preeclampsia (blood pressure condition). It was a condition that could have been resolved with better health care resources.

"Sixteen mothers die each day in Uganda from maternal related issues," he said. "These are preventable issues."

While recognizing multiple needs, Mulindwa, a married father of four, always circles back to food.

"All that I studied now makes sense to me," he said. "I realize there are so many people making mistakes because they lack food. I am grateful that God is using me not in narrow, expected ways, but in multiple ways."

(2023, Uganda)

Ghanaian African American*

I was certain she would hate me. I said so out loud.

To the puzzled look of my Ugandan driver, Tony, as our car wove up the short, steep, dusty hill to the Ankrah Foundation property, I explained: "I'm white. She's Black. White Americans weren't kind to Black Americans back in the day. Some still aren't."

She—Professor Eleanor Maxine Ankrah—had every right to be vitriolic about her days of cleaning Caucasian homes and about experiencing segregated eateries, education, toilets, even churches. Born in 1934 in the deep south of North Carolina, she lived on United States soil after the official abolition of slavery in 1863 but before the civil rights movement 100 years later. She addresses discrimination in her 2018 autobiography, *A Life without Baggage*.

Three weeks later, as my husband, Mike, drove us to a vacation on the Atlantic Ocean's Ocracoke Island, I looked at her book and my four hours of notes from an August 31, 2022, interview. Along the smooth North Carolina roads to our destination were neat houses with occasional US flags, barbeque and peach stands and people seeming to go about their lives just as they do in Ohio. I struggled to think of a time when Maxine's great-grandparents were among more than 300,000 slaves in this state and later when Maxine's parents and children were "free niggers" serving whites here.

At age 88, Maxine doesn't struggle with this memory. That, along with the 2015 death of her husband, Ghanaian native Kodwo Esuman Ankrah, isn't something she dwells upon.

"Keep busy," she said. "Don't think about such things."

On this last day of August and on two other occasions when I bumped into Maxine in the summer of 2022, this African American–Ugandan roughly two decades older than me was gracious, patiently reflective with my incessant questions, and even a bit on the sly humor side.

I could have acquired information from Maxine's 300-page book, but spending one-on-one time with her was delightfully magical and heart rendering. Magical seeing how a Black woman rose up, in her words, from "being allotted to the back of the room" to a noted scholar. Heart rendering as I sat in a comfortable, cushioned chair, next to someone who saw first-hand the brutality of Ugandan Prime Minister Idi Amin.

This, after participating in a couple Ohio Black Lives Matter events and reading books like *Stamped* by Kendi Reynolds, which Maxine also had on her Uganda Christian University (UCU) desk the first time we met officially in mid-August 2022. This, after two of my Ugandan neighborhood boys, about age 10, just a week before they proclaimed to me that Idi Amin "never killed anybody," something they knew because one learned it on YouTube and another learned Amin's goodness from a teacher.

In a planned two hours that stretched into four we ate sausages and sweet bread toast with butter and cheese, and Eleanor Maxine Moore Ankrah told some of her story, exhibiting a demeanor that fluctuated between British formality and southern American hospitality.

At times, I forgot she is Ugandan—Ugandan and African American, that is.

"I'm the only African American–Ugandan," she said, emphasizing her dual citizenship. "At least, I've never met another."

Maxine spent roughly 1/3 of her life in the USA with the rest in East Africa, settling in Uganda since 1974. She has degrees, including a PhD, from seven universities—pushing race, gender and economic boundaries in speech and research, especially with HIV/AIDS. On this day, she is pushing forth a UCU curriculum with two courses that emphasize African culture, including diaspora such as the forced displacement of Africans shipped to countries as slaves.

"There are 400 million of us worldwide," she said, referring to descendants of the enslaved like her.

This then, comes as a synthesis from my treasured time in Maxine's English-looking house

Eleanor Maxine Ankrah

on 15 acres in the heart of Mukono, Uganda. Shielded from our sitting room is the grave of her husband, Kodwo Esuman Ankrah, which is outside surrounded with purple flowers and near a gray bench. A sign reads: "Kodwo, Husband, Father, and Friend who sat here for years in conversations, reflections and prayers."

I had passed the area countless times for exercise either with my friend, Mary, or friend, Douglas, or alone hiking up what I knew as "monkey hill" for its vast population of primate red tails or "prayer mountain," so named for the loud, all-night Christian conversions of people living within and outside a bevy of nearby tents.

"Besania Hill—not prayer or monkey mountain," Maxine corrected as she proceeded to tell me a small slice of what I never knew about a woman I never in 10 years at UCU noticed living nearby.

She graduated at the top of her American segregated high school class, met her husband-to-be at Hartford Seminary (Connecticut) in 1958, had three children (one dying in the womb), lived in the USA, Ghana (1962–66), Kenya (1966–70) and Uganda (early 70s to now).

A portrait of Maxine's husband, gone nine years earlier to heart complications, looked over us as we talked.

Together, she said, they left Entebbe (Uganda's capital before Kampala) for a USA trip the day before the infamous raid of Palestinian terrorists in July 1976. While I was a reporter for a middle-sized newspaper and recording local opinions on Watergate and the Vietnam War in the mid to late 70s, Maxine and her husband were living an oftentimes brutal political war on the ground. Together, they shielded the eyes of their two children from bodies along the road they traveled in the late 1970s. Other children walked to school among the corpses.

At that, Maxine believes that Amin "was not stupid as many felt he was" and that some killings were the result of a power struggle not totally in the dictator's hands. Her personal challenge at the time was that because of her American accent, the rumor started that she was a spy as she lectured at Makerere University. She wasn't.

As Maxine sipped tea and I drank water, she shared some of her vast academic and activist achievements—significant for a woman and especially a woman of color.

Her interest in HIV/AIDS was personal at first. A friend of her teenage daughter died from it. Maxine became known for her research and wellness education in the area, traveling to 27 countries to share her studies.

Uganda, she says, doesn't need to be known for poverty. She is critical of taxes for NGOs and expensive ceremonies and how people from western countries travel more freely to Uganda than Ugandans do outside their country.

"Everybody finds money for weddings here," she said, asking rhetorically, "Why can't there be money for other things?"

We concluded our talk with mutual frustration over a woman's inability to get divorced in Uganda while their husbands freely have relationships with other females and my question about how she feels about racial discrimination in the United States in 2022.

"The problem in the United States is white people against other white people," Maxine said. "They have a mindset that they need to strike out because they feel bad about themselves. I feel sorry for people with that mindset."

As we walked to the door, she reminded me of her peace with giving UCU a no-cost, 10-year lease to use her Ankrah property for student housing and programs. Her children have their own lives and careers with no interest in the estate. The donation is what her late husband would want.

"Did she hate you?" Tony Kato, my friend and driver, asked as I climbed in next to him after dodging raindrops.

"Not a bit," I replied.

Once enslaved by issues of color, poverty and gender, Eleanor Maxine Moore Ankrah no longer has that baggage.

(2022, Uganda)

Hair

I have frizzy hair. Wild, crazy, untamed tresses.

Frizz is what happens when moisture swells the strands of hair. Apparently, about 3 of 10 women have it. But misery doesn't love company.

I long for smooth, shiny locks like my friend, Heather Baugess, or my niece, Trisha Eyler, back home. I think I had that once. When looking at photos when I was younger, it appears I had the bounce going for a few decades. I have it now right after leaving my professional hair stylist. If I don't sweat or shower, her work could last up to two days but the consequence of the first leaves me cranky because I like to exercise, and the latter doesn't endear me to anyone but the dog.

American actress Jennifer Aniston pays $500 a month to get a smoothing hair process called "Brazilian Blowout." I tried that with some success. But the salon's application expert gave me too many don'ts—don't swim, don't sweat. Just breathe. Conditioner is cheaper with fewer restrictions.

I would like to blame my hair on somebody—like my parents. Supposedly, fine hair like I was born with is more impacted by environmental elements. When I look at my pictures at age 5, I appear to be a boy with fine, thin wisps framing my face. Apparently, this is part of a hereditary condition called trichoptilosis—big word for "split ends" in which the keratin splits off of the hair strand. Mom and dad caused that.

My husband likes to blame it on me because a few times a year I indulge in chemical coloring and sometimes I use a hair dryer. I blame him because when he blames me, it causes stress, which stresses my hair. Or I blame Uganda because I live here a good part of the year, and it's hot.

Recently, a Uganda Christian University work colleague urged me to put my hair down instead of pulling it back. I complied but then she noticed what I already knew. The longer we sat together, the larger my hair grew into a mess of uncontrollable curls and frizz. Eventually, I pulled it back. Another Ugandan urged me to go to a stylist and get oil applied. The result from the stylist unaccustomed to working the muzungu (Caucasian) hair was a coiffure dripping like grease and no time to wash it out before attending a wedding.

Not willing to give up, I double up on the hair vitamin supplements I take. A regular daily dose has 833% of the daily requirement of hair healthy biotin. I figure taking 1,666% of what nutritionists say you need must do something. It doesn't.

Recently and from my room at Uganda Christian University, I did a Skype with my 88-year-old mother back in Ohio. She said I looked great. My hair, slightly wet, apparently looked okay when blurred with the across-the-Atlantic electronic transmission. We continued our conversation for about 30 minutes. At last, I thought, a person whose opinion I valued the most in the world, accepted and actually loved my rather wild look. It felt good.

Then, as we concluded and my hair had dried, mom remarked, "You look horrible…your hair…"

Frizzy hair is horribly or delightfully me.

(2017, Uganda)

Ik Tribe

Rain-washed pathways derailed an original plan to hike up to villages of the little-recognized, often-ignored and misunderstood Ik tribe that lives within Mount Morugole near the South Sudanese and Kenyan borders in northeastern Uganda. This information is based on personal research and a conversation with an Ik who lives and works down the mountain.

You leave one country for a better life. You adjust to how you make a living in that life until some neighbors make that adjustment too hard. You move to a place where nobody else wants to live. And then you're told to move out of there and back to the place of difficult adjustment.

Such is the over-simplified, decades-old story of the Ik (pronounced "eek") tribe that the United Nations has said is near extinction. The Ik migrated from Ethiopia to Kenya and then northeastern Uganda.

The Ik side of the story is that the Karamoja tribe came closely behind them and used their warrior strength to control the cattle business, often stealing from the less aggressive Ik. After forfeiting their cows, the Ik became "hunter-gatherers" who took to growing/gathering crops and hunting wildlife until 1962 when the Ugandan Wildlife Authority (UWA) said the Ik couldn't kill animals anymore. When the government designated the land a game preserve, now Kidepo National Park, the Ik lost 20% of their revenue.

The Ugandan government side of the story—side-stepping the Karamoja–Ik cultural tug of war—is that lions and other wildlife need protection.

Regardless of who is right, the Ik felt their survival dictated a move back closer to the Kenyan/Sudanese border and up 2,750 meters (roughly 1.7 miles) onto Mount Morugole. They grow crops up there.

Today, the Ugandan government is nudging the Ik to come down and live in the plains again. The message that they are valued is reinforced through a fairly recent, possibly token addition of an Ik, Hillary Lokwang, to the Ugandan parliament.

"The Ik don't want to leave," said Ik tribal member and UWA Sgt. Lotyanga Maxben. "They are peaceful where they are, planting in their gardens, making honey and crafting walking sticks. And they have a vantage point to see if anybody is coming up the mountain to disturb them."

The 41-year-old sergeant, sitting with his second wife, Mhtyang Betty, 22, also Ik, answered questions outside the Nakamarkol House bar in the Karenga village of the Karamoja region. UWA Lance Corp. Manyimanyi Gilbert, helping with some Ik-to-Swahili-to-English translation, completed the quintet with my husband and me. We sat in plastic chairs under the cement structure overhang on this early February 2020 day. A light rain fell on curious, barefooted children and a teenager carrying a dusty radio blaring loud music. (Note: While considered unethical for credible journalists in the

Ik husband and wife, at right, during interview assisted with a translator, at left

United States, I paid the translator and subject 50,000 UGX—$15 American—each for the interview and gave the wife ginger cookies and nuts.)

Sgt. Maxben said the Ik aren't buying the government argument that they would have better lives with more access to quality education and medical care if they moved down again. In the plains, they would be living with still-hostile Karamoja neighbors and not able to return to hunting wildlife.

"Some of them remember that the Karamoja would kill you so you wouldn't tell who stole their cattle," Maxben said.

People, books and the Internet are wrong when they estimate Ik at a dwindling 1,000 and when they categorize them as unfriendly when they are really cautious and can live up to 100 years. And unlike some Karamoja, there is no forced marriage, according to Maxben. It's clear he has answered those questions. Maxben quickly recites the Ik 11-clan population at an exact 13,936 men, women and children and asserts that both the wives of his seven total children, ages 1 to 15, wanted to marry him and came from warm and welcoming families.

While Betty, who speaks no English, and their son, age 4, and daughter, age 1, live up the mountain most of the time, Maxben visits for six days every three months. When he arrives, there is a celebration with a slaughtered and cooked chicken and brew made from sorghum. Regular fare are locally grown Irish potatoes, maize, beans and cabbage. Sometimes, there is dancing.

"Yes, they protect their land," he said. "They love nature. They take care of the trees, pruning them, and carefully using parts for cooking posho (porridge) and rice and handcrafting stools and walking sticks."

Like the Karamoja, the Ik often sleep on cattle skins. Unlike the plains-living Karamoja, phones are not plentiful. There is no electricity. Primary school teachers are from other more-educated tribes. There is no high school or hospital. Sometimes, they remove two front teeth to ease getting medicine into the mouth. Rarely is there malaria because there are no mosquitoes.

"We simply want peace," Maxben said.

He and Betty looked at photos of starving Ik in a book, *The Mountain People*, written nearly 50 years ago by the late anthropologist Colin Turnbull. They laugh. They recognized some of the names with the pictures, but said nobody looks like that—ribs protruding from emaciated bodies—today.

Maxben pointed to the word "Bam," which means "friend" in the Teuso or Ik language. "Friend of Ik is called "Iciebam." Friends of Ik, and a bit of understanding about them, Maxben said, is all they want.

(2020, Uganda)

Listening

Listening is underrated.

Somewhere between the Ugandan girl looking over my shoulder to see Lake Victoria from the sky for the first time and an Ethiopian native's sighs about his Nashville house seeming empty while his wife and children continue a holiday, it hit me. Listening might be the only thing we need to do to make the world better.

Listening is what I did most during my recent three months in Uganda. I interviewed 40 people. Their words reinforced what my early life as a journalist taught me. People want to be heard. The result of this listening project is a plan to improve the climate, culture and communications at Uganda Christian University.

When I was a reporter, friends would ask: How did you get a parent to talk about a child recently killed by a stray bullet, a man to apologize for abusing his wife, or make a seemingly routine story about someone's missing dog compelling?

The simple answer: Listening.

Researchers, journalists, psychiatrists, hair stylists and priests do it—or seem to—as part of their jobs. But everybody should.

Traveling from Mukono through Seeta and Kampala to Entebbe, I listened to Philemon, driver of a white car with a cracked windshield and cardboard floor mats. I listened to Judith, in her late 20s, as she lamented her lack of a job and love of singing over digging up potatoes.

My 19-year-old seatmate from Entebbe Uganda, to Addis Ababa, Ethiopia—barely able to contain her excitement about her first plane ride—shared her thoughts about marriage and a job as a nanny.

A 60ish woman wearing a black, gold-trimmed burka engaged me in conversation about the Manchester, England, suicide bombing of two days prior. "If you kill, you go to hell," Nadia said as we sat together before boarding a plane. She added, "Islam is not a religion of terrorism."

I met another Muslim woman and her baby, both in red, in the Addis waiting area. "I'm Canadian," she said. "Most people look at me and don't know that."

Between Dublin, Ireland, and Canada, and high above the clouds, an Ethiopian–American with deep-set eyes and a goatee told me about discrimination among the more than 70 different ethnic groups in the country where most of his family still lives. He goes by "Teddy," he said. Members of Ethiopian tribes not in power are subjected to human rights violations that include unemployment, homelessness, imprisonment and death.

The same is true with the South Sudanese who reside in Bidi Bidi, the world's largest refugee camp at Uganda's northern border. Since civil war broke out in 2013, more than 800,000—mostly women and children—have fled there to survive on United Nations rations. My friend, Diane, has been listening to their stories, including from teen girls carrying babies spawned through rape by men who killed their parents. She hopes more will hear.

On a tiny airplane screen and over the Atlantic Ocean, I watch a movie, *Loving*, which recounts the true story of the United States' 1967 Supreme Court ruling allowing interracial marriage. It's sad, Teddy and I agreed, that people think skin color makes us different.

I have taught listening as part of a college public speaking class. In front of students, I lecture about the types of listening—to learn, to evaluate, to empathize.

Yet, I am not always a good listener. As a reporter, I did false listening; I thought up the next question while someone spoke. As a wife and even in precious moments on the phone from afar, I am distracted. My husband asks, "You're doing something else while I'm talking, right?"

When I left for Uganda, I carried anger about a group of people at our local church who were engaged in biased listening. Instead of focusing on the congregation's shared love of Jesus Christ, they twisted messages of helping the poor and praying for victims of gun violence into political perceptions. They elevated their voices. They drowned out mine and those of others, including two pastors who were silenced into unemployment.

In the early hours back in the United States, and while visiting my mother, I met a new resident, Norman, in mom's assisted living community. Like me, Norman has Irish heritage. He told me how he came here in the 1960s and became a citizen in the 1970s. The Irish weren't accepted at first, mostly because they brought cholera from their ships and into the United States.

"A lot of people still associate immigration with disease," he said. "They don't understand."

If we did deep listening, if we really made an effort to get to know each other, we might not label people because of age, race, religion, poverty, ethnicity, gender or political party.

We might not change opinions. But we just might solve a problem or two.

(2017, East Africa)

Malaria

Good news: I don't have malaria. With the prick of blood from one finger followed by a 15-minute wait, I learned my results.

I got checked last Wednesday for five reasons: 1) I had stomach discomfort for three days; 2) I was sweating more than normal; 3) it was the rainy season; 4) I have mosquito bites; and 5) my husband was arriving in Entebbe. On the last one, I know you can't catch malaria from humans, but after four months of not seeing each other and his nearly two days of sleepless air travel, I didn't want to be the sickly wife in his arms.

Turns out it was a simple case of constipation. My friend, Mary, told me to unblock my colon by eating carrots, which I did with success.

The malaria question is the most frequent I get from Americans curious about the 473 days of nine trips over 10 years I've been in Uganda, Africa. The disease that was eradicated in the USA the year I was born is always included in questions about clean water and terrorism safety. You ask about the weather, about giraffes, food and more.

So, my curious American friends, on a dark, rainy morning in Mukono, Uganda, and sitting cross-legged in pajamas before preparing for church, I'm typing a short list of Third World country myth-breaking, one-sided (mine) information. With absolutely no claim of high-level research, here's my brief, informed but biased perspective on the top 12 questions (in order) I get from you.

> 1. LIFE-THREATENING DISEASES. Yes, there are more cases of malaria here than just about any place in the world. Anti-malaria pills decrease the impact if an infected female (yes, it's all about the girls) mosquito bites you, but they might cause nightmares and if you take the medication too long, the drugs can damage your liver. I don't take anti-malaria pills anymore. I have never had malaria, probably because I always sleep under mosquito netting, use insect spray as perfume and seldom venture out at night when most of the biting occurs. HIV/AIDS, another life-threatening condition, is still an issue. When it comes to Ebola, it doesn't exist in Uganda in 2018.
>
> 2. MEDICAL CARE. If you get malaria in Uganda, the health care workers will know what to do better than those in the States. The medical facilities are classified as levels I to V. It was a Level III clinic where I got my lab results. If I tested positive for malaria, I would have been treated in a IV or V facility. Don't come here for open-heart surgery. Doctors, some of whom got their degrees in their early 20s, can't do a triple heart bypass.
>
> 3. WEATHER. Uganda has two seasons—wet and dry. Being on the Equator, Uganda can be hot, like 85 degrees Fahrenheit but seeming hotter in some places like the north. But evenings can cool down to 60 F and in the hills, like in southwestern Kabale, it can be downright chilly. On Mt. Elgon, to the east, it actually snows at the top.

4. FOOD and WATER. I can eat and drink on $1 a day here. That's not a typo. Most of what I consume consists of water, rice and vegetables that I fix myself on a tiny hot plate. A 7,000-shilling (about $2) bag of white rice will last me for months. When boiled and mixed with fresh tomatoes and peppers (about 10 cents each), this makes a pretty good and cheap meal. A restaurant meal with tilapia and fries is 14,000 shillings ($3). Bottled water and sodas (at 50 or 60 cents each) are available and generally safe unless you buy them from a vendor who came to your window while you waited in traffic. Then, and because you don't know if the containers have been sitting in effluent, you should use a straw. I buy three to four bottles when I arrive and re-fill them with boiled, cooled water. This, despite a free university breakfast of eggs, chapati and toast four days a week, results in a wonderfully slimming diet. I generally lose 10 pounds per trip.

5. MONEY. Just when I tell you I can live here on $1 American a day, remember that I came with my own clothing and medicines, that I'm not supporting anyone but myself, that I'm relatively healthy, don't have a care and don't pay for a place to live. I am an unpaid volunteer. While most people don't ask what I do in Uganda, I'll sneak it in here. I am a literacy consultant and professor—writing, editing and teaching English composition and research to students and faculty. The staff members that I work with—including employees with salaries paid by some of you who have contributed to my work—make anywhere from $100 to $600 a month. People in rural areas are lucky to get a dollar a day.

6. RELIGION. I mostly interact with Christians because I am one, but there are some Muslim students and lecturers at the university and in the surrounding Mukono village. The Muslim prayer chants occur morning, noon and night—audible from the local mosque loudspeaker. But the Christians like in the Cathedral close to my apartment are actually louder for longer periods with their amplified, repetitious, all-night song and preaching vigils. The Somali-based, extremist Al-Shabaab sect made threats towards this university awhile back but they are quiet now. While Muslim and Christian views of God are different, believers pretty much stay in their own lanes and get along.

7. GOVERNMENT. Uganda President Museveni has been in power for more than three decades. When someone runs or speaks out against him, they are often jailed. He and members of his Parliament make more than the average upper-middle-class American wage and definitely more than me. When the news media reports something he doesn't like, they can be shut down, and printing presses can be removed.. The members of the military are among the lowest of the low paid and some can be bribed. This is one of the most corrupt countries in the world. If you think the USA is in peril with Donald Trump, take a look at Uganda.

8. TRANSPORTATION. I hear that India competes with Uganda for having the worst roads in the world. I've never been to India. I can attest to Ugandan roads being the worst of any of a dozen countries I've visited, including my own. Here, the roads close to the President's home village, the ones leading up to where

kings reside and where wealthy ex-patriots (internationals) tend to hang out in the capital city of Kampala, are better. The worst is outside the rich Kampala areas. What looks like a 30-minute trip from where I live in Mukono to Kampala can be three hours in and three hours for the return. They call it "jam." Once, it took me five hours to return home with traffic lights and stop signs nearly non-existent and traffic cops stopping people for under-the-table payments.

9. CEREMONY. Ugandans are big on it. If you are an Anglican Christian, you probably revere bishops, their robes and their titles, and you call the arch-bishop the "Most Reverend." Introductory ceremonies for a couple about to marry are long; filled with loud music, speeches, gifts, food and jokes; and, for the bride-to-be, include multiple changes of ornate clothing. Before the wedding, the groom must donate cows, goats and chickens to the bride's family. When someone dies, people often pray around the house for days before the funeral and burial that can be in someone's backyard. Everybody in the community comes to these events, even if they don't know the people.

10. SEX. If you are Christian, you aren't supposed to have it before marriage. That said, if your family needs the money and your parents are illiterate, all bets are off. A young girl can be forced into a relationship with an old man. While homosexuality is illegal, when it comes to public displays of affection, it is okay for two men or two women to hold hands with each other but not acceptable for male-female hand-holding. And while men are supposed to be loyal to their wives, even Christian women look the other way when a man has another partner or wife.

11. PEOPLE. Uganda is known for having the friendliest people around the globe. They smile a lot and are laid back, often making them late for work or other appointments, especially if it rains. I've experienced this part of the culture as well as one location where the people are the least friendly—Bwindi. In three trips there, the native Batwa (pygmy) tribe seemed either sad or angry. I'm convinced it's a combination of all the rich people descending on their village to plop down $600 each to gorilla trek and sometimes engage in illegal, big-game trophy hunting. More than 10 years ago, hunters were forced out of their Impenetrable Forest natural habitat in order to save the gorillas from poachers.

12. WILDLIFE. Birds as well as primates, elephants, lions, leopards and giraffes are the reason most Americans come here. Generally, the wildlife is endangered and needs to be protected, but sometimes the population has to be culled to balance nature. Years ago, the Uganda Wildlife Authority was forced to kill massive numbers of elephants and hippos to protect the greenery and landscape around Murchison Falls, the country's prime resort. Here on the UCU campus, monkeys sometimes become too aggressive and have to be shot from the trees.

I don't have malaria or yellow fever, the latter of which everybody has to be vaccinated against to get in Uganda although I don't know anyone who has had yellow fever…

(2018, Uganda)

Mission

A clock on our kitchen wall is the most frequent and obvious reminder of a country in the heart of Africa. Operated by battery, it is set on Uganda time, which is seven or eight hours (depending on U.S. daylight savings time) ahead of Ohio. Within a small circular area next to a golden elephant ridden by a hunter-gatherer-looking man, the plastic clock hands move unsteadily with a double, audio "tick tick" followed by a full second of silence before sound repetition. Oftentimes, it is the only noise in our house.

Joy Wambuzi gave me the clock at the end of my 2012 trip. The groundnuts she provided and we consumed earlier in the week were not enough, she felt. After all my luggage was packed for the trip back to the states, Joy shoved the clock into my hands.

"It's an old thing," she said. "But it's from my house, and I want you to have it."

Realizing the delicate nature of the appliance, I carried the clock on my lap during the bumpy van ride to Entebbe and then on the plane to London to Chicago and Columbus. I wondered what I would do with it in a house filled with electrical, digital clocks. My husband, Mike, hung it on the kitchen wall. Joy's clock has become a symbol of the people we love, of experiences, of faith and, frankly, a simpler life than we have in the United States.

Mike and I are among Americans who are part-time missionaries in a Third World country. I logged two trips to Uganda before Mike decided he would go to see what the fuss was all about. For whatever reason God has called us to serve as much as we can and when we can with one foot in Ohio and the other in the East African country of Uganda.

This is part of my story about how I became a part-time, international missionary and why I continue to do it.

I became first hooked on Uganda in 2009 when leaving the snow-covered Midwest with about two dozen people from Ohio and Pennsylvania. My official mission in this country on the equator was to teach teachers. In the villages of Mukono and Busia, Uganda, my new friend, Sue, and I focused on strategies to teach reading skills to an average of 30 adult pupils each day. I learned to speak in five-word phrases to allow an interpreter to translate to the Luganda tribal language. While instructing, I had to overlook the distraction of hungry children who peered in and clung to window bars like flies.

It would be easy to focus only on the poverty in a place like Uganda. It is visibly evident in the people, the housing and the roads with ruts too deep to even slightly resemble an American pothole. One of three Ugandans uses pit latrines, doesn't have access to safe water, makes less than 400 American dollars a year, sleeps in a bed surrounded by multiple family members, and is illiterate. The images of children with worm-infested bellies and adults doing hard labor in fields and ditches are enough to break the hardest of hearts.

But because of my American poverty upbringing (we didn't have running water until after I entered first grade), my interest in U.S. women's rights issues in the 70s and my family work ethic, I gravitated naturally to the sustainability model of mission work. Helping Ugandans help themselves is the promise for Uganda.

The biggest gap in that promise is the education of girls and women. In Uganda's patriarchal society that values education for boys more than girls, females lag behind. The problem becomes greater after girls reach puberty for reasons that include lack of school facilities for personal hygiene, concern that a smart woman won't get a husband (and a dowry for the parents) and, in many cases, child rape and forced early marriage. Education for women is especially important in Uganda's polygamous society in which women are considered property that can be pushed out of housing and off of property with their children when a husband dies or takes on another wife. With increased literacy, women improve the family income and health and education of their children. Ultimately, the country's entire welfare benefits.

Being highly relational, my part-time mission work on the ground and back home involves considerable networking with many who care about the work—a nonprofit in Texas, a non-profit in Pennsylvania, a couple pastors, women's groups, a French–American working in Kampala, and a Californian doctor with a clinic in Bwindi, to name a few. Like me, they understand that overseas mission trips allow you to see and meet people first hand and go beyond statistics.

Thirteen hard-working, intelligent Christian women in Uganda are integral to my work. Ranging from their 20s to their 50s, these 13 are:

Sarah Nakayima, Joy Wambuzi, Esther Salaamu, Rachel Isabirye, Eva Najjuma, Agnes Kadama, Damalie Nakiku, Babirye Jamirah, Sarah Lagot Odwong, Monica Chibita, Judith Nabwire, Evangeline Ekiyingi Nalugya, and Melody Kukundakwe.

Among them are a journalist, teacher, college professor, artisan, government worker, women's prison advocate and more. Suffice it to say that all have had hardships that they continue to work to overcome. Each of these women merits a story. The first relationship I developed was with Sarah Nakayima, a now 20-something educator.

While I am a double-degree educated, middle class American in a job with no raise in salary since 2006, I landed home from Uganda in 2009 unable to shake the promise of the teenage daughter of Esther and Moses. Through Sarah, God spoke to me. I could not simply chalk up my one overseas mission trip and go back to my full-time, government communications job and part-time university teaching. Barely 90 pounds in weight, the Sarah I met five years ago worked alongside "muzungu" missionaries in construction of a church and a room where women were taught to use pedal sewing machines. Under my sponsorship, she became the first girl to go to college and the first to graduate with a university degree in 2012. Her first job involved work with a poor school in the village of Banga—not the best place to live, but, as Sarah stated it, "God does not make mistakes."

My female friends in Uganda tell me the joys of new babies in the family and experience with me the laughter and dancing to their music. We touch, hug and talk about the struggles. One has a mother in constant pain due to fractured breast bones from pounding and lifting in a stone quarry. Another is supporting her children and those of relatives by working two jobs. One aches for women in prison—at least half wrongfully accused, many imprisoned with malnourished babies and a couple pregnant with the babies of guards who raped them.

I help the women by selling their handmade products—necklaces from paper, baskets from the banana plant—and sending proceeds back to them. I assist by raising funds and putting them through college to enable them to have better jobs to support themselves and, later, their families. As a writer and a speaker, I work to tell their stories.

Approximately one-half of my disposable income goes to Uganda. I am humbled when I see the impact of more materialistically rich contributors to poor countries in Africa. My work could seem insignificant when compared to that of celebrities like Oprah Winfrey, George Clooney, Bono and Bill and Melinda Gates until I remember the Biblical story of the widow who gave all she had (Luke 21:1–4).

My 13 (with the number delightfully going up) women friends are a snapshot of Uganda's promise. They issue large smiles in spite of hardships, always ask about my family and me and remind me to "put worries in the hands of God." When they say they are praying for me, they actually are—and hard. My Christian friends in Uganda talk about God the way most Americans discuss the weather. They live the scripture from James 5:13 (NIV) : "Is anyone among you suffering? Let him pray. Is anyone cheerful? Let him sing praise."

When the other two digital clocks connected to the kitchen oven and microwave falter from an electrical outage, Joy Wambuzi's less-modern, battery-operated clock keeps ticking. It makes me smile.

(2014, Uganda)

Painter

On a not-even-a-bit overcast morning and with a student whistling "Jesus Paid it All" from Uganda Christian University's (UCU) nearby business incubation center, Joshua Kabitanya talks about the significance of stickers inside chewing gum wrappers, why a misshapen tree is more interesting than a symmetrical one and details of a mural project on the UCU Mukono campus.

Sitting at the base of the painting that covers a once-gray cylindrical water tank, Kabitanya's all black attire and subdued demeanor contrast with the bold colors, messages and images of the mural. He admits his introversion with people and extroversion with his craft.

"I hear music, I sense nature, I feel God," Kabitanya said of his artistic process.

Kabitanya is an artist and a Christian.

On this late August day, sunshine envelopes Kabitanya. When asked what he sees when looking around him, specifically which of two trees in front of the School of Business center he is most drawn to, he picks the misshapen, asymmetrical one.

"It's the tree that isn't uniform that's interesting," he said.

The mural, sandwiched between student dorms up a hill from the university library, was the idea of two Americans, Mary Chowenhill and Jack Klenk. Both had previously acquired Kabitanya's works depicting African life.

Kabitanya tells a story within the mural. His representation includes rays of light reflective of God's work, musical keyboards, dancing and mud-and-wattle huts.

"Some have asked why we didn't depict our culture in more modern terms," Kabitanya said, explaining, "Even today, people are more joyful when they go home to visit where they were born."

Home for Kabitanya is Mukono. He is one of nine children.

Kabitanya's earliest recollection of others noticing his passion and talent for art was when he was in Primary 3. Chewing gum packaged with stickers of sports stars was all the rage. He took to copying images from those stickers. Other children and teachers were watching.

"I became the one who teachers would ask to draw things on the board during lessons," he recalled.

Kabitanya identifies himself as quiet and oftentimes distracted from normal conversation by being drawn to his own imagination about his surroundings—traits commonly described by artists. He meditates and creates.

"It's how God made me," he said.

While certain of a destiny to art, Kabitanya learned to "hustle" with other work, making bricks and collecting stones for cement to pay for some of his clothing and school needs. After getting a diploma in electrical engineering from Kyambogo University, he decided to get serious with his artistic passion.

With Uganda's two-year lock-down during COVID, survival became even harder. For Kabitanya, he reminded himself of the message from Joshua 1:9 (NIV) to "be strong and courageous" and to not "be frightened or dismayed for your Lord God is with you wherever you go."

"The mural is more than just a painting," Klenk said of what was once a gray tank. "This project was about entrepreneurship, which is the point of the hub (also known as the idea incubator) next door. It's about how something ugly can be beautiful."

(2022, Uganda)

Joshua Kabitanya, *Dolls in Trees* book cover artist

Prison

In the United States, our prisons are like fortresses, ascending multiple levels with chain and barbed wire fencing to heights of 40 feet (12 meters), generally located away from residential areas and with multiple steel gates that click each time visitors or prisoners pass through. In Uganda, the fencing enclosures are about one-fourth that height with a single gate to what resembles a house, often located close to where non-incarcerated families go to market and within beautiful green fields of crops and near such natural wonders as the River Nile or Lake Victoria.

More than 35,500 of Uganda's population are in 223 prisons around the country. The U.S. population is more than eight times that of Uganda (316.8 million compared to 37.8 million) with 60 times more prisoners. While the United States might not be a fair comparison because it is geographically larger with more people and with the highest prison population in the world, the USA is the frame of reference I have. I was born and still live in the state of Ohio, which has about 50,000 of the 2 million prisoners in the 50 United States.

It would be easy to look only at these data and what you see when driving past Uganda prisons and assume all is well. That assumption would be false. The real story is within—the convicted and alleged rapists, robbers, thieves and murderers.

Before coming to Uganda, I made arrangements for two visits to a Ugandan women's prison in Jinja. The first visit was with my husband, Mike, and others affiliated with a Pennsylvania-based Uganda Christian Solutions organization. The second visit was with two writers—a Uganda Christian University (UCU) Mass Communications student and an intern with The UCU Standard. Each time, we engaged in singing, prayer and a Bible study with 50 women and up to a dozen babies and toddlers inside.

While we were not permitted to take notes and individual conversations with prisoners were discouraged, observations, prayer requests from the incarcerated and comments from outsiders combined with research to help fill in the blanks.

We laid hands on a woman with eyes nearly matted shut from infection or lack of bodily nutrition or both. I prayed that she might be provided a visit and medicine from a doctor or at least food better than the posho/maize, beans and porridge that is a prison staple. Nearly blind, she is led around by another inmate or simply sits alone on the floor. There are six doctors for all the prisons in Uganda.

We prayed for a 16-year-old girl, thrown in prison after a neighbor was found dead. With officials unwilling or unable to determine the culprit, her entire family of 12 was incarcerated in various prisons. Three months ago, she was an average schoolgirl.

We prayed for a woman six months pregnant after being incarcerated for 12 months; she claimed she had been raped by a male prison guard who saw her working in the fields. When I asked a social worker what action would be taken against the man, she simply shrugged.

The children, including a tiny girl just born inside the walls during a second visit, are growing up in a sea of yellow prison smocks with milk mostly from suckling that could be from the breast of an HIV/AIDS-infected mother. The older children are intellectually stimulated by a faded poster with alphabet letters and creatively stimulated by kicking in the dirt outside the housing. If they are lucky, an older child could be taken to live with a relative while the mother hopes that child will not be abused outside her watch.

My humble gift of underwear and sanitary pads for the prisoners at Jinja ended up as unintended gifts for the guards as did some of the eggs and sugar my friend brought. Although it is a weak defense, the guards are not rich.

Official reports validate these anecdotes. The Human Rights Watch and the Commissioner General of Uganda Prisons Service confirmed issues of overcrowding, guard abuse and lack of due process, hygiene, nutrition and medical care.

I realize some of the women are better off inside a prison. Here, they have a bed, food of some sort and safety from husbands who beat them. And there are women prisoners who should be punished for crimes.

But the fortress is too unkind.

(2013, Uganda)

Rat in Toilet*

The reason I didn't watch America's vice-presidential debate live as it was happening was because of the rat in my toilet.

I suspected the rat was living with me four days prior to the CNN on-air broadcast of Democrat Tim Kane and Republican Mike Pence sniping at each other in 2016. But I never expected it to be where I deposit my body waste.

But there it was—male or female, I don't know. So, I call it "it."

At 4 a.m. Oct. 5, 2016, Ugandan time, or 8 p.m. the evening before in Ohio, a black, roughly 10-inch rodent was inhaling and exhaling, baring teeth from my white porcelain privy.

The day before, I thought I saw the tail waving from the bedsprings.

I suspected that Meri, the cat I was watching here for an American priest back in the States, saw it, too. Blonde tail swishing, Meri's eyes seemed to be studying dark corners of the tiny apartment for days. But she took no action to validate her species' mouser existence.

I thought Meri and I heard it—in the kitchen, in the bedroom, in the room with the tiny TV.

My Ugandan friends, mostly faculty members on the East African university campus where I lived, shrugged. My journalism friend, Douglas Olum, said East Acholi people eat large rodents called "grass-cutters" as a good source of protein.

"It's just a mouse," most Ugandans said. Much smaller than a rat.

We had mice—tiny critters in our basement mostly—back home. Once, while my husband was in California with his ailing mother, I had beaten some baby ones to death with a large spoon.

I consoled myself that even if rats were bigger than mice, they had redeeming value. Rats

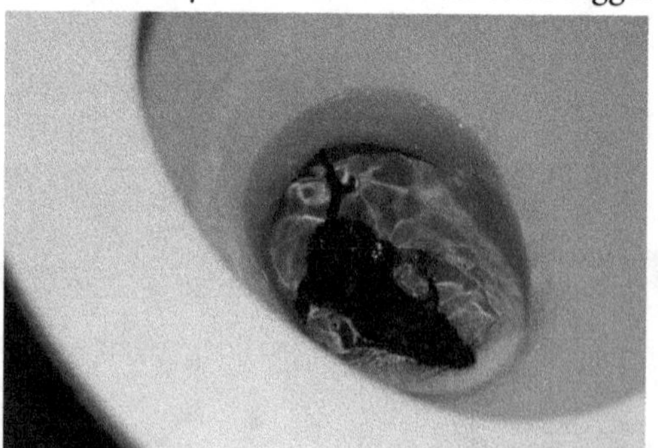

have been trained to sniff out landmines in Cambodia. In Tanzania, they detect tuberculosis.

Proverbs 30 references the value of all living things. Would I be a disappointment to God if I didn't find some saving grace for this rodent?

In the few days before the toilet discovery, I went to bed, somewhat assured that I wouldn't wake up half eaten or with rabies or worse yet—that I wouldn't wake up at all.

After all, seeing is believing, so sight unseen, the rat might not even exist.

But it did.

The night of that vice-presidential debate, I was so convinced that my imagination had the best of me that I got up once in the dark, probably about 2 a.m., to relieve myself. (Knowing what you know now, let that visual settle in.)

I climbed back under the covers until the two hours later time for the televised debate.

Just as the running mates for Hillary Clinton and Donald Trump were being introduced on TV, I entered the bathroom and turned on the light for a pee. It was then that I saw it. Long and big and brownish-black, trying to climb out of that white bowl.

I took a photo. I squeezed disinfectant in its face and tried to flush. My husband, on the phone and back in the States, accused me of waterboarding and wasting precious water in a country that needs its water.

By now, the United States vice presidential candidates were halfway through their solutions for the economy and world peace. I hadn't absorbed any of it.

With my bladder near explosion, I went outside and woke up a security guard. He came reluctantly, reminding me that pest removal was not part of his job. He likely wondered why Uganda allows rat-fearing Americans to take up residence here.

Together, we sized up the critter that kept sliding back from the rim. I held a black trash bag while the guard tried to nudge our rat into it with a stick.

It wanted out. We wanted it out.

As the USA candidates provided closing remarks in an adjacent room and no success with the bag and stick strategy, I pushed the toilet lever one more time.

With a final grasp upward of one claw and the gurgle of the swirling water, the rat swirled away into the sewage system where it could, should or would emerge…and be someone else's rat.

(2016, Uganda)

Rocks

Spoiler alert: Ugandans eat rocks.

Several days ago, as I purchased two tomatoes and two green peppers for 1,000 UGX (26 cents American), a woman next to me bought a rock. She carefully selected one hardened mineral from a box of about 50 others and gave 500 Ugandan shillings (13 cents) to the boy selling my veggies. While I positioned my four items in a bag with eggs and apples and before the woman and her friend departed, I readied a question.

Me: "Why did you buy a rock?"

Her: "To help my stomach."

Me: "Do you eat it?"

Her: "Yes."

In 14 trips since 2009, I never knew Ugandans ate rocks.

Certainly, I thought, this must be some kind of scam, uninformed opinion, superstition, witch doctor advice or a combination of the four. Always curious—a trait I tell writers that I think is paramount to our trade—I set off to learn more.

I went beyond the journalism "two-source" rule. While scanning the Internet and engaged in more serious work on the Ugandan Christian University campus, I worked the rock question into conversations with about a dozen people. Most are highly educated. All seemed surprised that I thought rock eating odd.

Just like the gender difference with ice cream (males don't eat it) that I learned on my trip here earlier this year, men don't eat rocks. Women do.

Clarification. Pregnant women do.

More clarification. It is a clay-based rock called bumba.

Three undergraduate social work students, trapped with me as we waited out the Ugandan rain last night, were among my chosen 12 with the rock query. They said that while they haven't consumed bumba, they would consider it when pregnant someday.

Me: "Won't it break your teeth?"

One of Them: "No. It softens in the mouth as you chip it off."

Another of Them: "It makes your teeth healthier."

Today and with the help of interpretation by a granddaughter, an elderly neighbor outside my door admitted she used to eat rocks.

"But never after the baby is born," she said.

I'd like to say this rock-eating information is new to everybody. It isn't.

Credible media like the BBC have done stories. One story from 2019 talked about women (not men) controlling nausea by eating clay rocks as well as by licking the sides of buildings and eating ant hills.

By some accounts, rock eating is not just about pregnancy but associated with an eating disorder called pica. That word, pronounced in English just as it looks, gets its name from a bird, the Eurasian magpie (formal Latin name of Pica pica) that has a reputation for eating strange things.

I also found some on-line companies who sell the rock in the USA for $7 each, plus shipping. The same company sells something for the guys—sex enhancement through an African root called Mulondo.

(From the rock advertisements, not my words)

"No side effects."

"Eat clay. Seriously, do it."

"It's a natural way to boost the diet with minerals."

Medical doctors don't recommend eating rocks or clay.

Just now, a friend working in the public health sector in South Sudan, emailed, in part: "Some adolescent girls are accused of having pregnancies when they turn to eat clay soil in hidden places. Other people say (the rock eating) is a lack of mineral deficiencies in the body. But public health experts discourage it, claiming that it is harmful to mothers and babies."

My husband, who learned along with me that Haitians eat dirt when we went to that country together in 2010, normally doesn't tell me what to do. But during a Zoom chat this morning, he asked that I not eat rocks. In a rare move to obedience, I probably won't try.

Clay-based bumba rock

Probably.

(2022, Uganda)

Shepherd

In last Sunday's shepherd-and-sheep sermon from Ezekiel 34, my mind wandered. As the woman behind me unintentionally kicked my chair—one of those schoolhouse wooden ones—I heard the pastor mention that bad shepherds take care of themselves and good ones take care of their flocks.

"I don't want to be a shepherd," I later that day told my first Ugandan daughter, Sarah, during her visit here from Dubai. As we shared ice cream, I asserted, "I want to be a sheep for a while."

My faith that is usually restored when traveling here has been tested.

I started writing down my reflections in my small Mukono, Uganda, apartment as some sort of critters that a neighbor said were rats scattered above the ceiling.

I'm finishing my thoughts here in Entebbe.

Mission work is hard—especially when you're doing it away from home.

Hours before a middle-of-the-night flight home and while sipping white wine from an elegant-looking glass, savoring the taste of tilapia wrapped in lemon grass with rice, and feeling the Lake Victoria breeze, I reflect on how easy it's not. At my familiar, decompressing site called 2Friends Hotel Entebbe Uganda, and while listening to the slosh of waves under a handmade, anchored boat, I am thinking about the struggles I've had this past two months.

After 11 trips in 10 years, perfection (if it ever was) eludes me.

Perhaps, it was that I didn't allow myself to rest between trips, and I've been working 12-hour days.

Maybe it was that after two months and 100 pages of documentation and less than two days on the ground eight times zones away, I got the government email that mom's Medicaid application was denied.

Possibly, it was because my flight over here was rearranged, causing me to rush and leave things I considered important behind or that my flight back was canceled, causing me to spend 90 minutes over three days to find an English-speaking, Turkish air agent to re-book.

Western world tourists express excitement about boarding the small boat I am watching, tethered and rocking from the waves. They find the chipped red paint and ruggedness of no personal flotation devices enchanting. They don't know or care about the 30 lives lost in a tragic accident on such a boat near here last November.

They haven't been approached twice a week with people pleading for money to eat or buy medicine.

While focusing on a single American tourist abducted and rescued on safari, they likely aren't aware of the more than 200 Karamoja people hospitalized because the World Food Program gave them outdated cereal.

The need is great.

(2019, Uganda)

Shoe Boxes

Today, I unsubscribed from Samaritan's Purse Operation Christmas Child emails.

It's not that I don't support poor children getting gifts at Christmas time. I do. It's simply that I know those shoe-boxes—ones that I have filled in the past, dropped off at my church and felt good about—don't always get to the intended recipient. And when they do, they often have gifts that have no meaning to these financially challenged children.

Case #1—In Kampala, Uganda, men, women and children are on the streets, selling items out of the shoe-boxes. Where do they get them? Some greedy person intercepts them illegally in customs, pays a corrupt official there for some boxes and then sells them singularly to individuals like these on Kampala's busy streets. I don't have data on how often this happens, but I know it does.

Case #2—A friend, Marna Lombardi, in California sent me an article today about a child who got a box with a slinky inside. He didn't know what to do with it. It's a toy meaningful to the developed world but not so much to a child in need of food and clean water and accustomed to playing with twigs, stones and old rubber tires. Again, the ratio of this mismatch frequency to when a shoe-box has items that are valuable to the poor is not a figure I have. But I know this unintended consequence does occur.

It's times like these when I question if I am more informed than the rest of the world or if I'm becoming a missionary snob. With the exception of a few like Mother Teresa, Pope Francis and martyrs who allow themselves to be burned to death instead of denying God, missionaries are not holier-than-thou people and can at times be outright arrogant.

In 2017, I spent six months in Uganda—the longest I've been out of the United States at one stretch ever. At that, some more "full-time" missionaries have told me, "Oh, you're part-time" and proceed to provide me facts about their service in the Peace Corps, how they raised their families in a developing country, how they got federal grant money to do their work and how much they sacrificed more than me. One missionary friend said she was better able to give fully because she was unmarried. Another missionary questioned my treating myself to a nice meal and retreat in a hotel when so many are not as fortunate.

Be not deceived, missionary groups—often known as NGOs—are a competitive lot. They are loving, caring people but can sink into criticizing each other to elevate themselves or their organizations.

With these same people, I have caught myself laughing at the "mission tourists" who show up for two or three weeks and leave. One problem with these short-timers is with medical supplies that get left behind and expire without being used, and doctors and nurses who administer care without educating locals to do the same. Another problem is the mission vacationers who fly in to build churches and schools without teaching locals how to build themselves.

At the same time and when spending one of those "luxury nights" with my missionary friend, Sheila Hosner, at the Kampala Sheraton, I openly slammed one of the best examples of mission work in this decade—the story of Katie Davis Majors, who founded Amazima Ministries in Uganda.

"This book depresses me," I told Sheila as I finished the last page of *Kisses for Katie*. Katie gave up her boyfriend and a college education to become a mom to 12 orphans. She exposed herself to jigger fleas and malaria and never got either, and ended up marrying the right guy anyway.

"Everything she tried ended up perfect," I said. "That's not how it is."

Being a bit of a hypocrite back in the United States, I was repulsed during a recent visit to the Columbus Zoo in Ohio. Especially depressing was the lion. Behind the glass, he locked eyes with me and other visitors, including our granddaughter. I felt sadness about his huge size (no lions are that big in the wild) and lack of movement in an enclosure where he no longer got to hunt for food, but simply waited for a human to deliver it. Likewise, with the cheetahs, who twice a day are on display to cheering crowds as they use their speed to chase after meat they didn't have to stalk.

The point of all this, I suppose, is that we all have to make choices regarding where, to whom, how, and how much to give. I tried to explain this to a Democratic Party caller just a few minutes ago, telling him about the work I do in Uganda and the girls I have in school there and how I couldn't afford to support my party. But he only wanted to stick to his script. I kept thanking him. Finally, I hung up in the midst of his pitch.

I began to be irritated with Samaritan's Purse when its religious leader, William Graham, chose to use the organization as a platform to support Donald Trump more than a year ago. I suspect my thoughts for this group are a bit tainted by that. But my eyes and ears regarding the shoe-box charity don't lie.

While admitting my own human frailties (yes, I drink wine, consume a lot of dark chocolate, buy snacks in Uganda that most Ugandans can't afford, and am no candidate for sainthood), I pray for groups that get so large, they lose focus. I pray that I accept the missions of others. I pray that others accept mine. I pray that all of us find our greater purpose.

And I pray for facts.

(2016, Uganda)

Teachers

Daphine Oitamong talks about Sophie who walked to school two kilometers (1.3 miles) barefooted with rat bites on her heels. Nannyanga Restetuta talks about Dora who went from "jolly and active" to being withdrawn after her parents left her in the care of a sexually abusive uncle. Nancy Ongom, who mentions the name Jafa, grapples to pick just one.

There are so many.

Daphine, Nancy and Restetuta, who prefers the name Resty, are Uganda primary school teachers with over 100 students per class. While they barely know each other and work in different schools, the young women share the distinction of being Teach for Uganda fellows, having Uganda Christian University (UCU) degrees and owning a passion to serve "the least of these," as they know from Matthew 25:40.

The three UCU alum are among 226 men and women engaged in two-year fellowships helping the poorest of the poor ages 4 to 10 in Uganda's Kayunga, Mayuge, Namutumba, Mukono, Buikwe, Namayingo and Bugiri districts, according to Decimon Wandera, who serves as a coach for the fellows.

Charlotte Iraguha, co-founder and managing director for the seven-year-old Teach for Uganda NGO, says there are 40,000 students in 151 public schools where fellows are assigned. Uganda has nearly nine million elementary school children. Charlotte, a former teacher, explained that her organization's model has government teachers working alongside fellows to build a "full child—not just focusing on grades." Fellows with degrees in various programs teach children and, as time permits, engage with parents.

"When I first came here, I thought I had arrived in another country," Daphine said of the primitive, rural Namutumba area of the Kamudooke Primary School where she teaches. "I grew up in Kampala and never traveled here."

Namutumba is more than four hours from Uganda's capital city as well as four hours from where Resty and Nancy teach in Mayuge district. The often-rugged roads leading to all three schools are lined with brick and mud-and-wattle homes, children carrying jerry cans of water from bore holes and fields of bananas, maize, cassava and sugarcane.

According to Decimon, 70 percent of the fellows stick it out despite that most didn't grow up the way the schools' students are.

Resty, 26, and Daphine, 29, who graduated with UCU Bachelor of Arts in Education degrees in 2021; and Nancy, 29, who got her UCU degree in law in 2017, are part of the retention data. For them, what started out as sh550,00 ($150) per month for a job vs. no job at all has become a mission for positive change and a reminder of the biblical lessons from UCU.

Quoting Luke 6:38 (NIV) "give and it shall be given unto you," Nancy said she interprets that verse to include love, compassion and skill that could break the cycle of poverty she sees every day. She entered her teaching post at Kaluuba Primary School with no formalized pedagogical training but a drive to "go deep in humanitarian action," to challenge herself and to learn what she could from trained government teachers.

Resty and Daphine applaud the teacher training that came with their undergraduate degrees, citing the value of psychology, discipline and teaching methods they gleaned from the classroom. At the same time, they point out practical experience gaps—especially when working with children in high-poverty, rural areas. These children come to school dirty and hungry or not at all as they are needed at home to plant and harvest food. One frequently absent student explained that her belly is full if she climbs a tree to eat mangoes near her home but empty as she sits at a desk at school.

"The school provides porridge as the main food for children during lunch but only for those whose parents can afford to bring some maize so we still have a lot who go the whole day without a meal," Nancy said. "It breaks my heart."

Resty and other teachers at Kigandaalo Primary School, start each day with a 7:45 a.m. hair, teeth, body, and clothing cleanliness check. Discovery of lice means the child goes home.

"Many days, it helps to remember the servant-hood, diligence and Christ-centeredness that was part of our UCU character building because that is what we do," Resty said. "At the same time, I see now that our university life was too soft. We weren't prepared for work this hard."

Hard means understanding a non-native language from children and parents with little to no knowledge of English in a country with as many as 70 different dialects. Resty and Daphine have Luganda mother tongue in schools with children speaking Lusoga and Ateso, respectively. Nancy, who speaks Acholi from her native Gulu, is surrounded daily by indigenous Lusoga speakers.

Dr. James Taabu Busimba, Head of the Department of Literature and Languages, UCU School of Education, agreed with the value of academic application in real-world contexts. "Knowledge gained is as useless as pride if filed away and never applied," he said, repeating a quote often attributed to several writers and politicians.

On one day in July, Resty was using phonics and memorization to teach English while Nancy was teaching numbers and how to add them together. Crammed at desks in the two school locations, children were sounding out the words "poison" and "chicken" for Resty and adding the numbers three and four and two plus five to equal seven for Nancy.

For the three UCU teaching alums, the work doesn't end with a school day among small children. Their afternoon hours may find them seated with a child's custodial parent, helping the secondary girls make and understand how to re-use sanitary pads, preparing lessons for the next day and fundraising. Using their UCU alum network, they have raised money for food and clothing for their neediest schoolchildren.

"I learned the value of helping others through UCU's Save the Buddy program," Daphine said. "At UCU, we would be looking around, especially at exam time, to see if we had extra money to help classmates pay fees so they can sit for exams."

According to Daphine, Nancy and Resty, the challenged home lives of the children seated before them who live amongst latrines, filth, and dust provide many life lessons and reminders of how Jesus might have lived.

Like Jesus, Daphine feels she is going deep and "testing my strength." Resty believes that the work in the schools, no matter how difficult, is preparing them for other opportunities. Most days, the three are exhausted but ready to give more.

"If God gave his only son, we can give this," Nancy said.

(2023, Uganda)

Terrorism

For a brief 90 seconds during what appeared to be a bomb explosion last weekend, I huddled, crouched low behind a rather flimsy bamboo wall with a half dozen people I didn't know. Two minutes before, we were in our own Internet worlds, typing on iPads, laptops and phones, relishing in the fairly strong Wi-Fi at Café Cosmo, Arua, Uganda, and the connection it afforded to our families and work colleagues around the world.

The boom shook the tables and us. Immediately and seemingly from instinct, we left our money, passports and electronic devices for where we felt was the safest place within the mostly open cafe. We—an American (me) and others from, I think, China, Denmark, England, India and Australia—didn't speak until quiet engulfed us for that 90 seconds.

We softly speculated "a bomb," "a car backfire," "gunshots." Then, in the immense quiet, we got up, shrugged and went back to our vacated possessions at plastic tables and chairs. From my MacBook Air, I checked in on a magazine project back at Uganda Christian University in Mukono. Minutes later, my French–American traveling companion, Patti, returned from a restroom visit and calmly asked if I knew the source of the commotion. I didn't.

Our driver, Tony, arrived. We ordered food and drinks. I had fried tilapia fillets and mashed potatoes—the real mushy ones like I was used to back home. I sipped wine (a rare treat because alcohol isn't allowed on the campus where I work). When bringing the check, the waitress gave an update on the earlier incident; she said that a pipe under a sauna next door had exploded.

"Did anyone die?" I asked.

"I think one man," she replied.

"Oh," I said, taking a last sip.

Days later when back in Mukono and in a fleeting thought, I tried in vain to find a news account of the Arua incident in the news. In the northern Uganda area sandwiched in by fighting at the South Sudanese border on the north, by lines of trucks transporting fuel and other supplies into the Democratic Republic of Congo on the eastern border and populated with United Nations workers from two refugee camps, a single death and a momentary disruption of business for me and others didn't make the media cut.

I was even nonchalant when mentioning the incident to my American colleagues, Mary and Sylvia, en-route to Jinja, on the following Saturday. They were quiet. Then Mary spoke.

"You should write about that," she said.

I certainly can't compare my recent small brush with perceived terrorism to the recent mass shooting by an American in Las Vegas, Nevada; to the Al Qaeda-owned, horrific tragedy on Sept. 11, 2001, in the United States; to Boko Haram's kidnapping of 276 Chibok schoolgirls in 2014; and to the atrocities committed by the Lord's Resistance Army and Al-Shabaah. Unfortunately, the list goes on and on. Again, no comparison to my less than two minutes in Arua.

As a journalist, I have been trained to compartmentalize such experiences—processing them later and mostly through writing. I did my master's level research on crisis communications, so in a smaller, less-worldly sense, I'm not completely naïve to unexpected, life-threatening incidents. As a reporter, I've covered my share of fatalities, documenting family anguish and grief.

I don't thrive on putting myself in danger although it might seem so.

My husband, Mike, and I flew into Uganda in the midst of Al-Shabaah rumors against Christians here in 2013. We traveled to Paris with Sarah, one of our Ugandan daughters, changing planes in the eerily vacant Belgium airport after serious threats there in 2015. In March of this year and while seated with Uganda university students getting information about possible careers, my young intern leaned over to show me a trending news story from her phone. Assistant Inspector General of Police Uganda Andrew Felix Kaweesi, scheduled to speak in this large, outdoor campus area in an hour, had just been brutally murdered, reportedly by Muslim extremists. He wouldn't be coming.

I am certainly no expert on terrorism. I live a relatively normal life both in North America and Africa. I don't sit around thinking about how I might be attacked or kidnapped. But my exposure and reflection related to my international mission work since 2009 and during six months outside of the United States this year gives me an added perspective and opportunity to stimulate my own thoughts and, hopefully, that of others.

The three terrorist groups I know the most about are Boko Haram, Al-Shabaah, and the Lord's Resistance Army. What they all share is ignorance, excessive greed, disrespect for human life and stubbornness to accept lifestyles and opinions other than their own. Boko Haram (literally translated to English as "western education is a sin") and Al-Shabaah are alike in that they became active within the past 10 years, don't like the Christian faith and, once aligned with Al-Qaeda, are now claiming association with the Islamic State of Iraq (ISIS). Although never personally making attacks on American soil, the Lord's Resistance Army and Al-Shabaah openly share a dislike for the United States.

Boko Haram is mostly doing bad things in West Africa, namely Nigeria, Cameroon, Niger, Chad, Benin.

The Lord's Resistance Army incidences of rape, kidnapping and murder have been concentrated in Uganda and Sudan/South Sudan. Whether the leader, Joseph Kony, is dead or alive is debated in 2017. What is broadly accepted is that this group's attacks against people have shifted to an even more vulnerable population—elephants, which the Army reportedly kills just for the ivory tusks.

The jihadist fundamentalist group known as Al-Shabaah targets Islam enemies in East Africa, mostly behaves badly in Somalia and Yemen with the exception of the mass killing in a shopping mall in Nairobi in September 2013. Because Uganda is in East Africa, it is in the line of fire with rumors about Al-Shabaah attacks. Because Uganda Christian University promotes faith-based learning about the teaching of Christ, this institution is often rumored as a target.

Sitting cross-legged in an apartment on a Sunday filled with Christian music wafting up the hill and blended with chirping birds, it's relatively easy for me to write about such a sensitive and much deeper topic like terrorism. My walks through the campus are met with the delight of monkeys swinging in trees and cheerful smiles and greetings from students and faculty. The perimeter is fenced with guards.

I'm not deceived that I'm living in a dangerous world, that Uganda is one of the most corrupt countries around the globe and that President Yoweri Museveni is a dictator who, unlike Donald Trump, doesn't have United States-style democratic checks and balances for his bad decisions.

As I prepare to return home to the States in just over two weeks, I'm watching the news more closely but filtered through CNN and BBC international lenses. From what I learn here and have verified this morning through the 2017 Index of U.S. Military Strength, Russia is the biggest threat to America, followed by Iran, North Korea and, yes, China. Except for Iran, no U.S.-terrorist-labeled countries are on that list.

I'm inadequate to give advice related to this lengthy discourse, but here it goes anyway: Be open to educated opinions of others, make decisions based on compassion, responsibly enjoy the life you've been given, give to others.

Try not to be ignorant, greedy, and disrespectful of human life and avoid being stubborn— at least try to understand lifestyles and opinions other than your own.

And for God's sake, if you can't help somebody, at the very least don't hurt anybody.

(2017, Uganda)

Third World Hospital

When the young doctor told me he believed the reason for my three days of vomiting, chills and no appetite were related to the hand tremors I've had for 25 years, I suspected I was in trouble.

I knew I was in deep shit as I explained that the shaking the young men in the white coat observed was an unrelated hereditary disorder. I spelled the condition "familial" connected to how I genetically possessed it. He carefully wrote it down.

This was AFTER I left one health care clinic because the blood analysis equipment was broken… AFTER one doctor wondered out loud if my over-60 age was a factor with no remedy… BEFORE the results of my worst-ever blood draw with the needle piercing my right wrist, stinging to my fingertips and disengaging feeling for five minutes…BEFORE results of my urine test that I provided from a room with a single hole in the floor at the end of a dark hallway…and BEFORE the doctor shared that he went to medical school in Gulu, which, in spite of the fact that I know a super intelligent guy there, I also knew had one of the highest illiteracy rates in the world.

In the end and with the help of understanding by my friend, Elizabeth Bacwayo, the doctor concluded I had a bacterial infection that I picked up from God knows where. I got a shot of something in the butt and some antibiotics given through a window filled with dust and left with paperwork barely readable as generated from a low-ink printer.

Thus was my first trip to a Ugandan hospital in 10 years of coming to this country..

After writing a half dozen stories on the Ugandan health care system over the past five years, I had, in August, the patient experience. To be fair, I don't like USA hospitals either, and a visit here would have been many times more expensive than the 70,000 shillings ($21) I shelled out in Uganda. But the World Health Organization ranks United States health as 37 and Uganda's as 149 of 190 for good reason. (France is #1.)

In Uganda, you become a doctor with five years of education. The quality physicians with specialties are few and far between.

The good news: In 24 hours that included prayers, food and close attention from amazing Ugandan friends, I got better. One Ugandan friend even offered to clean my nausea-tainted bathroom.

I've always said if you have a tropical disease, you'll be fine in Uganda. I'm sticking with that. For anything else, all bets are off.

One of my Ugandan daughters described how this summer she was in labor, walking and holding her stomach for 90 minutes to a hospital, delivering her baby and then leaving an hour later with herself and the infant on a boda (motorcycle) ride to her mother's home.

A French–American friend shared how a Kampala hospital botched the supposed "fix" of her fractured wrist, necessitating a scheduled trip to Paris for a re-breaking and repair.

Come to Uganda. But don't come sick or get sick there.

(2019 Mukono, Uganda)

Traveling Sweater

It was 65 degrees Fahrenheit (18.3 Celsius) when I saw Rose this morning (August 16, 2018). She wore a smile and a mostly-black sweater. In Uganda, such weather is cold. My arms were bare. In Ohio, temperatures like this are refreshing.

Sitting with me at the Uganda Christian University Touch of Class canteen, she apologized for the sweater—a used man's sweater, she admitted, and one she bought from her brother's shop. I encouraged her to see the garment's beauty. And I asked her to keep it close to her over the next four months.

You see, my young friend Akongo Ruth Rose will on Friday take her first-ever plane ride on her first-ever trip to the United States. Her emotions are mixed. She is honored— the only African chosen for a semester of writing courses at The Kings College in New York City. She is anxious. While the college is Christian, she will be living in the liberal community of Greenwich Village. She feels guilty knowing how much the scholarship she got could buy for her family, friends and village.

While holding her hands and praying with her today, I reminded her that God gives us gifts like these, that she is a gift, and that others she meets in New York City will surely see her that way.

I met Rose when teaching journalism with Professor Angella Napakol last year at Uganda Christian University. Right before I left, I matched up Rose and two other students for a one-week internship in northern Uganda with two professors (Diane Ross, Pegi Lobb) from Otterbein University (Westerville, Ohio). Like many, they enjoyed her eagerness to learn and help others. If that wouldn't seal the deal for wanting to hang around with Rose, her deep dimples on both sides of her cheek did.

This morning as Rose removed the sweater in embarrassment and clutched it in her hands, I insisted she pack it in the small green suitcase I gave her. I told her the story about the "traveling pants." I suggested she write about her traveling sweater. I hope she reads this and that she does.

(2016, Uganda)

Akongo Ruth Rose with her traveling sweater

Water*

From my luxury tent at Mhingo Lodge (Lake Mburo National Park, Uganda), I hike about 30 minutes in the dawn to a place called "The Hide." I duck inside the crude construction of bamboo, twigs and palm leaves to take my place on a wooden bench, where I hide and wait for zebras, bushbuck, waterbuck, impala, buffalo, warthog, anything.

Nothing. I sip from my 500 ml of Rwenzori water while birds aware of my hiding place mock me with their trill. The "o-lee-oh-lee" and "ta-tweet-ta-tween" also might be jeering at their larger neighbors who can't fly to a lake or swing through trees to drink morning dew drops from leaves. Before me are two bone-dry craters that should be watering holes.

Water. I swallow a large portion of it from my bottle. Liquid makes up about two-thirds of our bodies. When we lose just two percent of it, we feel thirsty. When we lose more, we can't eliminate toxins through sweat and urine. We eventually won't be able to walk or even breathe.

Dehydration. That afternoon, when coming up for air in a swimming pool, I see the same two craters but from further away. When you have mild to moderate dehydration, you experience dry mouth, dizziness and fatigue. Severe dehydration results in confusion, lower blood pressure, rapid heartbeat, fever, sunken eyes and, in some cases, unconsciousness. The immune system is under attack.

Survival. In early evening as dusk descends, I taste a chilled cola in an enclave above the pool, even further from the stagnant craters. Red-tailed monkeys get dangerously close before lodge employees shoo them away. When resources are scarce such as in a drought, animals and people conflict and compete.

Hope. Seated with my husband and next to two Australian businessmen, the lodge manager points to five zebras coming to the dry holes. Through a telescope, we view them. I sense the horror, as each zebra turns away and walks slowly back into the forest. "They have more hope than the others," I say out loud, remembering that animals are better at storing water than humans. "They are dying," one businessman replies.

Death. Along the red road from the lodge is a dead klipspringer. Dehydrated animals are weak. Stronger animals attack and kill them. Vultures finish the job. As we near Kasersero village, our driver slows to show us a baboon, hanging by a rope from a tree, likely beaten by villagers upset about having their gardens robbed. I learn later that more than three dozen zebras died from anthrax ingested from vegetation they wouldn't normally touch except in severe drought, and large numbers of cattle are being relocated to Tanzania, where water is more plentiful.

Drought. On the Uganda Christian University campus where I teach, I can fill a plastic bottle with clean water at several locations. But outside our gates in the village of Mukono, animals and people don't have enough. In January of 2016, around 640,000 of Uganda's Karamoja citizens faced food shortages due to drought. In late October, up to eight million people in East Africa were starving. Rainfall saves lives and reduces poverty.

Rain. As temperatures rise, moisture evaporates. When there is no rain to replace liquid on land, a drought occurs. Rising heat reduces the likelihood of rain, creating a feedback loop that goes from bad to terrible. Droughts have been getting worse since the 1970s. Scarcity of water is one impact of the earth getting warmer. Moreover, 97 percent of the earth's liquid is seawater, of which there is not a drop to drink.

Climate Change. Around 97 percent of the world's climate scientists agree that global warming is human-caused. Yet, even with all the snowstorms, floods and hurricanes in the United States and with the many starving people I have seen in villages of Uganda and Haiti in the past decade, I was not an early adopter. I never fully connected the role of atmosphere to animal and human suffering. I didn't want to change my habits—even in simple ways like taking shorter showers or reusing water bottles.

It took this four-day break from teaching to wake me up to the inseparable link among plants, animals and human beings. Clearly, I have some catching up to do.

(2016, Uganda)

Writer

Timothy Wangusa used pieces of dried grass stalk to write on his thigh because his primary school was short of slates. Plus, paper and pencils didn't exist for his class back then. That early inscription disappeared in his sweat while he slept each night.

Not to even vaguely compare my life to the recently turned 80-year-old Wangusa in Uganda, it reminded me how in my 20s I used to jot notes on bar napkins with ink blurred from chilled glass condensation by the time I pulled them from my purse the next day.

Finding ways to write and things to write upon is what writers do.

Wangusa's right hand, bearing a scar from when a teacher's whack drew blood 70 years ago, held a pen as three months ago, he scripted a message to me in his book, *Lost in Wonder: An Autobiographical Tale*. That book, along with Wangusa's *The State Is My Shepherd*, traveled in my luggage across the Atlantic from East Africa to Ohio in mid-September.

I first met Wangusa on April 21, 2016. We were in a parking lot next to the Uganda Christian University library. On that day and standing next to some cars, he wrote "To Patty, a kindred spirit in the word" in his 2015 book, *Betwixt Mountain and Wilderness*, which he then handed to me. Standing too, I wrote something to him in one of my books, *Kid in the House*. We were both hurried that day but assured each other that we would connect again and for a longer period.

Six years later, we did. On September 7, 2022, we talked for two hours about our craft. Mostly his.

Wangusa is a big fish in the Uganda literary pond. So big that scholars working on their doctoral research in his country study Wangusa and analyze his works. Nobody (thankfully, I think) has done that with my writing.

We both once gave up our true passions for creative writing to churn out oftentimes dry, uninteresting things for the government.

Wangusa said Uganda President Yoweri Museveni "picked me for my facility with words." I was plucked from a newsroom to be the Public Information Officer (PIO) for State Superintendent of Public Instruction Franklin B. Walter because a friend who was leaving the post recommended me. I was bored that day and said "yes."

Wangusa and I both have taught our trade at universities—me mostly to undergraduates required to be in my class, and Wangusa mostly to post-graduates who listen intently with hopes that someday they will be like the esteemed professor before them.

Wangusa is kind of my idol, too. Other authors who I once held in esteem—William Least Heat-Moon and Tracy Kidder—fell from grace because of their arrogance when meeting them. Not so with Wangusa.

The September 2022 setting was within Wangusa's gated compound surrounded by poorer neighbors in the eastern part of Mukono town. There were three chairs—two for our respective sitting and one to hold some of the books Wangusa authored—and a small table. Margaret, a mid-40s woman with an education in commerce and technology and who met Wangusa a decade prior as she was selling clay, brought us juice and freshly made, cubed sweet breads.

After assuring me that the water in the juice was clean, Wangusa affectionately referred to Margaret as his "wife of my longevity." A first wife, who died in a car accident 10 years into their marriage, was "the wife of my youth." A second wife, still living in Kenya, is "the wife of my prime."

Wangusa puts his number of children as seven. Counting non-biological children would bring it higher. Wangusa is hard-pressed to assign a number to the many pieces he has authored. Wangusa's collection—his works and others—is in a small garage converted into a library, attached to his house.

With a neighbor's squealing pigs in the background, I sought to learn where Wangusa's talent began, what made him tick and, selfishly, how I might become better in the passion we share.

Had he not become a writer or, in the words of his autobiography, an initiator of "learners into the world of books," Timothy Wangusa could have been a rain disperser or a circumciser. His father had the gift of making it rain to improve crop yield, and an uncle was known for his skill of circumcising adolescent boys as is still the custom in Wangusa's maternal clan of BaNaŋanda BaNantsumbya in eastern Uganda's Mbale region.

His story is mostly woven in poetry and prose influenced by the world around him. It could be a mountain, romance or politics. His topics tend to center on culture, education and Christianity with some creative disobedience with the latter as exemplified by his *The State Is My Shepherd* version of Psalm 23.

In part, Wangusa pens, "The state is my shepherd, I will not want; it makes me to lie down in a subsidized house…"

Some of his work is influenced by Idi Amin Dada, who Wangusa regarded as a "primary one school dropout" and "comedian" before Amin's "protracted nightmare" of his "horrendous regime" of January 1971. Wangusa, a former professor of literature at Makerere University in Kampala, describes how he was geographically one foot away from the former dictator when Amin was the university's chancellor and Wangusa was one of Makerere's first two PhD awardees. Other than one brush, Wangusa was not in the company of Amin but always aware of being "close to being missing (i.e., killed)" for driving Amin's more visible targets and their families to escape across the border to Kenya.

When Yoweri Museveni became Uganda's president, Wangusa served in the Parliament. Prior to that, he served as Education minister in Tito Okello's government which Museveni overthrew. Dabbling in politics informed his true love—writing. Having been on the inside enables him to see that in Uganda the Parliament has gone from being the "limbs" of the President to his "walking stick, which isn't good."

"My career has been language," Wangusa, once a Fulbright Scholar living in the USA, said. "Right from childhood, I was intrigued by language niceties and oddities…I remember listening to sermons and wondering what would compel a congregation to come… Today, I wonder what it is that gets an audience to want to experience the same play over and over again…"

Like most writers—me and my friend, Dr. Alan Johnson, come to mind—he doesn't like the promotional or publishing part that seems a necessity for authors in the 21st century. Fortunately, some of Wangusa's children own a publishing company to help with that piece now.

Wangusa, healthy except for some hypertension, writes day or night. Recently, he churned out four books in a year, including "one on myself, which was hard." He's got at least one more book in him.

"Could I do better?" he asked rhetorically. "I think I could. When will I stop? Not as long as I'm in love with it. My legacy? I don't think about it."

Same here.

(2022, Mukono, Uganda)

Timothy Wangusa at his home in Mukono

United States

UNITED STATES

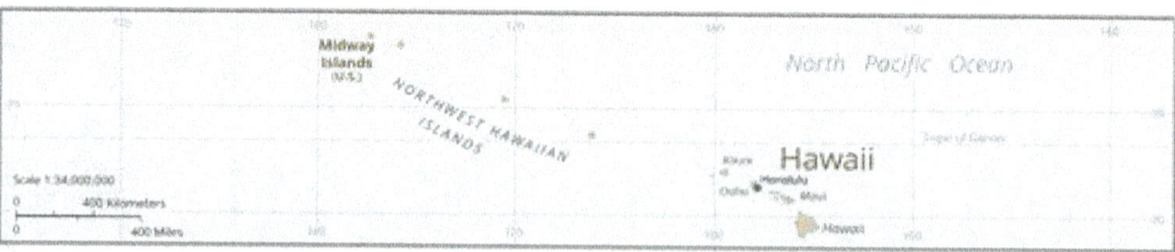

Map of the United States

"C" Word

On July 5, I had a "C" scare.

One doctor said it was "chronic," which is long lasting but not fatal. I understand chronic because I've lived quite well for two decades with a chronic, neurological disorder called familial tremors (also called dystonia). But my slightly shaking hands are not debilitating.

That same day, another medical person talked about what blood platelets do and used the word I won't type with a "maybe" disclaimer.

Another longer term applied to my body was thrombocytosis, which refers to a high count of platelets that can indicate a lot of things, including risk of clotting.

This was four days before my scheduled 11th trip to Uganda. I canceled the July 9 flight because, as my husband said, "We hope for the best while preparing for the worst."

As I sit at the Boston Airport this afternoon and wait for the first of two more re-scheduled flights to East Africa, I am pleased to report we think we got the best. On Tuesday, July 16, my oncologist reported this platelet thing appears normal. He shook my hand, wished me a good journey out of the USA and said he would see me again in October.

While psychologically and financially painful, these last two weeks have given me cause to reflect.

During a glass of wine with a friend, an afternoon lunch with my cousins and their new baby and my husband, I commented with humor about how much kinder people are when they think you're dying. Staff and caregivers in doctors' offices offered me water, touched my arm with warm eye contact, and complimented my wrinkled dress.

I recalled, too, how a woman shouted at my bicycle and me without knowing the freedom I felt just before that encounter, and how her words subsequently reduced me to tears as she accelerated angrily down the road.

(2018, Ohio)

Agree to Disagree

At 3 p.m. February 27, 2024, my friend, Steve Winegardner, and I were lamenting the murder of Georgia nursing student Laken Hope Riley. Just age 22, and while jogging, she was brutally killed by Jose Ibarra, 26, a Venezuelan unlawfully in the USA since 2022.

We are both saddened by the senseless February 22 attack and agree that Jose should never have been in the United States. He crossed the Mexican border near El Paso, Texas, and was released for further processing that never happened even in September 2023 when he was arrested for possible child endangerment and a car license violation in New York.

In a Zoom discussion with me in Ohio and Steve in Florida, we concurred that the American borders are too easily, illegally crossed. Too porous. We had a similar, virtual discussion in May 2021 when I was in Punta Gorda, Fla., and Steve was 60 miles away at the condo he lives in seven months a year in Naples, Fla.

The Homeland Security 2022 report (the latest available because federal data is always at least two years behind) shows just over 1 million persons, including 16,605 Venezuelans, with lawful permanent resident status in our country. In the same year, there were 2.6 million expulsions and non-citizen apprehensions with 206,000 from Venezuela.

Jose got through the cracks.

Steve and I sympathize with people trying to leave their native land for a better life, traveling with few possessions across bodies of water and rough terrain and paying the Mexican cartel to get to our southern borders.

I met a lovely Venezuelan family of five—escaping poverty (hourly minimum wage only enough to buy a gallon of water) and death threats from Venezuelan President Nicolás Maduro. They crossed legally and found a home in Ohio with the help of my church.

Steve finds the Mexicans (legal, he believes) who work on the courses where he plays golf to be "some of the hardest working people I've known."

We both understand that the USA was and is built by labor and ideas of people from many countries. But we don't want illegal immigrants or criminals here.

Steve and I agree on some things—like the border and that the 2024 USA Presidential election two main contenders, who are just under four years apart from late 70s to early 80s, should retire. They are too old for the stress of leading a country of more than 335 million people.

That said, Steve, a registered Republican, supports Donald Trump. As a lifelong Democrat, I support Joe Biden.

We respectfully disagree.

The Pew Research Center says only 1 in 5 people with differing political views believe that there can be some common ground.

Steve and I are in the 20%.

Among our common ground is that we both have degrees from The Ohio State University. We each had leadership positions in Ohio career-technical education. We like parties. One Christmas party, I remember my husband tossing Steve's middle child, a not-yet-age-two baby, Elizabeth (now 30), in the air.

Steve and I worked together for five years, lost touch and re-connected three years ago in my search to find calm conversation with someone politically polarized from me.

Biden, Steve says, has dementia and doesn't understand business. Trump, I say, has dementia, doesn't understand the government and says horrible things.

"I don't like the way he talks," Steve agreed about the former President. "But he says what he thinks, and he's full of energy."

Me: "Biden hit it out of the ball park with his (March 2024) State of the Union speech."

Steve: "It wasn't bad, but he read everything from a teleprompter."

"What do you care about?" I asked during our late February talk.

"Family, my health, golf and the country," he replied.

Steve has had a partner, Michelle, for more than a decade. Steve's two sons are 29 and 46. He has six grandchildren. He has had triple bypass surgery, both knees replaced and ankle surgery. He plays golf three times a week.

Trump, Steve says, cares about the country and is best to lead it.

I care about my health, dancing, my work in Uganda and United States democracy. In February, I'm recovering from a broken wrist.

Biden, I say, cares about America and is best to lead it over the next four years.

Among the Biden fumbles since Donald Trump left office in January 2021 are the Alaskan (Keystone XL) pipeline and the border wall that Steve says was 450 miles built with materials "bought and paid for" and then left unused to do more.

"The pipeline would have been more efficient than trucks going across Canada carrying fuel," Steve said. "The pipeline was to transport 380 million gallons a day to the area to be refined."

To me, the pipeline debate is over whether fossil fuels should be left in the ground in order to rein in greenhouse gas emissions and avoid damage from climate change

Steve looks at the oil that is trucked thousands of miles using hundreds of trucks.

"Which is harder on the environment?" he asks. "Hundreds of diesel trucks traveling thousands of miles a day to transport the oil while using a fossil fuel product for power or simply transporting it by pipe?"

Steve points to Trump's mid-2019 tariff threat to Mexico if that country didn't do something about the flood of Central America migrants into the States. He says we had 1.7 million migrant encounters (apprehensions for processing) under Trump compared to 7.3 million under Biden. The Pew Research Center verifies that the USA had a record number of encounters in December 2023.

"Biden wants more illegals here as a political rallying point in the 2024 presidential race," Steve says.

Not so, I say.

Steve believes the media, excepting Fox News, is part of the problem. I see Fox and CNN presenting biased information. We both watch News Nation.

As I write this on March 17, a Republican Facebook friend criticized my post of sympathy for a Gaza doctor suffering a broken hand by an Israeli soldier, assuming I'd forgotten the Oct. 7 Hamas attack. I had not and still haven't.

Broad stereotypes are seldom right.

At the same time, I texted a friend, Greg Farra, an ordained pastor, for advice on loving someone who supports a candidate (Donald Trump) that I consider immoral and incompetent.

Greg directed me to a recent sermon on YouTube. In it, he said, in part: "We all have Jesus as Lord…we don't see eye to eye…But if we start to despise people, we dehumanize people. We see them as enemies and not friends. When we look at them less than us and not worthy of God's love—to be mocked—we stop being graceful…"

Greg's message is that if we raise our voices in self-righteous indignation, three people leave the room—"the Father, the Son and the Holy Ghost."

Steve and I are Christians.

On February 29—two days after my last conversation with Steve, *The Washington Post* reported that violent crimes have fallen sharply during the Biden presidency. There is little evidence that immigrants, including undocumented ones, cause more crime than "home grown" citizens.

On March 18, Steve sent me a private Facebook message: "While illegals may not commit more crime, the point is that it (killing of Laken Hope Riley) is a crime that should never have happened because the person who committed it should never have been here in the first place."

Neither Steve nor I like that Jose was here to tragically take the life of a young woman he didn't know. On that we agree. Respectfully.

(2024, Ohio & Florida)

Boat Maker

Most of the 11.8 million registered watercraft in the United States come from the country's 4,000 manufacturers—not from the hands, the sweat and overall talent of an individual boat maker.

"Why would they want my boat?" Stevie Wilson, Ocracoke Island's only boat maker, asked. "Maybe because they took a fishing trip with me; they got to know me."

Or maybe the buyer of a vessel with Wilson's stamp knows that he or she is getting something uniquely made by a person who cares deeply about the product, its quality and the water it will operate upon.

Stevie, or "Captain Steve" as many have known him for three decades, is, in his own words, "a water man." Born here, or an "Ococker" as locals say, he is a master captain, master (scuba) diver, fisherman and a ship wreck historian of sorts.

Of the North Carolina Outer Banks estimated 3,000 sunken ships, often called the "graveyard of the Atlantic," Wilson says the ones he knows about are "non-grandiose rust buckets and piles of debris with sharks and turtles around them." He knows that most wrecks, naming a few like the *British Splendour* (British tanker torpedoed in April 1942) and the *Dixie Arrow* (American tanker torpedoed in March 1942), are 90 feet down.

On a blustery April day filled with gray skies and rain, Wilson works on his fifth boat and first skiff, which is best identified by its flat bottom, pointed bow and square stern. Inclement weather provides time from Wilson's other passions—Dream Girl Sport Fishing excursions and tending to his 400,000 oysters growing on a 10-acre, Pamlico Sound farm, a mile behind the island and near the campground.

While discussing his reason for making a boat and the process, he unapologetically points to the dust, wires and equipment surrounding his unfinished, 20-foot-long product inside a white tarped construction area on his Sunset Drive property.

"I grew up here on the water," he said. "I can't say why I'm infatuated with boats, but I have been since I was a child."

He credits his father, now deceased, and Ocracoke school teachers for his boat passion and skill. Less about academic learning and memorization, the informal and formal educators surrounding Wilson provided him with a push toward "critical thinking and problem-solving skills," he said. Such is how Wilson and his wife, Jennifer, a local postal clerk, today guide their children, ages 7 and 9, both inside their Back Road home and when away.

Wilson, whose titles include vice president of a Fish House Board that serves 19 full and part time fishermen, can't imagine a life outside of Ocracoke. Of his 53 years, only three—one as a high school exchange student in France and two at college (Elon University) he never finished—were off the island.

Creativity can be messy, time consuming, worthwhile and more.

His boat starts with an engineered mold from a traditional manufacturer.
The final step for the skiff is the motor. In between are the resin application, the battery
and its bay, bait tank, hatches, bumper rails, bilge pump, draining holes and more.
"The details inside that most don't think about are the most time consuming and
expensive," he said. "I'm the quality control…I'm here for every stage of the process."
With an assistant, Wilson could make a boat in two weeks. For this one and by himself,
"it's hundreds of hours" over a month or so. He is not driven by the money that could be
up to $40,000. Sight unseen, this Ocracoke skiff has "a few" interested buyers.

While Wilson plans on continuing his boating excursions, oyster farming and boat
making, he is aware that life can be fragile. Six years from this April 11, 2024, day, he was
recovering from a serious injury incurred when as he was fueling up at the marina where
he keeps his charter boat, his truck emergency break gave way, pinning him between the
dock and his vehicle.

"I'm in some pain every day," he said, pointing out the surgical scars on his back. "But I
like to be busy. It's important to keep moving."

While fishing, chartering and building, Wilson also is exploring a mentoring initiative.
Along with the Ocracoke school administration and Beaufort County Community
College, he's designing a course about boat construction and safety with the realization
that skills like boat fabricating are transferable to other careers.

"A student going into orthopedics would benefit," Wilson said.

(2024, North Carolina USA)

Boat maker Stevie Wilson

Breathe

"Is this reality? Am I dreaming? Breathing feels beautiful. Please let this feeling last…"
November 14, 2019, Facebook post by Robyn Petras.

When I met Robyn in early 2017, I secretly envied her raspy, sexy, Doris Day-movie star-like voice. After knowing her better, I told her so. She laughed and shared that what I was hearing was the sound of someone who struggled to breathe—someone with a disease called cystic fibrosis.

Until then, I hadn't thought much about breathing except to know that we all have to do it, or we die. My old junior high school science classes made me memorize that air goes into our lungs to remove carbon dioxide and add oxygen to the blood and cells for burning up what we eat and producing energy. But I don't sit around and think about it.

Robyn does. So do the more than 30,000 Americans who live with cystic fibrosis, or CF.

It's mostly about the mucus—a yellow or green and smelly secretion that we all get a little of when we have a cold virus. We get a small amount of yellow that we spit into a tissue or the sink. Robyn gets a lot of mostly green sputum that she captures in cups and jars and sometimes posts in pictures on her Facebook.

"I suppose some people are offended by seeing my spit photos," she says. "But it's my life every day, several times a day."

Whenever anything becomes personal, it's human nature to want to know more about that thing. So as Robyn and I became friends, worshiped together at David's United Church of Christ in Canal Winchester, and "liked" each other's Facebook posts, I read and listened. I saw words and photos related to mucus, breathing, exhaustion, sweat chloride results and, more commonly, messages about not holding grudges, being someone's sunshine, and letting go of hate and anger.

I got to know Robyn's mom, Becky, who makes great cookies and has a wonderful sense of humor; and Robyn's dad, Ed, who used to be involved in music before developing Parkinson's disease. I learned that Robyn's twin sister had died of CF 10 days after birth and that her older brother lost his life to AIDS. And I found out that CF is genetic and that Becky and Ed were carriers.

While most CF victims learn of their lung issues at age 3 or 4, Robyn was diagnosed with CF at age 8. For her, the childhood symptoms were less about breathing and more about eating. When you aren't getting enough air into your body and thick mucus clogs the pancreas, digestive enzymes are compromised. Food that can't be processed gets vomited up or comes out as feces that appear laced with orange oil. The body is malnourished.

At ages 10 and 11 and living in Mansfield, Ohio, she remembered a twice-daily routine—lying on a special postural drainage table before school while her mom thumped her chest to loosen mucus. At night and after a friend carried her home because she was too tired to walk, her dad did the tapping. Just to breathe.

Some of the mucus Robyn expelled so she can breathe

"I still remember the summer CF camps and all those tables lined up with kids spitting in cups while counselors did the loosening," Robyn said. "Not your typical kids' camp."

As she got older, Robyn used a mechanical device called the Vest to do her own mucus loosening. A black box that she wears in her pocket is attached to wires and tape to pump insulin every five minutes because scarring in her pancreas and elsewhere doesn't allow her body to do it naturally. Through IV medications and self-loosening, lung infection is held at bay. In her purse are capsules that she pops before each meal. Just to eat…and breathe.

An interest in Robyn got me doing a small amount of CF research on my own.

I learned that CF is one of eight major pulmonary diseases that include emphysema, which my late father had; asthma that a cousin has; and COPD, which a heavy-smoker friend has. I discovered that while procedures help with breathing, they also create scar tissue on the pancreas and lungs. I stumbled on words like "pseudomonas aeruginosa," learned a little about mycobacterial culture and the five strains of bacteria in mucus in our lungs, was enlightened by a CF infant sweat test, and concerned, but not surprised, that only 27 of 195 countries collect CF data. Uganda, the country where I live about half the year, has no data or treatment for CF.

Two days before Christmas at a local Panera Bread eatery, Robyn wondered out loud if the CF data is all that accurate when it comes to demographics that, according to the American-based, CF Foundation, has 90% of the CF victims recorded as Caucasian. We wondered if minorities and more economically disadvantaged people of all races and ethnicities might have CF but aren't documented because they don't access treatment at an accredited CF care center.

People with CF get married less often than the rest of the USA population, have babies less often, work fewer hours and years and are fortunate to live past age 30. Robyn is 53 with a great husband named Mike and an adopted daughter, Summer. With a bachelor's degree in education from Otterbein University, Robyn was forced by her health in her 20s to leave a Gahanna–Lincoln schools teaching job she loved.

"In the last 30 years, I have spent 38,000 hours doing lung treatments and I've produced and expelled over 225 gallons of mucus," she said. "But I've never been angry. God has always been at my side."

So back to Robyn's mid-November Facebook post, here's the good news she referenced: In October of 2019, the FDA approved a drug called Trikafta for 9 of 10 CF victims. Robyn started taking it in November.
While she had a setback with the flu, her lung capacity has greatly improved. Mucus is minimal.

On December 19, 2018, Robyn Petras of Lancaster, Ohio, posted this: "My sweat test showed a drop from 88 to 26 with anything over 60 in CF status…My lung function increased up to 69%…"

As 2020 starts, Robyn's nearly lifelong dream evolves. She is breathing.

(2019, Ohio)

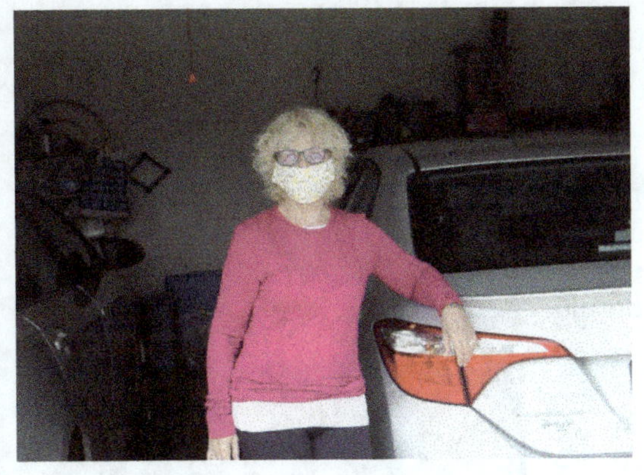

It's hard to put into words what COVID-19 means. Feeling healthy, it's easier to drop off home-baked pumpkin bread, send thinking-of-you cards, coordinate and participate in Zoom conversations, provide financial and face mask contributions and watch TV accounts of death. But as a lifelong writer, I write. This, then, is perhaps the best way I can give.

COVID Chronicles

In 2020, most of the world was hit with a pandemic called COVID-19, which is part of the coronavirus family that causes respiratory illness. Life as we knew it was shut down. These stories are a chronicle of 20 different times in nine months of the pandemic and through the lens of a woman living through it in the Midwest of the United States.

COVID-19 Journal Entry #1: March 16, 2020—Suicide

Somewhere among an unsuccessful trip to buy paper towels from empty shelves, putting down Ta-Nehisi Coates' page-turner *The Water Dancer* and acquiring a green Irish wig to stand outside my mom's window of her quarantined assisted living facility on St. Patrick's Day, my mind wandered to a pale pink dress.

Truth is that my thoughts about the dress re-surfaced during a delightful, surprise phone call on March 8—a full week before all Hell broke loose with physical distance restrictions and paper product shortages related to the coronavirus pandemic. I would have missed the 10:30 a.m. call had it not been for Uganda jet lag, the American Daylight Savings Time change and 3 a.m. insomnia that had me back in bed, oversleeping and missing church.

And I might have forgotten about the pink dress ... or whether it was blue.

While my detail about the color may be foggy and not verified by a 1960s black and white photo, the incidents surrounding the dress are clear.

In a Sunday morning phone conversation with Joe Dyser, a former high school English teacher—with words spilling as easy as they always did despite years and miles of distance—we recounted the mysteries, joys and growing pains of my teenage years. I remembered a boy named Hugh with a talent for pushing his shoulders back to look like angel wings, a girl named Beth who shared my passion for words, the start of a wrestling team as well as the sexual abuses, gender confusion and hushed pregnancies that nobody talked about.

I recounted my excitement as a freshman and being invited to the prom by a popular, athletic upperclassman. How I picked out that dress with my mother. How it cascaded beautifully and loose to the tops of my new shoes. How I smiled at it and me in the mirror.

And how older girls stole my joy to put me in my place on their turf or to keep me out. They told me that I had to cut the cloth off to my knees as a new "rule" they devised as the only way that younger girls could enter the dance. I said it didn't matter as I watched the cloth fall to the floor of a sewing shop, as I carried the lighter garment home and wore it, moving on the arm of this boy among the older girls who wore long, flowing dresses and—at me—condescending looks.

But the muffled tears in my pillow for many nights reminded me that how I was being treated did matter.

The female intimidation with labeling me what I was not, their demeaning glances and deriding laughter didn't stop with that one event. While I was popular by most definitions—a cheerleader, good student, and former Mayfair queen—I was a victim of bullying for several months.

I attempted to end my life.

The details of how aren't as important as what happened next—how I was put in a hospital for a week of sessions with electrodes, psychiatric interviews and clergy prayers designed to fix me—not the bullies. Clearly, I had to suck up whatever life was dealing me.

Luckily, I did; I am stronger for it.

Recently, the Ohio Suicide Prevention Foundation noted that for ages 14 to 25, suicide is the second leading cause of death. I have to think this would go down if we let others—especially youth trying to find their way—know how much we value them for who they are. And not try to fit them in a box or push them out of ours.

My former English teacher reminded me that I wasn't the only young person struggling to find their way back then. He saw the pain in the journals his students kept and that he read and graded.

"I often think," Mr. Dyser said in that phone call, "of what the world would have lost."

(Ironically, while writing this, journalism colleague Alan Johnson emailed me a clipping about Associated Press writing awards we received years ago. My prize was for a series on suicide.)

COVID-19 Journal Entry #2: April 9, 2020—Breathing

Deb Holm, my sister-in-law in Iowa, got me thinking more today about breathing.

Actually, a cystic fibrosis (CF) movie, *Five Feet Apart,* and an Ohio CF friend, Robyn, had me thinking about it but differently for the past few months. Truth be known, I thought more about inhaling roughly a year ago. It wasn't the inhaling kind that President Bill Clinton denied doing in 1992, but what happens when dust goes into your lungs.

"I want to write about dust," I said out loud and typed more than once in the past 12 months.

A Uganda Christian University science dean named Liz Kizito was polite but evasive. My 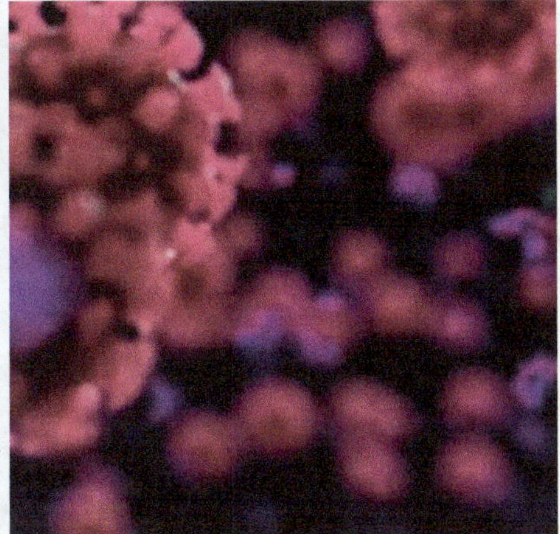 non-profit, Uganda-based organization boss, Mark Bartels (in Pennsylvania) was quietly supportive. And my Ugandan journalist friend, Douglas, was curious but skeptical.

Together, they accepted that constant construction, dirt roads and Uganda's dry season sends dust everywhere. We all learned to live with the fact that our lungs take a hit while residing, traveling and working in such grime. We don't think—or want to think— about the dead insects and other things going into our bodies from dust inhaled through our mouths and noses.

The World Health Organization (2018) estimates that 90% of us breathe polluted air. But not even close to 1% of the world's 7.5 billion people, including me, have conditions that cause us to think that much about breathing.

Until COVID-19: CO for corona, VI for virus, D for disease and 19 for 2019.

This deadly virus that started last November in China covered every continent except Antarctica in April 2020. It ultimately robs life by choking off breathing. Roughly 1 in 6 COVID positive people will have trouble breathing. Of those, .2% and 15% percent— depending on age—will die because they can't breathe. While I have none of the diabetic, cancer or pulmonary "pre-existing conditions", for my age range of 60 to 70, the death rate for COVID-positive people is 3.6%.

We're familiar with what happens with pneumonia and how small parts of the lungs struggle when inflammation blocks oxygen to the bloodstream and keeps carbon dioxide from being released. Since the 1940s, according to Mr. Sherwood, my high school biology teacher, we've been treating that with penicillin and other antibiotics.

The main difference between pneumonia and COVID-19 is that this new virus impacts larger parts or all of both lungs. If respirators don't do the trick to get the oxygen–carbon dioxide balance, all our other body parts stop working. Then, we take our last breath.

In short, on April 9, 2020, there is no coronavirus cure. The inability to breathe with COVID-19 has been compared to waterboarding, a form of interrogation torture also called "dry drowning."

Most of us take breathing for granted. Until maybe now.

When my Iowa sister-in-law posted a Facebook video this morning, I returned to my earlier thoughts about what we breathe in and out.

The Japan public broadcast video she shared is about droplets or, more accurately, infection droplets. This is the moisture expelled when we open our mouths to talk, sneeze, cough and just breathe. In the words of Kazuhiro Tateda, president of the Japanese Association for Infectious Diseases, these everyday droplets are the origin of COVID-19—beyond the bats that infected fish that infected people who bought and ate the fish from a dirty market in Wu-han, China, and started a pandemic.

When we talk, six feet apart is enough. When we cough or sneeze, droplets travel further and can float for 10 minutes in the air. The greater the airflow around us—open windows, being outside, etc.—the faster the droplets disperse.
The harder we breathe, the droplets become larger and travel further in what is known as "slipstream." A study out of Belgium and the Netherlands says for fast walking, we need to be 13 to 16 feet away to avoid contamination. For running or slow biking, it's 32 feet. When hard biking, keep a 65-foot distance.

I never liked science much. It didn't seem relevant to me. Now, it is.

Be healthy. Get your heart rate up. But be safe and practice distancing for a while.

And let's keep sharing to help each other.

COVID-19 Journal Entry #3: April 17, 2020—Hugging

Today, with 2.3 million coronavirus cases and 151,000 deaths worldwide, I address the simple act of hugging.

The last person I hugged was Jimmy Layton. Twice. First, we were in the office of the Mayor of Hebron, Ohio. That's Jimmy. Newly elected.

Then, we were outside in the sunshine, standing next to mom's open window of my car in the Hebron Municipal building parking lot.

We talked briefly. Me, mom, Jimmy. In 64-degree Fahrenheit sunshine. Interrupted only seconds by a long-haired, skinny kid who jumped from his dad's vehicle to go in and pay a traffic fine. Jimmy, a Lakewood High School classmate at least a foot taller than me, hugged me again before I got into my car, and he went back to his office to "spend some money."

That was 2 p.m. March 12, 2020.

Childhood friends, twins Joan and Jim Layton

That morning, I picked mom up at her Pickerington, Ohio, assisted living residence for an appointment with a doctor she's been seeing for some 20 years. We had lunch and an unplanned conversation with old friends at a place called Clays. We dipped grilled cheese sandwiches into cups of homemade potato soup. We licked scoops of chocolate iced cream with chunks of peanut butter. We went into a Dollar General store to buy packages of cheap cheese crackers, chips and popcorn.

We stopped to see a friend, Helen Artz, recovering at home from a fall that fractured her jaw.

Seeing Jimmy—a longtime friend with a twin sister, Joan, who lived in a house with a tree I jumped from and broke my arm at age 12—was our last stop before the 25-minute loop back to the place that mom has called home for four years.

"I want Jimmy to be the preacher at my funeral," Mom said.

Jubilantly and with me wearing a fun, green St. Patrick's Day hat, we made our way from the car to the outer door to a building that I knew well for its offices, activity room, library, cafeteria and 45 residences, including mom's. There and without a hug, mom was whisked away.

"You can't come in," said Kim, director of Abbington of Pickerington. "New rules."

Thus began my life controlled by COVID-19, the virus that by most accounts began on November 19, 2019, in a place called Wuhan, China. On the day of the first reported coronavirus case 7,000 miles away from Ohio—a day I didn't know about until three months later—I attended church in the morning and drank diet cola at a musical and auction fundraiser at The Pump House in the afternoon.

From November 19, 2019, to March 12, 2020, I celebrated Thanksgiving, Christmas, New Year's Eve, a wedding anniversary and my birthday. I traveled to teach in Uganda, Africa, and met and wrote about some members of that country's most indigenous tribe, the Ik.

At 6 p.m. Thursday, March 12, 2020, I met my husband at the Columbus airport. He was flying back early from a visit with his brother in France, where COVID-19 was rearing its head with a vengeance. We hesitated to hug. For a week, we slept in different parts of the house.

Now, on April 19, 2020, and in near isolation but healthy, Mike and I hug a lot.

I look forward to broader embracing.

COVID-19 Journal Entry #4: April 21, 2020—Nothing

Halfway to visiting the only county in Ohio with no COVID-19 cases, I remembered that I left my mask at home in the microwave oven.

Would Vinton County, namely the county seat of McArthur, let me in? Yes.

And the eight people I met in this least populous of Ohio's 88 counties weren't afraid of me—an outsider from a county with 102 identified coronavirus cases.

Two people in the Dollar General store, two in Mama Renie's tavern, three in Spring Street Sports and one sitting on steps next to a gas station were mildly interested that someone from Fairfield County would drive roughly an hour and a half to see Ohio's only virus-free zone. They relished a bit in their status. All agreed that the COVID-19 pandemic was real.

But fearful of my possible contamination? No.

On April 21, 2020, I convinced my husband to go with me to this least populous county in our state to breathe the air that might just be the most devoid of COVID droplets in the whole world. Okay, that's a stretch.

But I wanted to see some of what the media isn't covering in Ohio. A non-story can be a story.

So we headed out from our county, which has the 23rd highest number of COVID cases statewide, to the one and only place on the map of Ohio's 13,725 virus cases that has a zero. I wanted to experience nothing.

Past a wild turkey, a blue heron, several Trump/Pence signs, a mailbox proclaiming "Jesus is your hope," a creek and winding roads lined with trees and lots of American flags is Vinton County's center called McArthur. It's named for a long-dead Ohio governor and better known for a castle referenced in *The Rocky Horror Picture Show*.

While 22 of Vinton County's 13,000 residents have been tested and are COVID-19 free, and my conversations with eight people don't equate with valid or even credible research,

all but one of these people were skeptical of being zero.

The one—a large man with missing teeth—insisted Vinton County is protected by "the man upstairs who has his arm wrapped around us" and President Donald Trump.

Like most of us, the other seven wonder if enough of them and their neighbors have been COVID-19 tested to really know.

"We don't know," the 50-something clerk in Dollar General remarked while checking out my $1 each bags of crackers and chocolate and $4 bottle of wine. The man six feet behind me pushing a cart filled with bottled water smiled and said, "If we are (virus free), it's because there is nothing to do here but stay home."

Vinton County is mostly following stay-at-home rules of Ohio's Dr. Amy Acton and Governor Mike DeWine. McArthur's two restaurants have take-out only food. The biggest industry—a local explosives plant where an accident killed some employees 10 years ago—has moved from one shift to two for distancing. The downtown McArthur place making Vinton County virus-free status T-shirts calls itself essential.

Praying that the distinction of the "COVID-19 State Champions" shirts, like the one I purchased for $10 after sneaking into the shop, remains. And praying that the rest of Ohio and other states and people can move down to nothing as well. Zero is a good number.

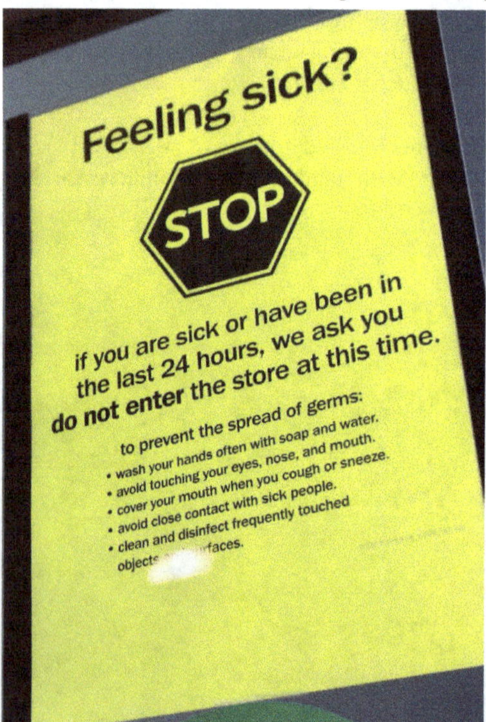

COVID-19 Journal Entry #5: May 4, 2020—Testing

On July 28, I vomited and shook so violently from chills that I couldn't control my fingers to send a "help" message on my keyboard; thereafter, I struggled to get warm with no appetite for four days. Six months later, in January 2020, my head throbbed, my nose was dripping, and I was sweating for two days. At 1:15 a.m. on March 17, body fluids were expelled from both ends for three hours, followed by five days of the worst headaches I've had in a lifetime, dizziness and no appetite.

Did I have COVID-19? I don't know.

On Monday, May 4, 2020—as we commemorate the 50th anniversary of the Ohio National Guard shooting nine protesters on the Kent State University campus—we still don't know exactly who fired the shots and why. And we don't know what is causing this dangerous strain of coronavirus or, for most of Ohio's 11.8 million people, if we had or have it.

The test—a swab inserted deep through your nostrils to reach cells where the nose and throat meet—isn't available to most of us. According to the Centers for Disease Control today, the United States has 97 public health labs offering the test. At least one of those and some private, slower and more expensive labs are doing it in Ohio.

Yesterday, I told my friend, Akena Luck, in Mukono, Uganda, that not even close to 1% of Ohioans have COVID as far as we know. But we don't. Here's some of why:

- Something called the COVID Tracking Project ranks my state 46th of 50 states when it comes to testing.
- As of today, only 1.3% of Ohio's population has been tested in two months with 13% of those, or 20,475 people, being positive.
- Supposedly, 1,800 Ohio contact tracers will be hired to determine who was exposed to the positive people, but as of today, there are only 680 doing that work.

What we do know is that the pandemic is real. For me, it's not just Ohio's daily press briefings that make it so.

An Ohio friend, Robyn, who went to a movie with me a week before my St. Patrick's Day illness, had it. She delightfully recovered and just donated 600 milliliters of her plasma to assist those still recovering.

Sarah and Manana, jamming from Uganda

As I type, a distant cousin is recovering in Iowa after contracting it during his emergency room work in California.

A 30-year-old daughter of a friend, working with COVID patients in Colorado, admits that her education and training did not prepare her for inadequate equipment and how to return cognition and physical abilities to virus victims. And it didn't prepare her for protesters targeting health care workers.

"It hits me in the gut," she said in a small group Zoom last night.

Today, a friend frustrated and anxious to get back to work, typed to me in an email: "I am not going to let this coronavirus take over 22 years of hard work building my clientele."

I try to "Be kind," as a Facebook piece rotating around now says. It says to be kind to people on both sides of wearing face-masks, social distancing, our national leadership and the urgency to return to work.

I get the work thing. I have been guilty more than once of going through a box of Kleenex while exposing co-workers to my germs. And I've been even guiltier of thinking sick people should suck it up with whatever fictitious illness they have and stop slacking at home.

But with this pandemic, what we don't know is more than what we do.

COVID-19 Journal Entry #6: May 12, 2020—Inconvenience

As much as I love dancing, I missed the Dougie 10 years ago.

In 2010, I was teaching public speaking to less-than-interested undergraduates at two different Ohio universities and spewing out boring government copy for the rest of my 80-hour workweek when everybody, including First Lady Michelle Obama, was doing it.

Today, thanks to COVID-19 and a Colgate Optic White Renewal Toothpaste TV commercial, I've got the Dougie (pronounced Dug-ee). I've got it because like many of the 327 million American citizens NOT among the 1.3 million confirmed cases of the coronavirus, I am healthy with more than usual time on my hands.

I'm not working in grocery stores or on the front line of the virus in hospitals. United States life for a two-month period of the pandemic for some of us put a halt on the fast-paced life, as we knew it.

For many, it has mostly been merely an inconvenience.

I binge watch Christina Applegate's *Dead to Me* on Netflix. I bake loaves of chocolate-chip pumpkin bread and deliver them to friends and neighbors. I conduct and engage in zoom conversations, prayer and even music time. I exercise and worship with YouTube videos. I press fingers against the glass to talk to mom, and wear a pink wig in a Mother's Day car parade. I do virtual interviews and exchanges related to my Uganda work, lamenting that I won't make a second trip there this year. I make more phone calls and send more cards and letters.

I take walks—lots of them—while dodging people without face-mask protection. Last week, I encountered a neighbor doing the same on his birthday; I sang to him across the street.

And I think—about teenagers rejoicing that there is no prom because they wouldn't have been invited, about large families crammed in isolation with not enough food on the table, about people living alone with no physical contact, about people hoarding toilet paper and about a President who cares more about money than lives.

The day after Mother's Day, the United States was closing in on 80,000 coronavirus deaths of 284,000 worldwide. Among these is the father of a Facebook friend. She mentioned his horrific two-week battle to live and the inability to have a memorial due to distancing.

As he took his final breath with no family at his side, other people were posting photos of moms surrounded by children and grandchildren not in isolation and of large groups laughing and drinking at graduation parties. I wondered if the smiles belonged to virus incubators.

At the same time, my husband and I sat, waiting among a snaking line of cars as workers wearing masks brought bags of take out orders from an Olive Garden restaurant in

Reynoldsburg. With pasta and soup in hand, we sighed, shook our heads and lamented poor management.

And our inconvenience.

Do the Dougie.

COVID-19 Journal Entry #7: May 19, 2020—Elderly

Last Friday afternoon, I did a short Zoom presentation on the ants that mom said were living under a plate in her room—namely a species called pissants that everybody, including mom, pronounces "piss ants." From the Internet, I had secured an image of an ant lifting his leg, although scientists say ants only poop and don't pee. I showed it via Zoom's "share screen."

Everybody laughed.

Mostly, the laughter was from 10 family members linking in from Ohio, Texas and South Carolina.

Mom and the other "residents," as they are called, were situated in wheel-and regular chairs placed on X marks six-feet-away around a room. Tired and hard of hearing, they squinted to see the brownish ant embedded in my PowerPoint and the images of us—their sons, daughters, grandchildren, brothers, sisters, nieces, nephews, friends. The residents stretch their necks to get closer to our words not always in sync with our mouths from their activities area TV.

At 2 p.m. every Friday for the past two months, this is how I connect to my almost 92-year-old mom who lives at a place called Abbington of Pickerington. At 2 p.m. on Wednesdays, I see her and wave during an on-line church service. A couple other days in the week, and after dropping off some of her favorite snacks, I lean outside mom's window for a look inside at her messy hair and a chat from my phone to hers. She sometimes mistakes her phone receiver for the TV remote and shouts over the *Judge Judy* volume that she can't figure out how to adjust. On non-Zoom and non-window days, we touched base from my home phone to hers.

This is how many Americans are connecting to the elderly during the COVID-19 pandemic. In Ohio, 30,000 of the over age 80 population are locked down in assisted living facilities in an attempt to keep the virus from them. Another 74,000 of the more

fragile elderly are housed in Ohio's skilled nursing sites. This vulnerable population makes up 22% of COVID deaths in Ohio.

The ignorant—including reporters that I otherwise respect at thrice-weekly press briefings—lump all these people into a category of "nursing homes" if, indeed, this older population is mentioned at all.

Let me state the data another way: One in five coronavirus deaths in Ohio are elderly living in skilled nursing and assisted living facilities. These aged 80 to 100 citizens are sleeping and eating in buildings that are located down the road from bars re-opened within the last week and populated with alcohol-consuming, potential, albeit asymptomatic, disease-spreading younger people.

I fluctuate among depression, anger, and helplessness. I am not alone.

As the Abbington Zoom Volunteer coordinator, I get emails and phone calls from shutout caregivers like me. What they say makes me feel less isolated.

"Mom seems to have mostly moved on—she doesn't ask about dad, and I think she is okay with him being in heaven…but I am struggling."

"I don't think I can handle talking to mom anymore. She's so negative—not like she used to be."

"Dad doesn't even have an outside window. I can't even see him. He doesn't understand why."

"Mom only understands and hears me when I touch her. And I can't touch her."

"I sometimes wonder what mental condition they will be in by the time we are able to be with them again. It's just all so sad and difficult."

And from the owner of a therapy dog: "Fiona (the dog) is unhappy because she's not working."

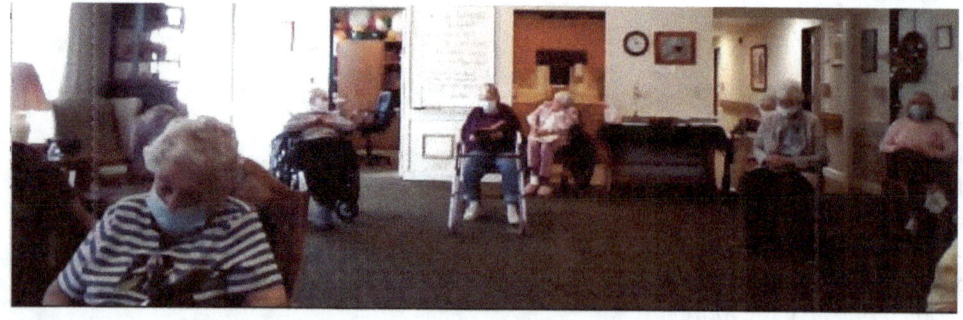

Inside and outside these facilities, and while appreciating the health care workers who are our hands and feet, the sons, daughters, grandchildren and friends struggle. And we worry.

Escapism is my coping strategy. I cope by keeping busy with both worthwhile and useless tasks.

The worthwhile—helping one student here and one in Uganda with dissertations, baking cookies for friends and neighbors, assigning and writing stories for an NGO Web site, conducting on-line conversations, taking walks with my husband, uplifting my mom.

The useless—ordering books I don't read, binge watching Netflix's *Dead to Me* and *After Life* and searching the Internet for something called orange wine... that I really want to drink.

I long for the balance of working with young people in Uganda while spending time in person here with mom and her friends. I long for lunch out and a mother–daughter hug like the last one we had on March 12.

Of the 12,000 species of ants world wide, 1,000 are in the USA. Mom had one of the 1,000—pissants—last week. They were on the table next to the chair where she naps more than usual and next to the window where I press my hands and watch while someone other than me eradicates the problem.

COVID-19 Journal Entry #8: May 28, 2020—Truth

My high school friend, Julie, thinks Trump is an idiot and immoral. But, she says, he's not as evil as Bill Gates who went over to Wuhan, China, to help create the coronavirus so he could develop a vaccine and make a lot of money. And all that isn't as disconcerting as the Black people who are rising up against the white people in South Africa and will eventually come to the United States and "wipe out the whites."

She spoke from my phone through my car's Bluetooth speaker. I called Julie (not her real name) after dropping off individually wrapped cheddar cheese sticks for my mother who I can't see at her isolated, elderly residence.

"Just checking in," I started. Heavy smoking, which Julie does, puts her at high risk for COVID-19.

She coughed. Then, she proceeded to explain what has caused the pandemic and what will ultimately eliminate the Caucasian race.

Julie isn't a bad person. She's a good human actually. She worked tirelessly for the government for 40 years, raised two wonderful now-adult children, and served as my designated sober driver on more than one occasion. The one and only time she was in an airplane, we flew to Chicago where together we listened to blues music and defended Obama in front of two other high school friends who detested him.

Julie, in 2020, is simply misinformed. In this technological age of open-season "news," she is among a growing number of people who not only gather information from unreliable sources but also believe it and share it with others. Julie puts her trust in YouTube, a 15-year-old video site with no editorial oversight, and some middle-eastern news channel I've never heard of. She thinks the *New York Times* is full of lies.

Disclaimer. I get a bit prickly about attacks on what has been coded "MSM," or Mainstream Media like the *NYT.* I spent half my career in journalism and the other half in communications, including the last 20 years teaching research and writing. I have two university degrees in these fields.

At that, I'm open to exposing myself to people like Julie who claim to know a "truth" that isn't mine.

The problem in 2020 is that non-credentialed, un-experienced journalists, scientists, doctors, nurses and researchers like my high school friend are too plentiful and vocal. These uninformed people are especially manipulative and manipulated in a U.S. Presidential election year. Plus, in the midst of a pandemic, these ex officio specialists are indirectly killing people by discrediting experts and making claims that the virus is a hoax.

One of the worst in the past week is a propaganda *Plandemic* video discrediting Dr. Anthony Fauci, director of the National Institute of Infectious Diseases, and crediting a study that has been debunked more than a half dozen times. As quickly as YouTube takes the video down, it pops back up.

One of the worst in the past year is an information campaign that demonizes Democrats like me as "baby killers."

In the old days, journalists learned and practiced the two-source rule. What this meant is that any rumor had to be verified by two sources, generally two credible people.

In today's world, "sources" are often merely services. Something on Twitter, a communication service, is repeated on Facebook, also merely a service.

In past times and now, we should ask about the source, why we should believe it, and if the information is current, complete, tested or vetted.

And in the age of accelerated confirmation bias—that is, the practice of looking only at something that confirms your existing beliefs or theories—few seem interested in using credible truth detector sites such as factcheck.org,

PolitiFact, Snopes or The Washington Post Fact Checker.

While no MSM is perfect, that nearly 100,000 Americans have died from COVID-19 as verified with their names, ages and cities in the May 24, 2020, *New York Times* is not a lie.

At age 17, hearing over the PA during first period Algebra that my friend, Julie, was in a car accident, I cried. When I heard she recovered a week later, I rejoiced. More than four decades later, driving in the rain, I listen to her voice.

Julie is a good human really. It is just that, like a growing number of people, she is tragically misinformed.

COVID-19 Journal Entry #9: June 4, 2020—Racism

The first time I saw a Black person I was five years old. I don't remember it, but I recall my father telling me about it. It was the late 1950s. We sat on the porch of our tiny house in the poor section of Buckeye Lake on an end-of-summer, still hot day—watching streams of cars go by with brown arms and faces dangling out. I asked if I could go and hang out with those kids.

"No, honey," Daddy replied. "You're not allowed. It's Colored Day at the park."

Years later, I learned, it wasn't me not being allowed. It was those Black kids and their parents.

African Americans were only permitted at the (Ohio, USA) Buckeye Lake Amusement Park one day each year. On that day, I was told, only chicken was sold because that's all Black people ate. They weren't allowed in the pool because it was "closed for maintenance"—every year and just on that day.

I graduated from high school with three images of darker-skinned people: 1) from my American-written history classes taught by coaches who exuded excitement about the next game over anything in the past; 2) one after-church family drive to see the corpse of a tuxedo-wearing, Black slave on display in southern Ohio; and 3) on that one day a year when some of Ohio's then 6% African American population came to the park where white people laughed, rode the coaster and bumper cars, swam in the pool, roller skated around an indoor rink and ate chicken, candy apples and caramel corn on all the other summer days.

If I hadn't gone to college and been exposed to multiple cultures and literature other than John Griffin's required *Black Like Me*, I might have remained locked in that narrow box. I say "might" because the only time I saw my less-educated, yet loving, church-going father cry was in 1963 when John F. Kennedy was assassinated.

"He was our best President," my dad, Frank Huston, said more than once before he lost his battle with cancer 23 years ago. "He loved all the people."

So, despite my Hebron/Buckeye Lake small-town upbringing and limited access to media telling me what was happening outside the 687 square miles of my native Licking County, Ohio, I knew that I wanted to be one of those people who loved "all" people. Martin Luther King Jr. carried the message of "love" over "hate."

Working two jobs to put myself through college while paying my rent and food bills was an excuse for not taking buses to demonstrate for justice or even to experience dating African Americans as my roommates did.

For four decades, I had lunch, studied and worked alongside some of the best and brightest people of all skin tones. We talked and strategized about how education and wealth could be equalized across race and poverty lines. Together, we lamented these inequities, and that Black people are arrested and imprisoned more than white people. We got angry, but then went on. I smugly thought being passed over for a position due to affirmative action was doing my part as was understanding the value of international students coming here on scholarships.

Too little too late, perhaps, 11 years ago and admittedly more out of curiosity at the onset than putting my Christian faith into action or reparation for my African brothers and sisters, I set out on a mission to teach and serve in Uganda, Africa. In a country where many five-year-olds are seeing in me their first white person, I am taught and served beyond what I give.

Former Buckeye Lake Amusement Park

At the same time, when back in Ohio, I went deep into white privilege curriculum thinking because I grew up poor that I wasn't ... but realizing that I am.

Fast forward to May and June of 2020.

In the midst of the COVID-19 pandemic, the United States rears its ugly head with African American discrimination that has been here since the 1600s. Likewise there is ongoing, lesser attention to the unfair treatment of Native Americans (my post from October 2019) by European Americans, documented as far back as 1492. Adults wrongly taught children like me that Italian Christopher Columbus "sailed the ocean blue" to create a better life for all. At that, he really only cared about himself and (white) Europeans.

On June 4, we have Ahmaud Arbery's blood on the hands of white vigilantes in Georgia and George Floyd's last breath taken by a cop in Minnesota while a white woman in New York engages in "murder by cop" language against an educated, Black man calmly suggesting that she control her dog.

In my anger, sorrow, embarrassment and yes, defense (not all of the 800,000 American cops are bad; women like me are discriminated against all the time; and injustice happens all over the world, right?), I'm trying to relate and do something about this mess.

Last week, I reached out to six people of color with an apology, my acknowledgment that I can't know how they feel and advice for what else I can do. Their responses ranged from "stay angry" to "talk to white people I can't reach" and "stop going to Uganda and fix the problems here." In a lengthy response, my friend Andrea consoled me with "I don't hold you accountable for the evil and vile things of this world." She added painfully, "My heart hurts…America has lost its moral compass."

Emmanuel Acho, former NFL linebacker and now ESPN analyst, on CBS *This Morning*, said Caucasian people shouldn't "feel bad," but, he advised, "keep educating yourself…I'm not saying your life hasn't been hard, but it hasn't been hard because of your skin color."

This then, is a small part of my story, written while virus-protection social distancing at home. I find hope in that so many young people—some who didn't vote when our latest President was elected—are engaged in demonstrations.

"What can I do?" I wrote in anguish last week to one of my daughters, Sarah, in Kampala.

"Write," she replied.

COVID-19 Journal Entry #10: June 11, 2020—Hunger

In an unplanned phone call this afternoon, a longtime Miami, Florida, friend named Ron said, "Remember, the hungry people are YOU."

821 million
people go to bed
hungry every day

- UN.org

I had been thinking for days about the word "hunger."
I was pretty sure that the topic for week nine of my COVID-19 journal was food—more specifically hunger, food security, malnutrition and starvation.

But me, hungry?

When we were growing up poor, and we had mayonnaise and bread that my dad teased was a "special treat," I wasn't hungry. As I grew older and forgot to eat or drink anything in the midst of a busy workday and felt faint, I called it low-blood sugar. Friends taunted me when all I had in the refrigerator of my single-woman-no-kids home was Coca-Cola and M&M candies, but I wasn't hungry.

Not me.

Hunger was what I saw in *National Geographic* magazine and later in person when visiting Ugandan villages where children had bulging, worm-filled bellies and elderly men showed protruding ribs. Hunger was the tearful story of one of my Uganda Christian University students who gratefully accepted a power bar while we worked together in the library. Her stepmother fed her scraps meant for dogs when her father was out of town.

When I asked one of my Ugandan daughters why her older sister married a man who mistreated her and that she didn't love, she explained simply that "she was hungry." Yesterday, a 30-something Ugandan father of two sent me a personal Facebook message describing hunger as "one of the most painful experiences…worse when you have dependents looking up to you." Another girl in Mukono said being without food goes beyond "the belly to your head …you sense hopelessness and that you're worth nothing." My friend, Dennis Wandera, now living in Iowa, recalled a Ugandan childhood "learning all day on an empty stomach" and "feeling like my insides are all crunched together."

Cars lined up for food in Florida

In my pajamas, eating sliced oranges and watching the morning news on Tuesday, I received an email from a Ugandan university colleague. Working without pay, she humbly writes that her "cupboard is empty." When her country shuts down and orders isolation, there is no transportation to food distribution centers if they exist at all.

So I'm pretty tuned into information about hunger that occurs in countries labeled as "developing." I'm a bit too smug about it, eating chocolate covered almonds and drinking iced tea as I type and research from the comfort of my front porch.

Arif Husain, the chief economist and director of research, assessment, and monitoring at the United Nations World Food Programme, says that 130 million of the world's 7.6 billion people are classified as "acutely" hungry mostly because of war and climate issues. He estimates the starving population could rise to 300 million because of COVID lockdowns. Two thirds of the world's malnourished are in Southern Asia and Sub-Saharan Africa.

But not in the USA, right?

Wrong.

Two friends, Mary and Kathy, speaking during a church Zoom chat last night, pointed to "food islands" and "food deserts." Ohio families living far from food sources and without transportation or jobs, don't have access. They worry about economically disadvantaged American children if there is a "snow day" on a Friday or Monday because some of these kids won't have food for three days instead of two. They worry about summers devoid not just of education but food.

As if racism with cops isn't bad enough, African Americans face hunger at a rate more than twice that of white, non-Hispanics. The 10 counties with the highest food insecurity rates in my nation are at least 60% African American in a country that is 12% to 14% Black. Seven of the 10 counties are in Mississippi.

This evening, my friend, Alex Taremwa, in Kampala, is writing to me about hunger. He describes it as "when someone throws away food because it is poorly cooked and someone else somewhere hasn't tasted bad food in days, even weeks…"

In his country and mine.

I know about wasted food. I've seen it. I've done it. During the coronavirus, American farmers dumped milk and euthanized chickens because there were fewer factories to process it and not as many open restaurants to serve it.

My friend, Ron Ishoy, in Miami is telling me over the phone about people "in nice cars like yours" lined up for food early each morning and in different locations. These are people who used to go to bars and buy expensive dinners. These are people of all colors not able to work and get food except for what somebody else loads into their trunks. The virus that rages and takes lives equalizes us all.

"Remember, the hungry people ARE you," he repeats.

Microphone drop.

(Sources: *New York Times*, *New Yorker*, *Miami Herald*, CBS, CNBC, Waste360, United Nations, friends in the United States and Uganda)

COVID-19 Journal Entry #11: June 17, 2020—Letter to Uganda

Dear Ugandan Family and Friends:

Greetings from my Canal Winchester, Ohio USA, home that I share with bushy-tailed squirrels, tiny striped chipmunks, furry moles, bandit-looking raccoons, rabbits, various species of birds, and an occasional mouse. These mostly rodent family animals share the outside. My husband, Mike, shares the inside.

I type this letter to you on the same laptop computer you see me with in Uganda. I sit cross-legged on a couch within a screened-in porch as my neighbor—a no-nonsense, gun owning, granddaughter-loving woman of my age—drives a green and yellow mower over her lawn that always looks better than ours.

Nicely manicured grass is important to Americans even in times of a raging pandemic and resurgence of racism.

These then—the topics of a deadly virus and Black Lives Matter—are mostly the reasons I write this correspondence to you as daily I see your Facebook posts about what's happening over here, and get your private Facebook messages and emails with questions of "how are you," "is this all true" and "when will you return." Nearly all of you have expressed concern for my safety, offered your prayers for my wellbeing and articulated a longing for me to come back on your soil.

Only one of you—a young East African woman trice rewarded with North American scholarships—has messaged me with a request "to divest your money from Uganda" and its "Black Africans" to "start being part of the solution to the problems" of "Black Americans." Her words diminishing my 11 years of contributions to your country are hurtful, but understandable in this United States climate where Black men are unjustly treated.

How I am is this: Angry about wrongful deaths of Black Americans, frustrated with USA national leadership that cares more about money than people, embarrassed about United States statutes and history books making heroes out of villains like the Christopher Columbus one in Ohio, saddened about our mounting numbers of COVID deaths, disappointed that I can't travel back to see you this year and depressed that I can't touch my isolated, 92-year-old mom.

I also am blessed. While a trip to the doctor last Friday determined I am slightly anemic (a condition common for 3 of 10 adults), I am otherwise healthy. I have a roof over my head and food in my cupboard. Once every week or so, my husband and I leave that roof to take a long hike and camp in a tent in the woods. We eat beef stew, roast marshmallows over an open fire and sing old songs.

I read. I Zoom (including one delightful music exchange with one of you). I bake chocolate chip cookies and pumpkin bread. I exercise, including yoga from a mat in the middle of a lake—albeit poorly—and water surfing on an electronic board (also dismal but an adventure). In collaboration with the Uganda Christian University Dean of the School of Research and Post-Graduate Studies, I'm creating my first on-line dissertation writing and research course. I'm engaged in getting my children's giraffe book that is now in Luganda and English translated into Spanish. I'm doing regular outside-the-window visits with mom and another virus-protected, isolated elderly woman.

I write—like this COVID-19 weekly journal entry #10—a letter to you. I reflect on what I have learned since the "official" word that coronavirus was here three months ago.

Things like:
Netflix likes me and knows me; it sends me emails, recommending shows for me several times a day. TV commercials about drugs to make you better have more negative health side effects than benefits. Bottle caps from my Raspberry Snapple Iced Tea are educational resources for learning; my latest one reads, "Plants, like humans, can run a fever if they are sick." Americans hoard toilet paper.

Things like:
The COVID virus is real. Right now, the USA has more than two million cases, which is higher than anywhere else in the world, including in your country. It's a horrible disease that leaves even survivors with damaged lungs. It will get worse as mostly young people ignore wearing masks and social distancing.

Things like:
Racism is real. The police killings of George Floyd (Minnesota), Breonna Taylor (Kentucky), and Ahmaud Arbery (Georgia) represent the tip of the iceberg. The civil rights movement ended when I was a teenager and resulted in forced school integration and affirmative action job hiring and college scholarships. At that, white peoples' resentment, disrespect and fear of Blacks persists with the greatest injustice and wrongful treatment from our law enforcement officers

Things like:
Protests are making a difference. We have more white people hand in hand with Black people this time. The looting and destruction of property take place, but peaceful movements are the norm. Some cops, mayors and governors support demonstrations.

Things like:
Poor white people living in the Appalachian Mountains of Ohio have "Make America Great Again—Trump" signs in their yards. Poor Black people live in cities and don't have yards.

I am seeking, as always, to know how to make my world and yours a more loving, compassionate place and to use the gifts God has given me to grow the next generation here and there. I'm watching. I'm listening. I'm praying. I'm assessing how in the midst of bad times, the best and worst evolve.

I hope it is safe for me to travel back to you in early 2021. I am grateful you are in my life.

So how are you? How is your family?

Be blessed.

Love, Patty

COVID-19 Journal Entry #12: June 22, 2020—Color

"Blue Lives Matter." I spoke into my phone and pressed "send."

"Blue is beautiful," Barbara shot back.

Yes, blue. From Canal Winchester, Ohio, and Punta Gorda, Florida—1,100 miles apart—we read *The Book Woman of Troublesome Creek*, a fact-based, fictional tale focused on a blue 19-year-old. Certainly, I thought, this information about people with light blue skin and darker blue lips and fingernails must be some sort of sensationalized tabloid fiction.

Through the story and our own individual Internet research, Barbara Cotner and I became aware of the poverty-stricken, shunned, blue-skinned people once living in the harshest of the Appalachian Mountain region near the Hazard, Kentucky, coal mines. I say "once" because it seems the last blue person died in 2013.

Starting in 1820 with an orphan who arrived in the USA from France, they all had methemoglobinemia, a condition that I can't pronounce but means they lacked an enzyme called diaphorase (that I'd never heard of). Their skin—that 20-square-foot body organ that holds everything else in for all of us—was blue. Their blood was chocolate brown. They were physically healthy.

I say "physically" because the psychological damage for having blue skin was significant. They had names, mostly ending in Fugate. People who called their own skin white reduced the identity of this enzyme-deficient group of people to "blues" or "bluet" or "colored" with ridicule and rules about what toilets they could sit upon and gatherings they could attend. A Fugate or Karason sneaking a window peak inside a dance hall or walking alone in the woods could be beaten, sexually assaulted, imprisoned and even killed.

For roughly 190 years and based on Caucasian judgments, blue lives didn't matter.

Not just in the COVID pandemic, Black Lives Matter environment of June 2020 USA, but everywhere and earlier in time, some can't or won't get beyond what they see. Various shades of white, brown, black and, yes, blue are among the many hues worn by the world's 7.5 billion people.

On the Uganda Christian University campus, one co-worker, Pauline Atwine, says she is "unapologetically dark…darker than my twin brother." There is a hurtful stigma, she says, from some lighter-skinned families who say that dark-skinned people don't practice good hygiene.

Thus, just like the Kentucky blue-skinned people who endured vomiting and headaches from drugs that changed their color to white, normally dark-skinned African girls bleach their melanin pigmentation, ignoring such side effects as fatigue, memory loss and kidney failure. According to the World Health Organization, as many as 4 of 10 Africans—many from Nigeria—will bleach their skin at some point.

The bleached color is not to be confused with that of an Albino. One in 17,000 people, mostly in sub-Saharan Africa, lack pigmentation to the point of having albinism with frequent eye problems. Some in the most ignorant of dark-skinned communities will kill an Albino out of a belief that their white hair and pink eyes have magical powers.

On the flip side, many Caucasians of all ages want to make their skin darker. In my 20s-early 30s and despite known dangerous side effects of skin cancer and early aging, I frequented ultraviolet radiation beds in winter and endured hours under the scorching sun in summer—just to add a deeper tan to my beige skin.

Most researchers believe that 1.5 million years ago, we were all black with lighter skin evolving as humans moved from Africa to climates with less sun. The dark skin got lighter over the years as it adapted to allow absorption of more Vitamin D. Today, the fairest skinned people are in Iceland, Ireland or Scotland while the darkest are in New Guinea, Mozambique and South Sudan.

Dennis, my Ugandan friend living in Iowa, sent me a photo of his baby daughter born to him and his white American wife the day before Father's Day.

"What color is she?" I typed, looking at a new, tiny human who seemed to be pink.

"One would think she's white without Black DNA," he replied. He laughed and surmised the newborn would "darken as she grows." Regardless of ethnicity, a baby's complexion is reddish purple for the first few days as the human circulation system mobilizes.

My friend, Barbara, says her skin is "speckled tan with a few freckles and age spots." Mine is much the same but so thick that nurses struggle to find veins when I give blood.

The Kentucky people with methemoglobinemia were led to believe being blue was their fault. They were told if they didn't marry so close to family—something allowed down to first cousins in a dozen USA states even today—that the blue tinge would dissolve in bloodlines.

The most famous United States "blue man" was known as "Papa Smurf"—a title I suppose we accept because our children love the comic character by the same name and one he earned from drinking a bogus health remedy that made him blue. Many believe he was the last blue person when he died seven years ago.

Last weekend and while taking a drumming aerobics class with 20 mostly Caucasian women, I couldn't help but notice that white is not white.

And I wondered how often we white people think about that.

COVID-19 Journal Entry #13: July 12, 2020—Death

Dignity Memorial, a place based in Houston, Texas, but with a reported 2,000 locations nationwide, wants me to die. At the very least, they want me to plan for it with a down payment.

They have been urging me—six times via email—to let them call me since this whole COVID thing began exploding in March in the United States. Like Netflix, which I have subscribed to for $8.99 a month since May just to watch that Christina Applegate series about death, they care.

"It feels good," I tell my husband, "to have so many people who care about me."

People I don't even know.

I'm reflecting on this over a glass of wine (poured from a bottle gifted by a Christian friend, Don, who makes it in his basement) after a day of attending a memorial service for a high school friend who DID die. Not from the virus, but from a heart attack.

Mike Nadolson—a gifted musician and lifelong friend—was memorialized for an hour on July 11 with stories and biblical scripture in a church in my hometown. I almost didn't go but was assured by his sister-in-law, Joyce, an even closer childhood friend, that everybody would be wearing masks.

They were.

If I didn't know we were in the midst of a pandemic, I would have thought I walked into a hospital intensive care unit instead of a place of worship.

My left-wing friend, Bob, was there with his white mask covering all but his red hair. My conspiracy-theory friend, Geri, and my Christian sister, Donna, were likewise masked. Jimmy, my classmate who is now mayor of the town where I grew up, spoke through his face covering into the microphone, telling a story about how he, Mike and two other classmates started their own basketball team in our senior year after some dustup with the coach.

"I wonder," I told my husband during our regular evening walk, "why somebody isn't making money teaching people how to talk and communicate wearing a mask."

In spite of the fact that nobody but me was wearing face coverings in a restaurant I visited after Saturday's memorial service, this mask thing is going to last for a while. In Ohio, if you're in a "red" county (which is mine—named Fairfield—so rated because of high numbers of virus-infected people), it's required. The memorial service was in an "orange" (not as bad as red) area of Licking County, but not "yellow," which is not without fear, but the best in our state.

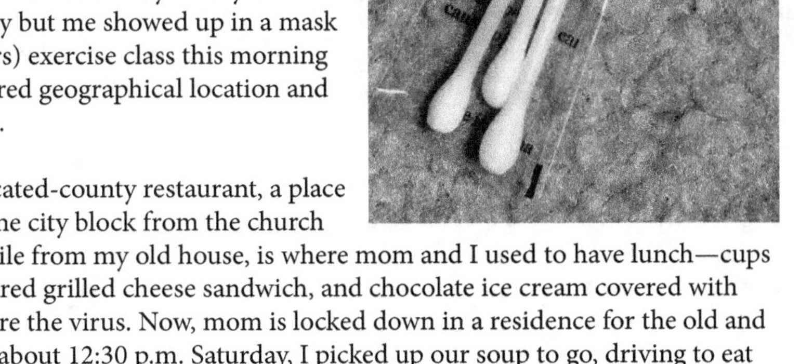

Our governor says, "Law is a teaching tool." Or something like that. More will obey if they are required. Yet, nobody but me showed up in a mask in an (albeit outdoors) exercise class this morning in a parking lot in a red geographical location and before the memorial.

The orange color-located-county restaurant, a place called Clays about one city block from the church service and a half-mile from my old house, is where mom and I used to have lunch—cups of potato soup, a shared grilled cheese sandwich, and chocolate ice cream covered with marshmallow—before the virus. Now, mom is locked down in a residence for the old and most vulnerable. At about 12:30 p.m. Saturday, I picked up our soup to go, driving to eat mine quietly alone on a bench near my father's 23-year-old gravesite in a nearby cemetery.

I got back in the car, and carried mom's portion in a white bag with a plastic spoon and crackers to drop off for her to eat alone in her room with TV's *Judge Judy* on high volume.

Last week and one day apart, mom and I had Q-tips stuck up our noses to determine if we are infected. She's not. Her results were immediate. While my blood antibody test from the week before came out negative (something that is roughly 70% accurate in determining if I had the virus and likely won't get it again), I'm still waiting for my snout result that still won't mean much.

For mom, her nose was checked in her isolated room that she calls a "dungeon." For me, it was my second try (first was overcrowded, so I didn't get in) from my Corolla. To get there, I drove 27 minutes behind a truck with a faded Tea Party bumper sticker and a better-looking photo of Trump's head before that guy turned off from the testing site. I rolled down my car window in Circleville, gave my dirty nose Q-tip in a tube to a nurse, and accelerated away.

While our nation's President and his followers think corona is a hoax, the USA's over 3 million cases and 134,000 deaths are very real. I don't yet personally know anyone who has died from it. But I do know about those infected with and without symptoms.

The data says 98% "recover." This means that if you don't die, you'll just have reduced lung and muscle capacity for a long time. Maybe for the rest of your life.

A 30-something man I spoke with on, ironically, America's July 4 Independence Day, proudly announced he recovered a month prior. Nearby, his mother whispered that he still has trouble walking.

Lesser-known and discussed are those who die from non-COVID causes during the pandemic as well as the impersonal grieving by survivors of virus and non-virus victims. In addition to Mike Nadolson, I grieve a friend, Clark, who fixed my screen door last fall, and a friend named Pat who was the realtor for mom's house.

In today's America, we can't touch and say goodbye to the dying because of strict hospital restrictions. We worry about catching something by going to funeral services. If we go, we can't embrace other mourners. We wipe away our tears. Alone.

In the early morning darkness and with a glass of Apple 2019 #114 in my right hand and an illuminated computer on my lap, I grieve for friends known and unknown, including Black lives lost.

And I find comfort in Netflix's *Dead to Me* and other selections "just for you." Plus, Dignity Memorial is just a credit card away.

COVID-19 Journal Entry #14: August 2, 2020—Shit
(NOTE: Content is offensive, but imperative.)

BREAKING NEWS: Shit DOES matter.

I'm not talking about the kind we all need to get together, but real legitimate feces. Plus urine. Plus flatulence.

When it comes to COVID or the SARS-CoV-2 that caused the coronavirus pandemic, our farts, poop and pee matter. At least, they do in Ohio.

A week or so ago, the Ohio Department of Health, several universities and the U.S. Environmental Protection Agency in Cincinnati started testing and analyzing raw sewage in my state to help with predicting hotspots. According to today's Columbus Dispatch, excrement from Columbus, Cleveland and Cincinnati are being analyzed even as I type.

The waste from human bowels and bladders have something called RNA (ribonucleic acid) that provides data similar to the DNA that medical people have collected from our throats and noses, and comparable to the blood that lab technicians have drawn from our arms for the past few months. Nose and throat DNA give an indication if we have the virus; blood results give some hint that you once had it and likely won't get it again.

My personal data is part of Ohio's anti-body (blood) and infection (nose) database. It won't, however, appear in the wastewater study because we have our own septic system.

Truth be known, I scooped (pun intended) the media and maybe even researchers on the value of posterior emission's correlation to the virus. I brought it up to my twice monthly Faithful Friends Christian group. Sitting distanced in our own chairs at the close of our evening meeting at Chestnut Ridge Park, we pondered, at my request, the possibilities of COVID danger from infected, excess gas from the intestinal tract.

Out loud to five "friends" once labeled, like me, church "rejects" for liberal views, I wondered about the coronavirus dangers of farts. To my husband only, I confessed my sin of judgment that those who do it more (or louder) than others are perhaps a greater contagion threat. Perhaps, I said, those who exceed what medical experts quote as the maximum of 25 a day for a healthy person should be penalized.

At that, one of our Christian members scooped me by providing research on how possibly contaminated droplets can escape from the toilet if the lid isn't secured before you flush. This is little harm if the discarded matter is your own, but what if it is another person's or another's urethra discharge lingers in the air as you take your turn at the bowl?

One study involving mice validates this danger. Rodents inhaled flushed pneumonia from their cages held above the toilet; a quarter were infected.

As of last week, the Centers for Disease Control and Prevention says it is "unclear whether the virus found in feces may be capable of causing COVID-19," and "there has not been any confirmed report of the virus spreading from feces to a person."

At that, play it safe: Use your own toilet or a tree. Fart into your elbow. Remove your posterior covering (no mask debate here) only when absolutely necessary.

And by all means, if you smell something, do something.

(Sources, with some re-quoting other sources, are the *Columbus Dispatch, Gastroenterology Journal, Washington Post, BBC News, Forbes, Lancet Journal, Physics of Fluid journal*, Australian Broadcasting Corporation, *Journal of Physiology, USA Today*)

COVID-19 Journal Entry #15: September 28, 2020—Essential

Today, it was bittersweet being able to actually touch mom after 200 days of phone calls and yelling through masks and screens at her assisted living site. Bitter realizing the toll that lack of loving family contact has had on her. Sweet to be with her and have a conversation she mostly understood in spite of her diminished hearing and cognition.

Mom and I were restricted (i.e. Ohio COVID regulations for elderly in congregate settings) to a pick up and one-stop to mom's doctor. En-route there and back and from the car, we got dairy queen milkshakes and called two of mom's old friends. The voices of Betty Milligan and Helen Artz from my Bluetooth speakers were, mom said, "just like they were sitting in the back seat."

Mom is 92. Her world is smaller without me in it. And, most days, with frequent naps and *Judge Judy* blaring from her TV, she seems to be adjusting to the size. Better than her daughter.

While Mom has been well protected from the physical ravages of the coronavirus and her bodily needs are met by aides and nurses better equipped for that than me, the past six months' lack of family/friend contact has taken a toll on her, on the elderly congregate housing workers and on sons, daughters, grandchildren, nieces, nephews and friends on the outside looking in.

We are all essential but only those inside get the label.

COVID-19 Journal Entry #16: October 18, 2020—Healthcare

If I lived in Sierra Leone, I would be dead right now. So would my mother.

This is one of many fleeting thoughts during the nearly nine days I was at the Mt. Carmel East Hospital bedside of my ailing, 92-year-old mom. Most of the time involved documenting conversations and monitoring treatment with doctors, surgeons, nurses, therapists and aides while enticing mom to eat and drink to further heal her bladder that had a cancerous tumor removed and kidneys that had a stone. There was much fluffing of pillows, raising and lowering the bed, massaging feet and responding to questions about people long gone who mom thinks are still alive.

Mom readily recited her June 7, 1928, birth date for medical practitioners checking her cognition. But other details such as if she understood she was in a hospital and the current year in which we live were fuzzy. At times, she told us that Reagan or Bush was President. In clearer moments, she said the leader of our country is "that man I don't like."

Sierra Leone, a West African country that I've never visited, ranks the lowest, or 191st of 191 countries when it comes to health care. Uganda, which is my second home, is 149th, or the 42nd worst globally. The World Health Organization 2018 statistics show the United States at 27th from the top, but COVID-19 no doubt has caused that ranking to shift.

Regardless of diminished health care data because of the pandemic, the American College of Surgeons says the average USA citizen will have nine surgical procedures in a lifetime. In Sierra Leone, there are 22 physicians for every one million people. In the United States, 1 million of the country's 328 million people are doctors. Do the math. If I grew up in much of Africa, including Uganda, my thrice-broken right arm wouldn't be healed and my ruptured appendix at age 12 would have ended my life.

Except for two baby deliveries, mom didn't start her journey to hospital care until age 80 with one broken bone, followed by her failing eyes, kidneys, colon and bladder. While these surgical procedures improve the physical body, they take a toll on the aging brain. This time (Oct. 9–17), she is worried about her brother, Bob, who died years ago; feels guilty that she missed her mother's funeral, even more years ago when she was actually there; and wants out of wherever she is to live in her house that has long ago been sold to new residents.

The cognition toll is worsened during hospital COVID restrictions that allow only one family member to visit. The deteriorated brain function of the elderly, including my mother, is overlooked by residential facilities such as where mom has an apartment and hospitals that forbid daughters, sons, grandchildren and even spouses to touch the older person out of fear of virus transmission to harm the physical body. If an outbreak occurs, more will die and the facilities will lose money.

The hospital regulations allowed me to enter only once a day, required me to remain in mom's room the entire time, and insisted that I wear a mask without touching—the latter a rule I broke as I lowered my mask to connect via mom's one ear that is not hearing impaired, combed her hair, brought a straw to her lips and kissed her forehead. Health care workers looked the other way.

On Saturday, Oct. 17, mom, who tested negative twice for COVID in nine hospital days, went into a rehabilitation facility. She was wheeled through glass doors while her belongings were sprayed with disinfectant. She is quarantined with only window visits for 14 days. The people inside are caring and working to help mom regain her mobility so that she might go back to her assisted living apartment. At that, the aides are not relatives.

Into her phone today, mom cried and begged for me and other family to come inside. I repeat the coronavirus guidelines that forbid it.

The average lifespan in Sierra Leone is 54 years. In Uganda, the life expectancy is 62.5. In the United States, it's 78.5 years.

In a Thursday morning Zoom conversation, my Mukono, Ugandan friend, Dr. Miriam Mutabazi, consoled me as I wondered out loud about the quality of life as technology enables Americans to live longer. I complained about my exhaustion—my own caregiver fatigue. A medical doctor herself, Miriam lost her 87-year-old mother over the summer. She asked me to remember how my mother took care of me, including when I was age two and kept asking the same questions repeatedly.

"It's your turn," she said.

COVID-19 Journal Entry #17: October 31, 2020—The Heart

In the midst of my friend, Alex, messaging me from a taxi en-route to Mbarara; a too-close-for-COVID woman, half-masked, telling me how her husband physically abuses her; and an HGTV show about rich people spending money to get bigger, more expensive homes; Dr. Nahush Mokadam saved my husband's life.

In a small room off the fourth floor surgical waiting area of The Ohio State University (OSU) Richard M. Ross Heart Hospital shortly after 12 Noon on Friday, the cardiac surgeon gave me the exhilarating news. Mike was on a respirator but recovering nicely from a five-hour process to ease a cardiovascular disease we didn't know he had until five days ago.

The turn of events since Tuesday shook me to the core.

On October 27, we drove together in the dark of 5 a.m. for an outpatient heart catheterization and stent designed to open an artery to Mike's heart. In the same room where Dr. Mokadam delivered the good news three days later, Dr. Ernest Mazzaferri gave me the bad news. The arteries were too blocked for a quick wire-mesh tube fix. To save my husband's life, they would need to open his chest.

In short, Mike's heart was working too hard because arteries supplying blood to the four chambers were partially or fully blocked. Two arteries not needed as much elsewhere would be repositioned. Those arteries would be the ones that supplied blood to chest muscles. They would not come from my husband's arms to better protect his passion and skill with the guitar and piano.

The Oct. 30 double by-pass, open-heart surgery was done without a heart–lung machine. Led by an Asian–Indian heart specialist, Mike's team of healthcare professionals made the "off-pump" decision following multiple assessments of data on his heart, lungs, arteries, brain and his history, including that he had a stroke when I was in Uganda in 2011.

In this last week of October and driving back and forth daily to a campus best known for OSU Buckeyes football, I can't remember when I cried so hard, prayed so often and loved so deeply. A world without my best friend and life partner would not be a world worth living.

"If I didn't have you, it would be like two feet with one shoe," Mike said through his pain and from the intensive care unit today.

We reminded each other that Oct. 31, 2020, is the 30th anniversary of the day we met. It was a Halloween party at a small bar called Hey Hey. We shared sauerkraut balls and that we had no intention of a permanent, serious relationship.

Happy anniversary, Michael Bishop Holm

COVID-19 Journal Entry #18: November 26, 2020— Indigenous

On the morning of the day before Thanksgiving in a year (2020) that has pretty much sucked for most people in the United States, I took a delightful walk in the woods in 45-Fahrenheit rain with some friends. Masked up. On this Thanksgiving Day and for my Wednesday Chestnut Ridge exercise buddies over the past six months, namely Rhonda, Lori, Bonnie, Dave, Jan and Max, I am grateful.

I am grateful for Pam Jarvis and her calmly spoken four words—"You are not alone"— as I drove home from the hospital, sobbing into the phone and my steering wheel on October 27. Within the hour, she had assembled a team of women to not only pray for my husband's surgical success and recovery but to bring food and to lend and deliver a post-surgery sleeping chair to the house. For Pam, Kathy (2 of them), Liz, Linda, Judy, Donna and Neva, I am grateful.

As I angrily pushed the mounting autumn leaves around our yard and wondered how I would get them out of the house gutters before Mike came home, Sandy and Shell Scott pulled up and finished the job. For them, I am grateful.

For the skillful Ohio State University heart surgeon and many health care workers, including the nurse who gave us "just a few more minutes" to hold each other tight in a tiny hospital bed before Mike was wheeled into surgery, I am grateful.

For the conversation with Audrey as alone I sat outside the operating room for an excruciating five hours...

For Brenda who prayed with me before I exited my car in the OSU hospital parking garage... For two couples who dropped off flowers that awaited me at an otherwise empty house as I drove home in the dark and emotionally drained from the hospital...For Cindy and Jill leading free, dance-drumming classes that allow my escape and stave off depression...

For a church friend, Linda, who picked up groceries when Mike and I couldn't leave the house...For a neighbor, Sue, who kept asking what she could do, "anything at all," she said...For a childhood friend, Christy, who I hadn't seen for decades but pulled into the driveway with pizza comfort food on a Saturday night...For two family members who had fruit delivered...For Zoom friends who prayed and asked not only how Mike was doing, but cared about me...For Tom and Dave, who sat on our porch during Mike's two weeks of needing 24/7 attention to allow me a fresh air break...

For Joseph, Elizabeth, Mary, Sarah, Frank, Douglas, Alex, Eleanor, Akena and so many others in Uganda who not only said they were praying, but actually were…

For the many prayers, cards and messages from Mark, Peggy, Anne, Barbara, Penny, Trisha, Mike, Bob, Val, Gennai, Josh, Adam, Dan, Deb, Rose, Chris, Charlie, Robyn, Becky, James, Erin, Tim, Kim, Alicia, Paul and many others in person, on the phone and through Facebook, I am grateful.

Older and wiser about the American Thanksgiving Day, I'm not too crazy about celebrating the arrival of Europeans who three centuries ago shared a meal of deer and duck (not turkey) with Native Americans who were belittled for their culture, killed and robbed of their land. Both Columbus Day in October and Thanksgiving Day in November should be honoring America's indigenous people who continue to suffer injustice and discrimination.

And it continues to pain me that the COVID pandemic has relegated me to shouting in a phone and seeing my aging mom through a screen while a facility czar reminds me that I didn't have an appointment to be a daughter this day.

Yes, there is much to be thankful for.

"This year has shown us just how nasty people are," my friend, Sandy, recently said.

To which I replied, "But it also has shown us how good they can be."

Thank you, everybody.

COVID-19 Journal Entry #19: December 17, 2020—Reality

The last words Dave Cyphert said to me were about our sticky front porch door.

"I'll come back and fix that for you," he said, exiting with a necessary jerk to that entrance after a 50-minute, fully masked and distanced visit with my husband, Mike, who, like Dave, had open-heart surgery but more recent than Dave's.

That was November 14. Thirty-three days later—on December 17, Dave Cyphert died from COVID-19.

Dave Cyphert was one of four men that Mike jokingly called "babysitters" as they came to allow me a solo, fresh air walk during the critical post-surgery weeks that Mike couldn't be alone. I'm not sure what Dave and Mike spoke about without me, but the three of us talked about how Mike and I would watch Cyphert's dog when they took a much-needed vacation.

"Thanks for stopping by," I texted at 2 p.m. Saturday, Nov. 14, 2020.

"Any time," Dave texted back.

Even with my reporter hat on, the where, who and how of the virus that entered and never left our good friend's body (but not that of me, my husband or Dave's wife) isn't as significant as the now of him being gone.

When someone good is gone, you try your best to remember the last physical connection.

For me, I normally connected to Dave through Anne Darling Cyphert, who I knew longer as a journalism colleague. That professional connection moved to friendship during a fundraiser maybe 10 years ago as I placed the highest bid for a pool party at the Cyphert's home. Dave was this amazing host alongside Anne. Seamlessly, they knew how to work a crowd. They knew how to make each guest feel welcome and special. Easily from that time on, my husband and I fit into Cyphert's always-growing circle of friends.

Dave Cyphert, a victim of COVID

Most recently, the Cypherts built a party barn—a lot with Dave's hands—to better accommodate the family they adored and friends they loved.

We had a decade of laughter, collaboration to help others and, on occasion, tears. After Dave's heart surgery, I visited Cyphert's home with my Ugandan daughter, Sarah. On that day, I massaged Dave's feet and, at his feet, Sarah and I prayed for his continued health. We joked and got serious that among all our partying friends, we (me, Mike, Sarah, Anne, Dave) were the believers in Christ.

One other unforgettable moment with Dave was when sipping wine at the Canal Winchester blues festival. In the midst of music and chatter, Dave and I simultaneously noticed an obese man stumble from the back of a sausage food cart. We smiled at the irony as an even larger woman, cigarette dangling, emerged behind him.

"It just got better," Dave said as we clicked glasses.

Anne was one of the first to reach out when Mike had open-heart surgery in late October. In one of those early conversations about how she and Dave could help, Dave took the phone from Anne and reminded me to take care of myself while I was tending to Mike. He lamented, he said, that Anne didn't do enough for herself after his by-pass surgery.

Around Thanksgiving 2020, Anne alerted us that Dave had COVID. He was hospitalized—on and off oxygen for weeks. Hundreds of prayers, including mine, were seeking more time. Anne was doing her best to keep it together. She prayed from her car in the Fairfield Medical Center parking lot and, when allowed, behind a glass where Dave struggled to breathe in an Intensive Care Unit. In Dave's final days, they held hands at his bedside.

"Sometime this spring when Anne and I go away, maybe you could watch our dog," Dave said on Nov. 14. We were looking forward to that.

Several times each day since Dave's diagnosis, I scoured Anne's Facebook page in hopes of good news. I woke up thinking about her. She was the last person I thought about before closing my eyes each night. I felt anger for the Cypherts and all of us with each mask less, COVID denier I encountered.

The pandemic won't allow me to embrace my friend, Anne, in person or even honor Dave in a way he and his family deserve. With a virtual hug, I echo Dave's words: "Take care of yourself."

COVID-19 Journal Entry #20: December 21, 2020—Survival

With large snowflakes descending on my car windshield from a spot in a Columbus, Ohio, medical center parking lot, I read about my friend, Olum Douglas, and how at age 11, he was captured by an African terrorist group called the Lord's Resistance Army (LRA). In December 2020, Douglas, now age 34, is a first-time author of *The Captive: My 204 days with the LRA rebels.*

The stories of abduction, murder and sex slavery of 30,000 children since the LRA's start in 1987 are many. I know something about the LRA and three other main African-based terrorist groups—Al-Shabab, Al Qaeda and Boko Haram. The main difference with this story, which is published in e-version and paperback on Amazon and is every bit as compelling as the other stories, is that I know Douglas personally. And I know every bit of his story about his time as a child soldier is true.

I ate chicken and vegetables with his wife and children, ages 4 and 7, at their humble home in the village of Mukono, Uganda. I've mentored him as a journalist, reading and editing his stories about life at Uganda Christian University, where I have consulted and taught since 2012. Douglas has been a main contributor for the UCU Partners organization, based in Pennsylvania. We have shared laughter, political opinions and frustrations with life. On occasion, we agree to disagree.

I knew Douglas was working on his book before we met. On pieces of paper since 2011, he remembered and wrote while, in his words, "tears endlessly flowed out, dripping down." As he shared some of his draft manuscript, my first question was always about how he would feel being known for the indignities he suffered. Did he want to keep remembering that horrible time over and over again as an author?

"Yes," he repeated. He is on a mission to bring attention and elevate change about civil rights violations.

So it was in the darkness on April 4, 1998, that the LRA kicked open the door to where Olum Douglas slept in Gulu, Uganda, and brutally forced him and other children to become followers. I had been to Gulu as recent as January 2020. I knew the area was  surrounded by dense bush.

As the snow pounded on my car, waiting on my husband who had a medical appointment inside in mid-December, I thought about the heat of Gulu—7,400 miles away—as well as the terrain as I turned the pages of Douglas' book. I knew that Gulu was 468 kilometers (291 miles) away from what is now called South Sudan. Some say that Joseph Kony, the ringleader of the LRA, hides out in that region just across the Ugandan border still today.

Without my frame of reference, however, I saw how my author friend enabled even the most naïve about East Africa and terrorism to visualize and agonize with the LRA's kidnapped boys and girls. With captivating detail, Olum Douglas allows the reader to see him as a boy, hungry and wearing rain-drenched clothes, walking with bleeding, blistered bare feet and carrying on his small back the heavy supplies stolen from huts. He feared death for faltering.

Brainwashing starts on page 17 as the LRA rebels convince their abductees that they will help with a mission to save the Acholi people from Uganda President Yoweri Museveni's alleged plan to wipe them out. To do this, the LRA must kill and steal from people and abduct more children. Those too weak or trying to escape from this mission as called by "the Lord" will face death.

Throughout the book's 120 pages of 204 days in captivity, Douglas describes how he and the other children, mostly boys, are slapped, beaten, forced to sleep in the rain and deprived of food to reinforce their submission. The two most heart-wrenching parts of the story are how Douglas witnessed the decapitation of two girls and how he participated in killing a 40-year-old man.

I finished the book on that snowy December Ohio afternoon. Two days later, I interviewed Douglas via Zoom. My first question was about his feelings about being party to that brutal murder.

"It was survival," he said. "I knew many of the children captive with me, but I didn't know the man. If I could find his family today, I would ask for forgiveness."

My second question was about Kony.

"I never met him," Douglas said. "He's in his 60s, I believe, and still alive, probably living in the Central African Republic."

My third question was about anger. By his own admission in the book's conclusion that follows the account of his escape, Douglas got into fights with other children.

"When I get annoyed, I don't hit people anymore," he said. "I just get quiet."

In a Zoom discussion on a Saturday morning (for me in Ohio) and afternoon (for Douglas in Uganda), the author shared that he didn't write the book just for himself. For him, "When the sun comes out, and the plant has germinated, there is nowhere to run," he said.

For others who are still oppressed, there is "much education and many stories to be told," he added.

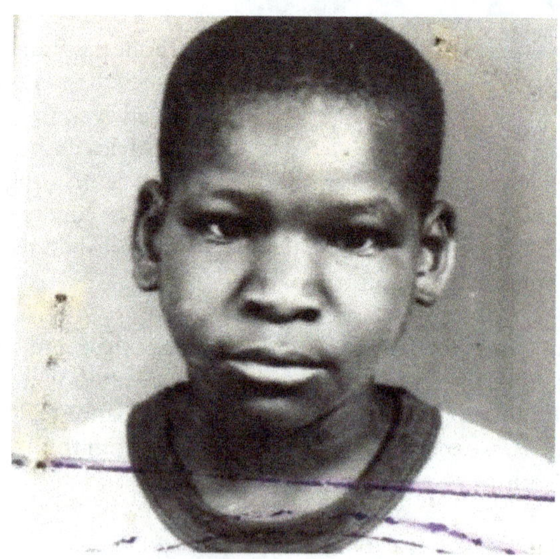

Douglas Olum as a child

Cross Cultural

Kasule Kibirige believes in Jesus.

A guy he met on November 15, 2023, believes in UFOs (Unidentified Foreign Objects) and Sasquatch, aka"Bigfoot."

After a quick handshake, the man, donned in a baseball cap embroidered with the Sasquatch name, asserted that USA government data verifies the existence of alien life (i.e., UFOs) and many videos from average people authenticate that a large hairy creature is walking his big feet around North American forests. Kasule listened without prejudice during the five minutes as the man in the cap espoused his views that were new to Kasule and what some more familiar folks consider fictitious and as the sun was setting outside the Sunset Inn in Cedarville.

Listening is what social workers, especially Christian ones, do.

"Social work has a value base similar to Christian faith," says Kasule, head of undergraduate studies in the School of Social Sciences at Uganda Christian University (UCU), since 2016. "Social work is a program of study that includes accepting others without judging them."

But the profession is much more. The Webster dictionary defines social work as a field with "activities or methods concretely concerned with providing social services and especially with the investigation, treatment and material aid of the economically, physically, mentally or socially disadvantaged."

The brief, unexpected encounter with the Sasquatch–UFO follower—who also might have shared his religious beliefs had he remained longer—provided an example of implementing social work skills outside the confines of a dictionary or textbook, according to Kasule, who learned of these topics for the first time in his three-week, November trip to the USA. It was his first visit to Ohio and his second trip to the United States. While waiting to have dinner with faculty at Cedarville University, he shared other illustrations, including his early recognition of how listening and observing make a difference in the field of social work.

"Most students come to universities directly from high school," Kasule said. "I didn't."

Without sufficient funds, or academic marks to garner a government scholarship grant, Kasule first enrolled in vocational training. Using his knowledge and skill in the trades, he was employed as a welder in a small-scale steel fabrication factory that made machines like the ones used in the agro-processing industry. He later saw social workers in action when working for a child-focused non-profit organization in Kampala, Uganda.

"Choosing social work was largely inspired by that life-changing opportunity of working with a non-governmental organization that helped disadvantaged, urban out-of-school children," Kasule said.

From 2001 to 2007, Kasule received his bachelor's and master's degrees in social work from the University of Botswana in Africa. Since 2008, he's been a social work faculty member at UCU and has participated in numerous community engagements that include both fieldwork supervision of students' practicums (jargon) and community service as well as researching and leading social work curriculum at UCU. In addition to these roles, he has collaborated with Lisa Tokpa of UCU's Uganda Studies Program (USP), a semester-long course of study for American university students. That collaboration is to create mutual benefit among the two university programs that includes research, co-teaching, supervisor training, and cross-cultural student groups.

"My major interest is to contribute to improving the quality of social work educational experiences for both students and faculty," Kasule said. "I continuously seek to engage with colleagues who share this passion through collaborations—in international field education, co-teaching and learning and applied research."

The main objective of Kasule's November visit to the United States was collaboration. He spoke and listened during the North American Association of Christians in Social Work Convention 2023 in Pittsburgh, Pa., engaged with educators and students at two USA universities that have been involved with the USP in the two decades of the program's existence and spoke with the Rt. Rev. Deon Johnson, Bishop of the Episcopal Diocese of Missouri at St. John's Episcopal Church, St. Louis, Mo. In Pennsylvania, he visited Grove City College. In Ohio, he spent two days at Cedarville University. In Missouri, he met with social work faculty at St. Louis University.

"My key initiatives are local and international," Kasule said. ""Locally, UCU social work and USP social work emphasis is through cross-cultural learning groups. Internationally, there is the exchange with universities outside Uganda."

Kasule has seen first-hand the academic and cultural value for American students spending a semester of study at UCU as well as a more recent collaboration that has UCU students studying at Hanze University of Applied Sciences in the Netherlands. He would like to see more U.S. higher education opportunities for Ugandan students and faculty.

"Cross-cultural conversations have infinite value," said Kasule, who has two children, ages 4 and 7, with his wife, Grace, a pediatrician currently engaged in clinical research. "We have our own perceptions about Christianity and social problems in Uganda. You have yours."

Besides its spiritual redemption and religious values for the majority of Ugandans, Christian virtues also are an important reference for promising hope; and a practical framework when integrated into curriculum.

While partnership benefits are readily acknowledged, money is a barrier for an equal exchange because Ugandans have fewer resources than Americans. But it's an obstacle that can be overcome.

"There is the possibility of grants, but we don't expect our partners to throw money at a problem," Kasule said.

David Hodge of Arizona State University is among USA social work partners who have come to UCU. In 2021, Dr. Hodge and Kasule co-published a paper addressing academic research inequalities between Sub-Saharan faculty and their counterparts in the West, and planned more related to how spirituality can be used in assessment until COVID drove Hodge home earlier than planned.

"Even for non-believers, Christian principles and similar intervention strategies can be applied," said Kasule, reflecting on some work he has embarked with partners fighting against child sacrifice (i.e. witchcraft), in Uganda.

Kasule sees Christian faith playing an integral part for worker efforts to rebuilding community resilience, prevention and mitigation of social struggles such as domestic violence, mental illness and children not in school. Loneliness issues for people of all ages also is a current focus both in Uganda and the United States, he said.

Enabling university faculty and students to experience multiple cultures is key, according to Kasule.

"We need to engage agencies as partners, teachers and students as learners," he said. "We learn so much from each other to help others."

(2023, Ohio)

Me and Kasule Kibirige in Cedarville, Ohio

Dancing

When I think of Molly Nantongo, I think of dancing. The tiny gap in her front teeth is one way I pick her out from the crowd. Both of those things—dance and space evident when Nantongo smiles—have played an important role in her still unfolding achievement.

For Molly, her journey into social work started with dance.

A 2015 Uganda Christian University alum with a Bachelor of Social Work and Social Administration, she received a Masters in Social Work from the University of California in Berkeley in 2023. Her achievement there landed her a full scholarship for a PhD in social work at Arizona State University. On Aug. 17, 2023, she started studies on the Tempe, Ariz., campus.

"I am aware it will be a challenging journey," she typed into an email from Uganda prior to heading back to the United States. "However, I am prepared for the difficulties and believe that with God's grace, I will persevere."

In 2002, Molly was one of four children living with a single mother, a former Hutu in Rwanda, in the Kampala slum suburb of Kirombe. Missing school and lack of food on the table were an accepted way of life that the then 10-year-old filled with "cracking jokes" and dancing. One such day, she and a girlfriend jumped gleefully onto a political campaign truck filled with music blaring from loudspeakers. They laughed and danced, oblivious to those seeing them, before jumping off to make the 35-minute walk to home.

Because of her dancing, she had been noticed on the truck. Because of the gap in her front teeth, she was found by an non-governmental organization (NGO).

That organization, now known as Undugu Society of Kenya, helped Molly finish primary school. Another organization, Empower African Children, got her to the United States as a member of the Spirit of Uganda (Various Artists—Spirit of Uganda: *2008 Tour Album* Reviews, Songs & More | AllMusic).

Molly never took her support and opportunities for granted. Working hard as she did in the years after getting her bachelor's degree was both rewarding and a way to give back. She got a meager salary from performances with a troupe at Uganda's Ndere Cultural Arts Center. She pieced together earnings from three jobs: a professional dancer, an occasional private dance teacher and teaching assistant and tutor for undergraduate students in the university's foundation courses. She helped students understand health and wellness and world views in the courses.

Alas, like for many, COVID was a hardship. A degree meant little without a place to teach, and dancing meant little without an audience to dance for. Molly started a passion fruit business to support herself and her mom who struggles from a stroke she had in 2017. A year into being a street seller, a friend suggested she apply for a scholarship opportunity through the American Embassy. Without much optimism as one of 60 candidates for one slot, she participated and was chosen to go to California despite the odds.

Once there, she applied for a $10,000 Davis Project for Peace grant—one designed to help Ugandan youth (ages 14–20) who are victims of COVID shutdown impacts, including pregnant-out-of-wedlock girls. The 15-week project, entitled Ntongo Skills4Peace, took place through mid-August 2022 with assistance for several thousand youth.

"I hope this email reaches you in good health," Molly wrote in early August 2023. "Thanks to my exceptional performance, I have been granted a fully funded opportunity to pursue a PhD program in Social Work at Arizona State University. Starting this PhD program, I am aware that it will be a challenging journey. However, I am prepared for the difficulties and believe that with God's grace, I will persevere until the end."

(2023, Arizona)

Molly Nantongo, left, and Kukunda Elizabeth Bacwayo, a university mentor for Molly

Disability (invisibility)

Sometimes, I'm a slow learner.

One case in point involves a friend I'm going to call "Julie" (not her real name for a reason I'll explain later).

I knew Julie virtually for three years before we breathed air in the same space.

In 2020, 2021 and most of 2022, we met almost weekly in separate Zoom boxes. No clickbait, astroturfing, catfishing or suspicious internet lure. Just clean, on-line Christian conversation.

Julie was first coming in from her house in West Virginia and then from Ohio. I was talking and listening in from Ohio, Virginia, Florida, North Carolina—even Uganda where I engaged when awake with the seven-hour Eastern Standard Time–East Africa Time zone difference.

Blame or applaud COVID for contactless meetings, but while the coronavirus pandemic was fraught with tragedy, I may not have met Julie without the virtuality. In her 40s, she was the youngest of the average one dozen mostly women in that Zoom. I found her comments in an Appalachian accent to be interesting, candid and often profound.

"I woke up at 3 a.m. today, thinking of you," I texted privately in the Zoom chat box.

"That's creepy," she responded with a smiley face.

"No, seriously, I want to interview you for my book," I wrote back. Insomnia happens to me frequently as I contemplate stories behind people.

"I'll think about it," she typed.

That was September 2022.

So, it was on a warm, sunny day roughly two months later that we met non-virtually, pulling breakfast food from a brown Panera Bread sack on her porch in Groveport, Ohio. Eating, talking and breathing in the same space.

Julie taught me a lot in that roughly 90 minutes of my bagel-and-cream cheese and her pecan pastry consumption and in the weeks that followed as we emailed back and forth about what I was trying to write.

Slowly, I learned.

Julie has a rare medical condition called Myalgic Encephalomyelitis/Chronic Fatigue Syndrome (ME/CFS). I can hardly pronounce the first two words. I kept trying to shorten it to chronic fatigue, which I knew something about.

"It can't be shortened," she said, directing me to Web sites that also try to explain the condition. "Horrible name, but that's it."

The Centers for Disease Control and Prevention (CDC) site describes ME/CFS as "disabling and complex" with "overwhelming fatigue not improved by rest." The CDC further describes ME/CFS as a thinking, sleeping, balancing deficiency with head and throat ache symptoms called "post-exertional." The CDC says up to 2.5 million Americans have it with one-fourth of those bedbound or housebound. While research conclusions are still out, ME/CFS is likely not hereditary and likely is related to environmental toxins or viral exposure.

"People think we're lazy," Julie said.

Scene outside Julie's home

Covering herself up from the 70-degree sun because of the ME/CFS-related skin sensitivity, she held up her water glass weighing about 8 ounces and elaborated:

"Some days, this is too heavy for me to lift. My vision comes and goes. Pain moves around with some days pain everywhere, especially in my back that gets spasms. Sometimes, I can't move at all and can hardly breathe. I lose my train of thought."

The 47-year-old, once-vibrant, middle-to-high school teacher has roots in West Virginia's Boone County, named for the American legendary Daniel Boone. She holds undergraduate and advanced degrees in gifted, administrative, music and math education from Marshall University and Concord College.

Her life as she knew it—the teaching, socialization and traveling that she loved—came to a screeching halt at age 30 when she was suddenly tired and hurting a lot. Doctors scratched their heads. A neurologist and hematologist ruled out multiple sclerosis and other more common conditions. The pain Julie experienced throughout her body was not visible and occasionally was discounted by medical and non-medical people.

"For a while, things got better, or so I thought," she said. The five-word condition that she hadn't yet heard of seemed to go away.

With a bachelor's and two master's degrees, she got engaged to be married and resumed work on her PhD in curriculum and instruction during that period of a few years.

Five different times in a decade, she chaperoned students on trips to Washington, D.C. From her early 20s, she did vacations and work-related trips to Hawaii, Kansas, Oregon, Texas, Florida and Tennessee. She came back into the school with strategies and new tools for herself and other teachers and into the classroom invigorated with ideas to help her students learn.

"I'd get them excited about literature and stage performances and show them connections to books and the world," she said of the middle and high schoolers she taught. "I encouraged them to come up with their own creations of poetry, songs and art." She cited examples like *Watership Down* with symbolism of humanized rabbit colonies to World War II; the *Les Misérables* movie and book; the *Titanic* and a mock trial against White Star Lines and its role in the ship's sinking; and the *My Fair Lady* musical based on George Bernard Shaw's 1913 play, *Pygmalion.* To name a few.

Julie and her students put together skits and plays with characters of Albert Einstein, Harriet Tubman and Abraham Lincoln. James Naismith, founder of basketball, got thrown in. Like me, Julie respected creative writing. While not among her formal academic credentials, literature was often woven in.

Julie, coming from a family of Scottish descent, had a father who played the saxophone and thus, as she got older, she took to that woodwind instrument as well. As a teenager, she was in three jazz bands that toured in Europe. Audiences of mostly university types in Prague, Vienna and Budapest were mesmerized by this American musical genre.

"I love to read," she said. "Still do, but it's harder. Now, I sometimes re-read novels. And no technical reading. That makes me pretty sick, pretty fast."

On good days, she drives to pick up groceries. Her energy level allows her to put away perishables first while items not requiring refrigeration remain in the car until she has more energy to bring them inside. Good days, like this day as we talked, her pain is a 7 out of 10 with the sharpest pain shooting up from her feet. Bad days, she can't get out of bed or take a shower, has chills, ringing in her ears, sensitivity to smell, gets her heart rate up too high and blacks out.

"Sometimes I can't think of anything but pain," she said. "People are pissed when I cancel or want to reschedule. I would freakin' love to work and go out to lunch, but this is my reality."

For 11 years, she has missed birthday parties and other events. People, not understanding, stop asking. She never got married or finished her doctoral studies.

"You're more than a condition," I argued.

Easy for me to say.

ME/CFS is chronic—and difficult, if not impossible to cure. Among the most common health conditions labeled chronic are heart disease, hypertension, arthritis and diabetes. Most of those don't happen at age 36. At that age Myalgic Encephalomyelitis/Chronic Fatigue Syndrome reared its unceasing head in Julie's body, forcing her to quit work, become homebound and lose friends.

Julie knows that others have it bad—like the people in Ukraine and people with dark skin who suffer discrimination. She watched the news in December 2022 as famous singer, Celine Dion revealed that she has the one-in-a-million diagnosis of Stiff Person Syndrome, similar to Julie's condition but not the same. While saddened that the pop star has had to curtail her performances, Julie knows that celebrity attention oftentimes accelerates research for cures.

Health care plan non-recognition of an illness puts sufferers like Julie in litigation for disability benefits. Thus, the reason for this alias of "Julie." She is working through the legal system to get help, even something as basic as a housekeeper. Stress, including litigation conversations with lawyers, worsens the condition. In short, it makes her sicker and requires more bedrest.

"Knowing that it's real, keeps me going," she said. "Knowing that there is very little chance, it will get better brings me down. Some people are completely bed bound. If it gets worse, if that's me, I don't want to be alive."

Conversation with a neighbor from their adjacent porches, and watching geese on the nearby pond along with her calico cat are Julie's stress relievers.

Days are mostly filled with music. While TV science fiction, cop shows and mysteries are a favorite, even those are a cognitive pull some days. Reality-based competitions like Amazing Race remind her of travel she misses.

"I know that my condition doesn't define all that I am," Julie said. "But going to the zoo—just being able to THINK I could go—would be nice. "

To Julie and others with daily pain we don't see, thanks for your patient teaching. We're learning.

(2023, Ohio)

Dolls in Trees

It took me 17 months and three trips to Ocracoke Island, N.C., to meet the doll lady.

At that, I met her virtually. I was on the island. She was about 200 miles away in Virginia and just days from getting a second hip replacement, she told me via Zoom.

"Nervous? No, I'm looking forward to it," Susan Dodd, AKA the doll lady, remarked about her pending hip joint replacement.

After dispensing with the niceties about Susan's pending surgery, I persisted with my obsessive—yes obsessive—questions about the dolls that I first saw hanging—yes, hanging—in trees outside Susan's house on Ocracoke Island.

From a computer screen on April 19, 2023, Susan laughed as I shared how in September 2021 and while riding on a paint-chipped, single-speed, rented bike during my first trip to the island, I came to a screeching halt at a property that had naked and clothed dolls and doll body parts hanging from trees. I guiltily took photos of the plastic and fabric figurines and headed back to the Ocracoke house that my husband, Mike, and I rented with Ohioans Paul, Alicia, Kevin and Debby.

Over the next five days, the six of us—with curiosity, speculation about this mysterious woman and an overriding concern about privacy invasion—went together and singularly to the house on Jackson Circle. We knocked with no response until Alicia, the wife of a guy I knew from college days, alone scored a brief meeting and a name after several attempts. Alicia reported that Susan Dodd was friendly and, like all six of us, a supporter of President Biden.

In the months before my conversation with Susan, group texts from Alicia as well as from Debby, a one-time roommate at The Ohio State University, asked about if I had yet interviewed the doll lady that they both had bumped into without me. I was envious that they got to see Susan wearing a fun, colorful tutu and walking her two Spaniels on a street in Ocracoke when all I got were photos of dolls in trees (some naked).

Later, I learned that Susan was more than the doll lady. She is a published author, was once married to former U.S. Senator Chris Dodd and was formerly a lecturer at five universities, including Harvard. As an undergraduate at Georgetown, she unsuccessfully challenged Bill Clinton for sophomore class president.

"I don't identify as any of those things today," Susan said. "I came to Ocracoke because it seemed like a good place to write. But I got tired of publishing and started to see writing as too isolating and didn't enjoy that."

Susan's published books are: *Old Wives Tales, No Earthly Notion, Mamaw, Hell-Bent Men and Their Cities, The Mourners Bench, O Careless Love* and *The Silent Woman*. The "bench" one—loosely referencing a church pew once designated for people grieving or seeking salvation from sin—is most related to dolls and maybe dolls in trees.

Now in her 70s, with macular degeneration and, as I write this, two new hips, Susan sees herself as a caregiver and a dabbler in art.

Looking out after others became her untrained but willing and natural role after 9-11 when she moved in with an ex-sister-in-law, who was a single mother fighting cancer in Kansas City, Mo. Following the lost battle, the daughter, now age 35, became the child that Susan never had. Likewise, in the aftermath of Hurricane Dorian in 2019, Susan assumed the role of caseworker on a disaster relief team for Ocracoke victims of the storm.

"I seemed to have a natural inclination for that," she said. "You don't plan it or realize it or do it until it happens or somebody points it out."

Regarding the artist part of Susan's identity, she said the craft of making things with her hands is "easier to get back to than writing that is hindered by interruptions." Inside her house are dolls of her own creation, often reflecting her social justice sentiments that include America's 2003-2011 involvement in the Iraq war. Some figurines appear trapped behind wires and nails. Other pieces are woven with beads, old jewelry and pottery.

"I don't think of myself as an artist," she said. "It's just something I do."

The partial- and full-bodied toys began emerging 20 years ago from her trees first at another house and now at Jackson Circle—both on the 16-mile island in North Carolina's Outer Banks. Even after two decades, Susan is hard-pressed to put her finger on any deep meaning about it now or at the onset. She is not a doll expert. She doesn't expound about the earliest documented dolls that go back to the ancient civilizations of Egypt, Greece, and Rome. Nor does she talk about doll manufacturing that has its roots in 15th century Germany.

Most of the dolls, attached to nearly invisible fishing wire hung from trees in Susan's Ocracoke yard, come from thrift stores where she also buys much of her clothes like the nylon-layered tutu that Debby saw her wearing. Her favorite hanging dolls include a Barbie-like, purple mermaid and, until it was stolen, a chicken head on a doll body.

"Some people add dolls," she said with more amusement than irritation. "Some take them."

While Susan admits that there might be a dolls-in-trees connection to the fact that she had few dolls when growing up in the 1950s, with my persistent questioning during our April conversation, she pointed to her widely recognized 1998 novel, *The Mourners' Bench*, as perhaps the biggest inspiration. From the beginning in this book, which is Susan's third novel, dolls are a metaphor for a theme of broken people. The main character, Leandra, makes a living mending broken dolls while trying to patch the lives of her mentally troubled older sister and the sister's husband.

Dolls are also a theme in her last novel, *Silent Woman*, based on Austrian painter Oskar Kokoschka's love obsession with Alma Mahler, widow of a composer. When the relationship ended in 1918 with the heart-broken painter returning from World War I service to learn Alma had married another, Oskar had a life-sized replica made of Alma.

"That story fascinated me for years," Susan said of her 2001 book.

While what I learned in 90 minutes reinforces that Susan, like her books, can't be read by her cover (i.e. biography), I found a kinship as writers, as possessors of hearts for the less fortunate and a seemingly misaligned fascination with life's shadowy people and circumstances like those in real-life crime and the fictional *Mourners* book that captivated me through all 270 pages.

"We must be related," she said. "I don't know what attracts us to that. Maybe it's a natural affinity for a writer to try to figure out the mysteries of life and what motivates somebody."

As Susan talked, a mismatch of bracelets, dangling from her right wrist, help tell her heart and dark stories. The bangles started with handmade ones never removed since made by some orphan girls she met during a mission trip to Honduras in 2018. A black one signifies her desire to abolish the death penalty, including for nearly 100 Missouri, North Carolina and Texas death row inmates she has met and visited with a discovery that "20 years later, they are not the same person" who committed a crime. Shortly after Dorian, she visited a man scheduled for execution in Texas; he got a stay of execution.

"Just recently, I became greatly worried about the hundreds and hundreds of death row letters I have saved," Susan reflected. "Never have I ever thrown one out...if I keep them, they will end up in recycling, an idea that is unbearable to me. So I have decided to have a (Ocracoke) beach fire in July and burn them in a little ceremony... this solution seems sacred."

Her novels represent human flaws, mental illness and death—a contrast to the lighthearted laughter of the woman still collecting dolls for her trees ("I have 40 more to hang when I get back to the island") and finding delight in smiles about her fashionably improper attire.

"During a radio interview about my writing, I was asked about my fascination with illness and dying in my work while in person I seemed to be vivacious with a good sense of humor," she said. "I said I was trying to learn how to do it...I have attended the deaths of a number of people and found them to be a gift."

While being "proud of accomplishment as a writer," Susan believes "I was just lucky... hundreds of good writers never get a break."

Returning to my fascination with her display of dolls flying magically through trees, Susan said that the reason for her habit or hobby or artistic expression might simply be for "my own delight."

(2023, North Carolina)

Eddie*

Dear Eddie:

I was thinking about you today as my niece's husband talked about the skyrocketing value of old cars. I wondered out loud why the value of people doesn't go up as we get older. Silently, between bites of a baked potato heavily lathered with sour cream and around a table with 10 other family members, I wondered, too, why it wasn't so with old dogs.

At 14 years, 2 months and 7 days, you are old. A Labrador Retriever (large breed), you are 88 in people years. Time is ticking.

So when I got home on this Sunday afternoon, I realized it was long overdue to tell you what you mean to me. Actually, the first impetus to write you a letter came a few days ago when in my usual insomniac state at 3 a.m., I received a private Facebook message from a friend losing sleep over being estranged from his kids and the grandkids he's never seen.

"Write your grandchildren a letter," I typed. My friend, also a writer, understood the therapeutic value of that for him in the present, and later for his kids and grandkids.

So today, I'm taking my own advice, realizing that we, Eddie, have always been close, and unlike my friend's grandchildren, you'll never actually be able to read this letter. In truth, this is for me and not for you. You get that because you've always been about me.

My husband says that you "just can't get enough" of me.

From the time you were little and you were overlooked because other potential owners didn't like the white spot on your chest, from when we named you after Thomas "Eddie" Edison because the famous inventor shared my February birthday and you were my gift, and through our many ups and downs, it was always you who loved and forgave most.

I'm sorry it took me longer than you to exhibit those Godlike traits.

I was angry during those potty and chewing accidents of puppy days. I resented times that I had to come home to give you dinner instead of going straight to exercise or meeting a friend after work and when I wanted a bit more sleep before letting you outside in the morning. I was embarrassed when you would jump on people in your excitement and when you were the most unruly dog in the obedience class. When you ate a baby rabbit, I ignored you for days.

Suffice it to say, my sins are much greater and would take longer to list.

To you, I would raise my voice or give you the silent treatment—often simply because I had a bad day. From you, I got patience and kisses. You persisted and insisted that I love you and know I was loved.

And love, we did. Together, we donned crazy hats on holidays. We wore flashing lights during our nighttime walks. We danced (a lot). We hugged. When I had a bad day—was less than kind to a human or had a human be less than kind to me—you were there. When I had a great day, you waited for everybody else to surround me and then embraced your moment with whatever I had left.

Because most humans found you harder to love than your calm, gentle and beautiful St. Bernard sister, I loved you a little bit more as I observed you wait and hope that maybe, just maybe, a visitor might like you and pet you, too.

You laid by my side when I was sick, soothed my worry with your nudge and lick, savored my scent. Through all the scolding, absence of affection and overall sin, you loved me. Correction. You adored me. Sort of like Jesus.

With this kind of affection that you taught me, I started overlooking your desire to eat unfavorable things. I was not disgusted that you started having a few in-the-house bathroom accidents about a year ago. Neither am I irritated with your loud, guttural cough as we watch TV, your increased snoring in the night or slobbery saliva on the carpet. Your fast-moving tail and head quickly consuming food belie your age and the arthritis we've been treating for more than a year with a daily pill you think is candy.

You are not just Eddie, you are my "Eddie-bo-beddie" and "Silly Billy" who, as my husband and I say, "can't control his lick-er."

Three weeks ago in the midst of a 25th wedding anniversary trip in New Zealand, we got the heartbreaking news that you were failing faster. Upon our return, you were there, but Dr. Libby Kinsel said, "We weren't sure he was going to make it." She prescribed stronger medication.

With your advancing arthritis, it must hurt your hips when you get up to follow me to my study, to the bedroom and outside. Don't think I don't notice the effort it takes you to lower your 78-pound body at my feet, including as you sit patiently on the rug and (don't be embarrassed) lick my arm as you always have as I take a bath. I notice. Please know, too, that I appreciate all this as well as when you use just two legs now instead of four to step into the house from the yard, to leap up to my side on the couch to nuzzle my arm and onto the futon that you were previously forbidden to use.

Eddie waiting for me to come home from Uganda

While your foggy eyes and never-still tail still show the excitement of our shared love of dancing, try as you might, I know you can't jump and sway the way you once did. Dr. Libby says that there will come a day when your hips will give out totally.

"He's willful," she said as my husband and I sat on hard-back chairs in her veterinarian's office six days ago. "But eventually, his hips will go. When that happens, he will be in so much pain, we'll need to put him down."

So in the midst of a Sunday afternoon family conversation about how we value cars and consuming a meal I know you would love at a place called Logan's in Reynoldsburg, Ohio, I thought of you. Truth is, you would love any meal. Truth is, you love anyplace I am.

Truth is, I think of you a lot more as I know our time together is ending. And those kisses I give you on your graying cheek are just a bit more often and heart-felt nowadays.

With sincere love and understanding from me and all dog owners who love and have loved their aging fur babies,

Patty

(written in 2018 before Eddie died at age 15 years, 5 months, 23 days on June 26, 2019, in Ohio)

Elderly

"Did you ever think," said my new friend, Carolyn Kvam, "that you would be riding down the road with an 83-year-old in a BMW convertible?"

Behind the wheel, traveling along Aqui Esta Drive in Punta Gorda, Florida, and with a smile, wind-swept hair and attitude that belie eight-decades-plus of living, Carolyn Kvam is all that. And more.

Carolyn is one of the growing numbers of senior citizens in Punta Gorda, a city translated from Spanish to mean "fat point," so named in 1887. Six of every 10 people in this city of nearly 20,000 residents is considered elderly by the state's legislative definition of those over age 60. Punta Gorda, located near the Gulf of Mexico, is second only to The Villages, situated in central Florida, with the huge number of seniors in the "sunshine state."

Florida is in competition with California, Texas and Maine for the largest percentage of older people. Florida usually wins because of warm weather.

Indeed, Sunday, May 23, 2021, was my first experience riding in a convertible with an 80-plus person behind the wheel. It was day 39 of my first time living in a community where the number of people in my age group are majority. And very active.

"Never place a period where God places a comma," Pastor Michael Ford said to me and Carolyn before the Congregational United Church of Christ service that day. In short, God—not people—decides when the work is done (Ephesians 3:20). Age shouldn't matter.

The phrases "getting old" or "slowing down" aren't used around here. Punta Gorda abounds with geriatric professionals who, a 74-year-old instructor at the YMCA told me

Carolyn Kvam…searching for life commas

in mid-May, emphasize the importance of doing more and not less for a healthier and longer life.

"Not like the doctors up north," the obviously fit and trim senior woman added.

Carolyn is active. Three times a week, she walks to her car with a new golden cane that she is not sure she needs and drives to morning therapy.

"I can lift my body weight now," she said proudly.

Once a week, she has lunch with the "Saltwater Swells," a retired, small group of singers. A 90-year-old friend, Charlie, picks her up for an early dinner every seven days or so. She swims when she wants to in her Colony Point Condominium pool. She reads two or three ebooks a week. Once a month, she connects to the Philanthropic Education Association.

Unapologetically, she says, "I take an afternoon nap."

Some nights, she invites a few neighbors to enjoy her favorite drink—a Manhattan of whiskey, bitters, vermouth and a cherry. Carolyn made one for me, my very first Manhattan in an ice-filled glass. Sipping our Manhattans with a view of the Peace River, I shared with Carolyn my biggest fear: the memory loss I watched with my mom.

"Me, too," she shared. "Take my body before my mind."

Carolyn, a former nurse who wanted to be a pastor in the days when women couldn't be clergy, lost two husbands and one son to cancer. None, fortunately, developed severe dementia. Her one remaining son and four step-children are healthy and have given her eight grandchildren.

Like me, she said she can be alone but not lonely. A dog would be nice but walking it would be a trip hazard and expose her to the bite of fire ants.

Together, we lamented ongoing discrimination against African Americans. Punta Gorda, like many USA communities, is thriving with 95% of its residents being white people living on land and in houses built by Blacks who can't afford to live among them. Also, like many of the nation's cities, the elected leaders engage in squabbles about tearing down African American historical markers because they don't quite fit into the landscape.

Carolyn and I agreed to keep searching for commas, not periods (final punctuation intentionally omitted)

(2021, Florida)

Fake News

Less than seven days after a recent return to the United States, a friend told me about the "plot" of Jewish people in Michigan and Black people in South Africa through separate movements to "wipe out all the white people."

She asserted that actions by these two groups of people were occurring out of anger about non-Jewish white people. Over a meal, she conveyed that this is happening because in the Michigan situation "you know the original Jewish people in the Bible were Black" and in the second the South African farms are operated by white people who employ "Blacks who don't like working for them."

My friend, with beige-colored skin like mine, spends much of her day gathering this information from the Internet. Her main sources are Middle East country Websites and YouTube videos—not "mainstream media that run fake news" and "are controlled by people with all the money."

"Check it out," she said, brushing off my probing questions that included whether she had actually met and spoke with any of the people she mentioned and why her sources are more credible. "You will see what I mean."

One-sided conversations like this leave me reeling. As a trained journalist, I try to employ nonjudgmental listening and engage willing suspension of disbelief. I know that wealthy people own most media houses as well as most of the businesses/industries around the world. I also know that these wealthy people are not as hands-on in the daily news gathering and reporting as many outside the world of journalism think.

As my friend requested, I did "check it out," but not from her sources. Among information from my sources, I learned that in the 1900s, automaker Henry Ford publicly stated that there was a Jewish plot to control the world. I learned that the term "white genocide" frequently crops up in South Africa.

Yet, there is no large-scale conspiracy. In instances like this conversation with a beloved friend, I feel like I have stepped into another universe.

The truth is that no person can be totally unbiased. I used to teach that possibility, telling students that the best reporters present both sides of the story without any viewpoint slant. I was sort of wrong. Try as we might, we all come into a situation with preconceived notions we can't shake from our words.

Four days ago, I gloated a bit in thinking I was above the rest as I listened to what I felt was a frivolous, 20-minute conversation of a couple trying to buy a waste basket. They victoriously walked out of a Bed, Bath and Beyond store with their purchase while I internally scoffed. Unlike me, they had no idea about a country (Uganda) where people didn't even have trash to put into a can, let alone money to purchase one.

Then, I related this to a friend who does interior decorating. She patiently explained the value of having balance among the things in a home. A simple trash receptacle actually helps a husband and wife function better as a family unit. I formed my opinion without all the facts. I was wrong.

At that, there are some biased opinions more dangerous than others.

On Christmas Eve, I spoke to a Jewish acquaintance about my childhood friend's assertions about Jews. He sighed about the world's ever-present anti-Semitism. We lamented the October 2018 Pennsylvania shooting by a gunman who believed a conspiracy theory that a migrant caravan from Mexico was the result of a Jewish plot to destabilize America.

This morning, I had a private Facebook conversation with a Ugandan journalist who said there are some incidences of violence by South African Black workers who feel they have "unfair conditions" imposed by white farm bosses. But nothing akin to a takeover…

Two days ago, a Facebook friend posted an urban legend about a reportedly averted terrorism attack by a dozen Muslims on an American plane. In providing this repeated, erroneous story from 2009, she warned us, "The Muslims are all getting very brave now."

God gave us dominion over the earth's other living creatures for a reason. The U.S. Constitution in the USA ensures freedom of expression. but we need to exercise that freedom with responsibility. It bothers me that negativity about each other—about people we have never met or even tried to know—is prevalent today.

It bothers me to write about it.

(2019, Ohio)

Falling

Yesterday afternoon, my 90-year-old mother proposed to me that we put her friend, Dottie Galliher, in a cage.

That, mom surmised as she described a wire enclosure to protect a person walking, would keep Dottie from falling. Dottie, a former roller skating instructor now in her late 80s, fell a few days ago. Consequently, she can't walk even with her walker without somebody at her side—at least for now.

My husband chimed in that "fat suits" might be a better solution for mom, Dottie and all the elderly in mom's assisted living residence. The inflatable suits, he explained to a doubting staff at Abbington of Pickerington, might not keep them more upright on two legs, but they would provide a cushion for falls.

Mom has fallen more than once with the latest being a face plant. Her bruised face and broken nose happened last autumn, she said, not because she was moving without her walker (which she was) but because of the shoes I bought her. Her solution was to give those expensive shoes to my cousin.

Fully healed and better today than Dottie and Bea Garrelts, another one of mom's friends who also fell this week, mom victoriously announced that she "snuck" a shower without an aide watching two nights ago.

"Don't tell," she said, smiling. "It felt so good to be in there on my own. I can do that."

Not just mom and her elderly friends are falling, but everybody is doing it.

My 40-something hair stylist fell on the ice and got stitches around her left eye two weeks ago. I read in today's *Columbus Dispatch* that a local grandmother was sled-riding with her grandchildren when she fell off; she died from head injuries.

To capitalize on the fear of falling, advertisements about "walk-in" bathtubs, railings, and fall-alert necklaces abound. There are canes; walkers with no wheels, two wheels and four wheels; and wheelchairs—all with more styles and price tags than you can count on both hands.

In the United States, falling is the second most common cause of death from unintentional injuries after motor vehicle collisions. Consequences of falling are the most often seen injuries in North American emergency departments. The U.S. Center for Disease Control and Prevention says that 1 in 4 people over age 65 are hurt annually from falling with one of these people dying from that fall every 19 minutes. As we age, low blood pressure and dementia cause dizziness; those and having a body that is less physically fit contribute to falling.

According to the World Health Organization, an estimated 646,000 individuals die from falls globally each year.

I have been part of the injury statistics three times. In sixth grade, two friends dared me to jump from the tree behind Joan Layton's house. I did, I fell, and I broke an arm. In my 20s, an out-of-control snow skier mowed me down, breaking my wrist. In my 30s, I did my own snow head plant at Pennsylvania's Seven Springs resort. My loopy speech and nodding head raised enough concern for Claudia and Karen to make sure I stayed awake in the back seat en-route to Ohio. I now wear a helmet.

Head concussions rank third to hip and shoulder injuries from falls.

Today, during my two exercise classes, and as I approach yet another birthday on February 11, I got to thinking about falling. I don't want to do it. Subsequently, I used one elevation in my aerobic step class instead of two, and decided to keep one hand on the floor during the yoga airplane pose. The older you are, the slower you heal.

In the final yoga relaxation pose, I wasn't chilled out at all.

My thoughts went to my friend, Bob, and how he fearlessly elevates his mountain bike over hills and through trees; about the woman who sat behind me at church and talked about her husband's slip at the mailbox last week; and about my 15-year-old dog who is afraid to step up a few inches on the new, soft pad I bought to ease the pain of his aging hips.

If it's not too serious, we laugh when people fall.

Yet, unless you are young and don't know enough to care, falling is not a laughing matter. As you age, broken bones don't heal as well, if at all.

Thinking of my upcoming trip back to Uganda—particularly the flight over the Atlantic from Toronto to Istanbul—I jokingly asked my husband what he thought it would be like if I jumped or was pushed out of the plane without a parachute. I would be falling into the sky. We pondered that it would be intensely cold, with little oxygen, and I might become unconscious or unable to breathe or both.

"But it just might be peaceful," my husband said. "Until you hit the ground."

(2019, Ohio)

Famous

I hadn't thought much about Ed Asner until yesterday, when he died. I wondered if, in his final moments, if he thought of me.

There was, after all, that glorious 70 minutes we had together in the back seat of a brand-new car borrowed from a dealership in Springfield, Ohio. I was almost 30 and he was around 50. We shared popcorn that he bought from a shop in the Columbus airport as I, a real-life journalist, asked him what it was like to be a TV journalist—first in the *Mary Tyler Moore Show's* pseudo-TV newsroom and then as "Lou Grant" in a simulated newspaper office.

Ed Asner was the keynote speaker for a conference of the Ohio Newspaper Women's Association. I think the year was 1981. After watching the smaller-than-life Asner exit from a now defunct, cheap Peoples Express airline, shaking hands as we stood eye-to-eye at our shared short stature and securing the popcorn, I recorded the interview for the *Springfield News-Sun*. Another reporter drove the borrowed car as Ed chatted and munched, and I took notes. Ed missed his mouth a lot. Kernels littered the car's carpeted floor by the time we delivered the star to his motel.

I wonder if Ed Asner remembered that day or knew that I collected the dirty kernels and had them embedded into a half dozen paper weights emblazoned with a gold plate that read: "Ed's corn."

Recently, as my husband and I breathlessly rode and then walked our bicycles up a hill to select our green burial sites through the Gambier, Ohio, Kokosing Nature Preserve, I thought about another famous dead person, Paul Newman. Four decades ago, for the *Mt. Vernon News*, I nervously interviewed the blue-eyed film star as together we stood in the sun on a hill at the nearby Kenyon College. That encounter was before Newman's role in the *Absence of Malice* movie about journalistic libel defamation but after he gained a reputation for telling reporters to "eat shit."

I wondered if the Ohio native Newman thought twice about that day. I wonder if Paul Newman didn't ask me to consume feces because he felt compassion. I wondered if he felt anything.

I thought about both media stars today as I walked the dog we're sitting with for some friends who are on vacation.

The deaths of Paul Newman at 83 and Ed Asner at 91 were on my mind as the young dog and I went past the house of a neighbor whose husband died of COVID several days ago. The not particularly famous neighbor who was about to celebrate 60 years of marriage with his now-widowed wife was 79. His funeral is Wednesday.

I wondered how my neighbor, Joseph, felt watching his wife and sons as he took his final breaths from a respirator.

Truth is, I don't think much or often about famous people who leave us. Disgust but not sorrow is whatI felt after seeing a crude YouTube post showing Asner in his casket with about 40 seconds of weird music in the background. Sadness but not grief describes my mood about Newman's life reduced to cremated remains a decade ago.

But I do think about the non-famous ones.

Joe down the street. My former skiing buddy, Claudia Speakman, whose life we celebrated alongside husband, Jack, now widowed, a week ago. Emily Buck, who died not knowing anybody. Mom.

(2021, Ohio)

Famous Politician

"I didn't do anything that anybody else couldn't do."

Surrounded by portraits of herself with famous people and accolade proclamations with her name, Fran Ryan, a Columbus, Ohio, icon, struggles to name one single thing that makes her stand out.

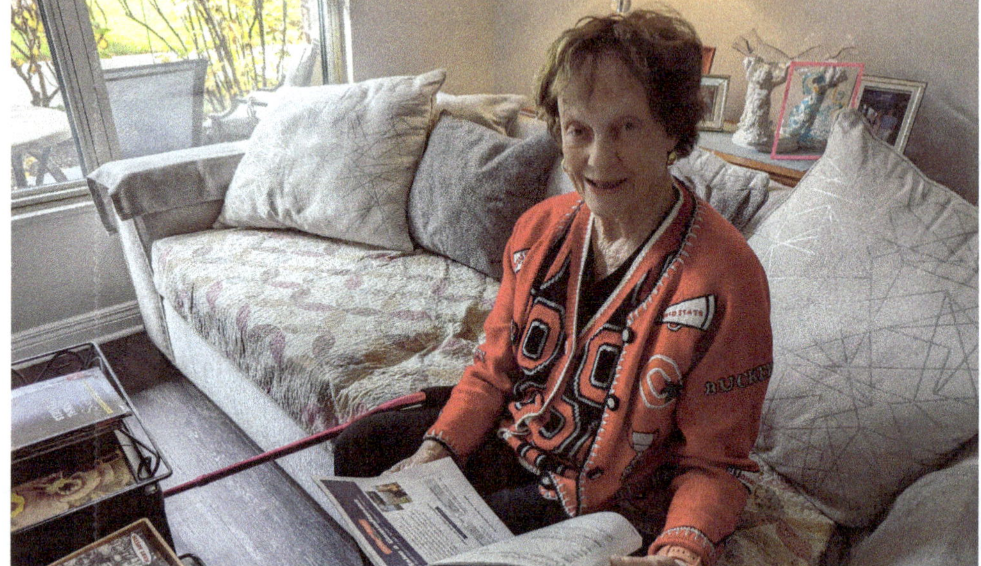

Fran Ryan

That is, perhaps, because there are so many.

"I never invented anything," she said. She sighed, adding, "My children want me to write a memoir, but it will be boring."

Boring? Hardly. A google search without "Ohio " pulls up Fran Ryan the actress, now deceased but once known for roles in the *General Hospital* soap opera and the TV western *Gunsmoke*. Columbus' Fran Ryan isn't THAT one. Adding her geographical location to an on-line search yields a very much alive woman with dozens of awards and affiliations with committees, boards and public offices. Many are female firsts.

City Council. City Clerk. Franklin County Commissioner. Chair of the Franklin County Democratic Party. Founder of the Franklin County Metropolitan Human Services Commission. YWCA's Woman of Achievement Award. 2010 Heritage Award for Caring. 2015 Outstanding Breathing Association Volunteer. The list, including that a community center bearing her name is being built for use by early 2025, is long and getting longer for the almost-90 Ryan.

"Following my children, my biggest legacy is public service," Ryan said. "The second is probably philanthropy. I am good at asking for money."

Public offices and fundraising beyond her pictures with former U.S. Presidents Jimmy Carter and Bill Clinton have made Fran Ryan a central Ohio household name. Such work and acknowledgements, she attested, often get a bad rap, including from jaded journalists.

"I've been written about at least 100 times," Ryan said.

Wearing an OSU sweater, she stood at the door leading to her apartment as her West Highland White Terrier, Louie, returned from a walk with Max, an 89-year-old dog walker associated with Seniors Helping Seniors, which is part of a national organization that has Fran's localized imprint.

"We're the best to understand each other," Ryan said about the purpose of the elderly-focused organization. "Plus, there aren't enough younger people around to look after us."

After Max left, and Louie, 14, blind and diabetic, settled into his bed for a nap, Ryan shared a slice of her life, getting the usual stuff out of the way quickly.

The former Francine Lottridge was born to "liberal parents" in a Puerto Rican part of New York City. She came to Ohio in 1950 and graduated with a degree in journalism from OSU in 1956, followed by a short stint writing for the former *The Columbus Citizen-Journal* daily newspaper. At age 23, she married Dick Ryan, an avid postage stamp collector who also was involved in local politics before he died five years ago. Fran misses him but doesn't dwell on it or her own advanced stage of life.

"Dick and I used to say that feeling depressed is cheating yourself out of a good vacation," she said. "Plus, I don't have time for a meltdown."

Fran, who plans to be on a cruise ship when turning 90 on Jan. 4, 2024, has a blue-lined notepad full of appointments reminding her and others that she's not done yet.

"Don't dare me," she said. "That's often why I do something."

At age 12, she wrote a "Parents are usually to blame" piece for a Pennsylvania newspaper. As a teenager, Fran played basketball in an era when most females were not on the court. As an adult, she broke gender barriers several times, most notably as the first woman to chair the Franklin County Democratic Party. She ran and lost her race for Congress, helped stock food pantries, lobbied to detect paint poisoning and control rats, sold cars and bought a share of a horse.

"Sometimes, I would show up with a child on my lap," she said of the engagements that came with her roles. "I was this crazy mother of five."

Fran's stories are anything but boring.

She started selling cars at Byer's Chevrolet on a dare—more like a bet in 1993.

"We were sitting inside the Clarmont Restaurant on a freezing cold February with three to four Republican judges when Frank Byers walked in," Ryan recalled. "I hit him up for some money for the St. Mary's church steeple, and he replied with a bet that I couldn't sell cars. No women were selling cars then. I went up there the next day."

She took the vehicle salesperson test, passed it, and put customers into the driver's seats of cars and trucks for 15 years.

Another more recent story is about buying a share of a horse.

"I loved to go to John Galbreath's," she said of the Kentucky horse farm. "When I found out I could have a share of a horse for $35, I did it."

Fran Ryan's stories continue to evolve as she shares her delight about her children, 11 grandchildren and eight great-grandchildren. Her calendar is filled with the likes of the meetings at the historical society and a brew emporium. Regardless of the formality of the setting, the almost-nonagenarian continues to be taken seriously.

When she gives an opinion like the closing of catholic churches ("It's especially hard on the seniors."), on President Joe Biden ("He's great and not too old for God's sake."), the media ("It's massive, working 24 hours.") and abortion ("The government can't tell me what to do."), people listen.

"I'm not ready to stop," she said. "I get my spinal steroid injection and my walker and go."

A cancer survivor with macular degeneration, Fran Ryan has drivers and a roommate, her youngest son, age 56, who works at Parks and Recreation.

"I love working with my seniors," she said. "When I totally break down and go to the boughs, and think back on everything, I guess that will be what I'm most proud of."

(2023, Ohio)

Gender Preference

Fifteen-year-old Evelyn DiSalvo is a minority—not because of the color of her skin, which is beige like mine.

She's marginalized by her sexual orientation that she calls "biromantic" in the sense that she romantically likes both males and females. Her partner preference that others call bisexual or pansexual (attraction regardless of gender) is unlike my non-marginalized heterosexual one.

The Center for Disease Control and the Pew Research Center report as many as one in four American youth identify as lesbian, gay, bisexual and transgender (LGBT) with 7–12% claiming physical and emotional attraction to both males and females.

But Evelyn is more than a statistic.

She's a writer, a singer, clarinet and saxophone player and a damn good speaker and teacher.

I heard her speak twice—once about addressing LGBT, immigration and abortion rights with offices of elected officials in Washington, D.C., and then when giving her bisexual testimony during a church service.

Just a bit older than my granddaughter and on a sun-filled June afternoon, she was a patient, candid and accommodating teacher, answering my questions about a lifestyle that isn't mine. As a writer, she understands the discomfort with the plural pronoun, "they" and respects its use. At that, Evelyn is comfortable with both "she/her" or "they/them" pronouns.

For 75 minutes and seated together on a rainbow-colored bench below steps of a United Church of Christ in Canal Winchester, Ohio, she talked about the confusion of her first sexual orientation realization at age 10, the pain of being bullied as a young teen and, approaching age 16, the satisfaction in acceptance for who she is.

I grew up seeing the rainbow as a symbol of joy and happiness after rainfall with memories of Judy Garland's voice about the optical phenomenon in the legendary *Wizard of Oz* movie. Evelyn gets that.

Evelyn also gets that the rainbow's red, orange, yellow, green, blue and violet colors became symbols of LGBT diversity about the time her parents were born. The bisexual flag is pink for same-sex attraction, blue for opposite-sex attraction and purple for attraction to two or more genders.

As Christians, Evelyn and I know that the Bible's first chapter of the Old Testament quotes God as labeling the rainbow as a "sign of the covenant" between Him and "every living creature." That's in Genesis 9 (NIV).

"We are all made in God's image," Evelyn said, referring to Genesis 1:27. "God created me to not just like but to love both males and females."

That realization doesn't diminish the teenage anxiety of being different.

"When I was 10, my friend and I were playing truth or dare. I remember she asked me, 'Have you ever had a crush on a girl before?' I immediately froze. I laughed and disregarded her question," Evelyn said. "Later I thought back to it. Why hadn't I given her an answer? I'd always liked boys before that, so how could I like girls? No, it can't be. I pushed it away for about a year. Then, I looked at one of my closest friends differently than I ever had before. I realized how pretty she was and how I wouldn't mind kissing her."

More recently, she experienced the anguish of losing a boyfriend whose parents forbid their relationship because they said Evelyn would be going to hell.

"He was my first true love," she said. "When he told his parents about my biromantic identity, they wouldn't even let us be friends."

At a previous school, peers called her "the F word"—disparaging "fag" or "faggot" words that she refuses to say out loud. She experienced taunting slurs from students because she wore a shirt with language professing gender acceptance.

We agreed that such insulting homosexual labels come from people ignorant and/or unwilling to embrace gender and sexual orientation differences.

"It doesn't mean that I have romantic feelings for all girls or all boys," she said. "Some of my friends don't get that and don't want to. Others do. "

Fortunately, her parents do. When she told them after first telling one of her two older sisters, they hugged her.

"They told me they loved me no matter what, regardless of who I liked," Evelyn said. "They did bring up the point that I was very young, and it could be a phase that I'd grow out of and change my mind. But I know I won't."

Despite her maturity and confidence, Evelyn is every bit a teenager in her fashionably distressed denim, crocs with high school mascot decals and decorated phone case. She yearns for the day that her braces come out.

On this day during a summer break from a new high school where she isn't bullied, she got up at 9 a.m., ate cereal, did a word puzzle and finished *The Devil Wears Prada* book with hopes to soon watch the movie by the same name. She is looking forward to a weekend trip to Nashville, Tenn., with the Capital University youth band and to her original *Christmas in July* production that is as part of a Columbus, Ohio, Young Writers Short Play Festival in July.

Evelyn says it's too soon to think about a life partner or family, but regarding children, she has dreams of adopting children. It also is too early to pick a career, but something in social justice is likely.

She's been on the injustice side and is sensitive to other prejudice like racism that she saw before switching schools.

She was surprised and saddened when I shared that globally, nearly 70 countries have laws criminalizing LGBT relationships.

Cruel judgment and treatment by others contributed to Evelyn's introduction to counseling and the world of antidepressants. She takes Zoloft and, on occasion, hydroxyzine.

"People are going to be triggered by different things but it's how we respond and deal with those that enables us to function and contribute," she said. "We're not all going to get along and all the time."

Evelyn DiSalvo shared that these days she has more nightmares than dreams. When waking up, she remembers them, and sometimes they are "realities mixed with dreams." Being accepted is important, but being accepted by every person is not a reality.

Walking to her mom's car, she laughed when pointing out that "some people like cookies, some like ice cream, and some like both."

Rhetorically, she concluded: "This isn't a perfect world, you know what I mean?"

Evelyn, however, just might be the perfect teacher to make it so.

(2024, Ohio)

Evelyn DiSalvo

Green Burial

Two women I never met—the late wives of Jerry Griffin, a guy I spoke to only once on Zoom, and Jim Kreimer, who my husband, Mike, and I had lunch with recently—will be my lifetime neighbors.

Yes, "late," as Jim's wife, Donna, and Jerry's wife, Judith, died in 2021 and 2018, respectively. And, yes, "neighbors" because both ladies are laid to rest six feet deep under the same ground that I have chosen as my final resting place.

Donna, Judith and I (not yet) are green burial buddies.

The place is Kokosing Nature Preserve, located next to Kenyon College in Knox County. The land with trees, prairie grasses and warm-weather Lavender Bee Balm, coneflowers, and Black-eyed Susans was once part of a golf course. It is one of 166 green burial sites in the USA and one of five in Ohio.

Green burials—also called natural and conservation interments—in the rawest form involve putting an unembalmed body directly into the ground to be naturally recycled. The "save the planet" internment like that of me, my husband, Donna and Judith enable our bodies to give back to the earth faster with less environmental impact than traditional casket burials and the increasingly popular cremation that sends a considerable amount of CO2 and pollution into the air.

Cremation aside, while we look at a population explosion above ground, it likewise is happening underground today in the USA's 144,847 graveyards and cemeteries as these formaldehyde-infused bodies in wood and metal caskets and vaults rot but at a slower pace than bodies making direct contact with soil.

The non-profit Population Reference Bureau claims that for every one of the world's 7.4 billion living people, there are 15 dead and buried six feet under us. The most crowded USA state with the deceased is California. The most graveyard space can be found in West Virginia.

Mike and I began researching natural burials six years ago. On March 19, 2016, we took a field trip with two friends, Paul and Alicia, to Foxfield Preserve in Wilmot, Ohio. This, we agreed after a green burial orientation that included walking on top of someone's grave and after a meal with wine and beer, seemed the right thing to do.

Other parts of the world already were more comfortable with putting a body straight into the ground than ours. Mike and I recalled, in 2013, a young man who we had just witnessed playing the drums in a Mukono, Uganda, church service being mowed down by a car as he walked home and how he was buried in his family's backyard.

Alas, after that 2016 green burial introduction in northeast Ohio, my life on earth went on with other priorities. Death was on the back burner.

Until June 28, 2021, when Mom died.

In the aftermath of grieving, Mike and I accelerated our plans to leave the world a better place as God leads us—both when breathing above the ground and settling in below it.

We visited Kokosing, which is one of two Ohio burial grounds rated higher for its conservation emphasis (Foxfield is the other one)—first on a hot summer day riding and pushing our bicycles up a huge hill in 2021 to compare this site to the other one from 2016. We were met by Amy Henricksen, who has titles of coordinator for the non-profit Philander Chase Conservancy and steward for the Kokosing Nature Preserve. She was accommodating without being pushy that day and on a chilly day a few months later when we selected our plots and sealed the burial deal.

The cost was $5,000 each with half the amount for a good-sized plot and the other half as a charity contribution to Philander Chase Conservancy.

Me and Mike on the burial plots we reserved

I have Burial Plot #2032 located next to Mike's #2033 on the GPS coordinate. We bought Kokosing shirts from a book store at the nearby Kenyon College. We laid flat on our plots and had Amy take our photo.

I wish I had known Jerry's wife, Judith. Her work at a university, her non-traditional way of looking at things, her highly social personality seem aligned with mine. Jerry shared how a friend of Judith's chose a green burial plan and sent around a shroud for friends to sign before she died and was buried in it.

Jim shared with me some loving notes and numerous photos of Donna, who at age 79 took her last breath three weeks after my mom took hers. Donna, who thought graveyards were "creepy" and cremation "scary," loved nature that presented itself in a green site. She was buried in her favorite red dress, in a biodegradable wicker coffin, covered with a spray of wildflowers. Donna's smile and eyes from the photographs are captivating. Her notes, typed into emails to Jim, spoke of "no regrets" and deep love.

My separate conversations with Jim and Jerry are likely a one off. Thanks to Amy and the willingness of these two widowers to share, I got a better feel for my own decision. We talked about the issue of handling one's own death details vs. leaving that task to others. We talked about the controversy and, to some, discomfort about the green-way of human deposition. Mostly, however, I listened as Jim and Jerry shared how much they miss their wives and all they were.

I listened, too, to Jacki Mann, an end-of-life doula (something I only learned about six months ago), in two on-line discussions about environmentally sustainable after-death disposal as well as the appropriate funeral rituals and ceremonies that can cost from a few hundred to a couple thousand dollars or more.

For those of us who are Christians, our forever home is with God. Our bodies are a temporary encasement for our souls. How we dispose of those bodies is an individual choice often tainted by religious and family tradition.

I don't plan on checking out soon, but believe the imprint we leave on others is as important as the imprint within God's earth, that will support the living when we ascend.

(2022, Ohio)

Heart

In the midst of my friend, Alex, messaging me from a taxi en-route to Mbarara, Uganda; a too-close-for-Covid woman, half-masked, telling me how her husband physically abuses her; and an HGTV show about rich people spending money to get bigger, more expensive homes, Dr. Nahush Mokadam saved my husband's life.

In a small room off the fourth floor surgical waiting area of The Ohio State University (OSU) Richard M. Ross Heart Hospital shortly after 12 Noon on Friday, the cardiac surgeon gave me the exhilarating news. Mike was on a respirator but recovering nicely from a five-hour process to ease a cardiovascular disease we didn't know he had until five days ago.

The turn of events since Tuesday shook me to the core.

On October 27, we drove together in the dark of 5 a.m. for an outpatient heart catheterization and possible stent designed to open an artery to Mike's heart. In the same room where Dr. Mokadam delivered the good news three days later, Dr. Ernest Mazzaferri gave me the bad news. The arteries were too blocked for a quick wire-mesh tube fix. To save my husband's life, they would need to open his chest.

In short, Mike's heart was working too hard because arteries supplying blood to the four chambers were partially or fully blocked. Two arteries not needed as much elsewhere would be repositioned. Those arteries would be the ones that supplied blood to chest muscles. They would not come from my husband's arms to better protect his passion and skill with the guitar and piano.

The Oct. 30 double by-pass, open-heart surgery was done without a heart-lung machine. Led by an Asian–Indian heart specialist, Mike's team of healthcare professionals made the

Me and Mike in Uganda – before the heart incident

"off-pump" decision following multiple assessments of data on his heart, lungs, arteries, brain and his history, including that he had a mild stroke when I was in Uganda in 2011.

In this last week of October and driving back and forth daily to a campus best known for OSU Buckeyes football, I can't remember when I cried so hard, prayed so often and loved so deeply. A world without my best friend and life partner would not be a world worth living.

"If I didn't have you, it would be like two feet with only one shoe," Mike said through his pain and from the intensive care unit today.

We reminded each other that Oct. 31, 2020, is the 30th anniversary of the day we met. It was a Halloween party at a small bar called HeyHey. We shared sauerkraut balls. We had no intention of a permanent, serious relationship.

Now, driving home solo in the dark, I pray.

(2020, Ohio)

Horse Therapist

Try as you might, you can't fit Kathryn King into a box. And for God's sake, don't try putting her horses in one.

Yes, for God's sake. Kathryn is a believer in Jesus and knows God blesses the five members of her equine family at Valhalla Hill Farm (VHF) along with other creatures living on the Alexandria, Ohio, property. Like the two dogs.

I was particularly taken with a large, white, and incredibly calm canine named Valkyrie.

All are spiritually anointed and using their gifts. From dogs to cats and horses, the living creatures on VHF are exercising servant hearts.

Kathryn King, 60, loves God and animals. The white board in her office has Biblical scriptures from John 15, Matthew 6, Proverbs 4, Romans 12 and Galatians 6 as well as instructions about what to do (listen to) and not to do (touch face, lips, whiskers) with the equine residents.

Unlike most profiles that I capture during one 90-minute interview, it took me three separate trips to learn enough to write about some of what happens at VHF medicine horse preservation.

One reason for the added time was that, as Kathryn openly admits, "I'm on the spectrum." She's autistic like the nationally known researcher and author, Mary Temple Grandin, who Kathryn has met and admires. Kathryn's responses to my questions didn't always align, so I returned to ask again.

The second reason that I journeyed to Kathryn's place three times is that what she and her horses do is incredibly interesting and unorthodox.

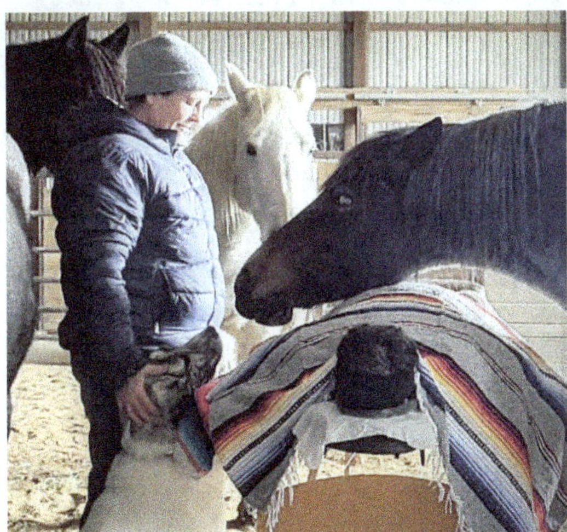

Kathryn King at her farm

In short, VHF is about healing.

Not the kind that used to take place at a farm about two miles from my house. For years and before it shut down, schools sent troubled youth to a farm on Alspach Road in Canal Winchester, Ohio, to learn love and responsibility. Not the kind found in Human-Equine Relational Development (HERD) models that I read about in a book entitled, *It's Not About the Activity* by Dr. Veronica Lac, a researcher in equine-facilitated psychotherapy. Not even the type of healing depicted in the restorative model from the Equine Assisted Growth and Learning Association (Eagala), where Kathryn got some certifications.

Like these, VHF IS about healing human physical and psychological conditions. It's just that the VHF "how" is closest to something called Horse Boy Method, which is a science-based intervention found to help people not only with physical pain but also with anxiety, trauma, attention deficit disorder and autism, a neurological condition that affects how people communicate.

Seeing is believing. Yet much of the world's healing or need to heal can't be seen.

Kathryn has believers and non-believers traveling down the winding lane to her barn just outside the 600-resident village of Alexandria, Ohio.

Horse healing isn't for everyone. One man, age 28, she recalled, "gave me the finger as he left." This didn't bother her.

Believers outweigh the naysayers. Believers include a 14-year-old boy healed of seizures, a 50-something woman leaving with no pain in her hip, another released of right shoulder discomfort, another with pain-free knees, many with long-held psychological barriers torn down.

Kathryn recalled one time when one of her horses leaned into a female visitor. She interpreted out loud that "he's saying that something is going on with your spine." The woman cried and admitted she has scoliosis. Two months later, Kathryn and the woman bumped into each other at a dinner, and the woman said she was healed.

Kathryn likened what she sees with her horses sometimes as similar to a scene from *The Green Mile* movie where a prison inmate resurrects a seemingly dead mouse.

Those who toe the line find discomfort in people who don't. They might see people like Kathryn a bit on the crazy side.

Look deeper. She's not. Kathryn holds a bachelor's degree in interior design and a master's in counseling. She is a certified Equine Assisted Psychotherapist and practitioner of numerous modalities of alternative healing, a lifetime horsewoman and student, and healer.

Chronologically, what she does makes sense. Her burgeoning love and respect for animals began at age five and focused on horses since she was 10. She describes herself as "an odd child" focused more on the "why" not taught in school with questions "annoying and irrelevant to most."

"As a child, I could hear the conversations going on energetically with animals," she said. "This became something that was embarrassing to tell anyone yet difficult to hide."

She connected with horses in particular, growing to respect them as 1,000-pound animals not just for working, racing and breeding but healing—as nontraditional medicine. For

Kathryn, there was never a time when she didn't believe sight seen or unseen. "They do the work," Kathryn says. "I am not a horse whisper, but a listener. I interpret, if needed."

Kathryn's horses—Leoti, Tatonka, Chief, Finn and Nick—are "the real story," she says. Leoti has the added prestige of being a movie star. He was featured in a 2021 movie called *Adeline*, based on a true story about how a horse saved lives in a community. All are Nokota, once wild and originating from North Dakota and connected to native Americans. All are revered by their owner.

VHF has additional powers because, according to Kathryn, it is located on "sacred ground" once occupied by the Hopewell and Shawnee Indian tribes. Visitors from throughout the United States travel to the nearby Ohio cities of Newark and Heath to view Hopewell Indian earthwork ceremonial centers—the largest set of geometric earthen enclosures in the world. The Shawnee have ancestral roots in Ohio and four other states.

Knowing this native American documentation strengthens the credibility of Kathryn's assertion of Hopewell and Shawnee presence at her farm. Juggling the financial needs of VHF and her passion and belief in equine medicine healing, Kathryn fluctuates between her focus on helping people through her horses and caring and respecting equine and the realization that a business model requires fiscal support. VHF has a combination of free and paid programming.

Kathryn says her horses are healers but so much more.

A text after the second visit states, in part, that the horses provide "a safe place with no judgment" as they mirror "the very things in need of change … all in a compassionate, loved-filled way."

Later, on Facebook, Kathryn shared that she "found this last year in need of healing myself." She became stricken with a tick-borne illness that almost incapacitated her.

She wrote: "Despite of the setbacks physically, it had become clear that I was experiencing the very things people have come here in the 25 plus years for... a safe place to just be and explore what the land and the horses have to offer emotionally, mentally, spiritually A place of no judgment, guilt, shame rather one that encourages, enlightens, and teaches love through observation, language and communication."

As cliché as it sounds, she says "love" and "community support" are the center of all existence.

This is the heart of the Medicine Horse Preservation at Valhalla Hill Farm (www. medicinehorsepreservation.love).

Totally in the box.

(2023, Ohio)

Humanitarian

While most of the world learned with angst of the April 1, 2024, Gaza drone attack targeting and killing seven World Central Kitchen (WCK) workers—and then perhaps moved on routinely after it occurred—for one resident of Ocracoke Island, N.C., the attack lingered and struck closer to home.

"I admire people like José (Andrés, WCK founder) and what they do," said Warner Passanisi, who recently returned to the house he has had on the island for over 25 years. Warner lamented that the Israeli Defense Forces bombed trucks that were clearly marked and approved by those forces to deliver essential food to starving people in Gaza.

"I worked alongside them in Ukraine and other war zones," Passanisi said of the WCK nonprofit and its workers. "Like many who serve others, they follow their hearts. This group provides essentials in a crisis."

Before his recent return to the island, Passanisi spent over 30 years as a senior relief/development manager supporting food, health, water and gender equity programs in over 50 countries, including Ukraine, Iraq, Somalia, Sudan, Syria, Liberia and Macedonia. His role and that of the non-profit, non-governmental organizations he assisted was not to take sides in conflicts but to mitigate loss of civilian lives by delivering meals, clean water, medicine and advice to prevent sickness.

When the Ebola virus epidemic occurred from 2014 to 2015 in Liberia, along with the neighboring countries of Guinea and Sierra Leone, Passanisi managed a response team of 400. Controlling the rare, contagious and deadly disease required working with religious and tribal leaders to restrict the spread through cremation instead of traditional burial ceremonies "with a lot of touching and hugging" that would cost more lives.

Ellen Johnson Sirleaf, president of Liberia from 2006 to 2018, is seated next to Warner Passanisi at a 2015 ceremony honoring the work of Passanisi's team.

"Dead-body management isn't something you hear a lot about, but it's a necessary part of crisis management," he said. "What piques the interest of Americans watching or listening in their armchairs is but a small piece of the thousand-fold balance of efforts and of unheard folks suffering."

Passanisi, born in England of Australian parents, has a curriculum vita that is pages long listing his academic credentials, his work and titles related to emergency preparedness, and risk management connected to more than two dozen nonprofits. He can pinpoint the most passionate, reputable organizations. He named WCK, Red Cross, Doctors Without Borders, World Vision, CARE, International Rescue Committee and the World Health Organization among those.

"Most of these people have seen somebody die in front of them," he said. "There is stress with anxiety and mental health issues with mostly nobody addressing this. It may sound exciting, but the tragedy and lingering trauma are overwhelming."

Groups and individuals focused on politics or short-term, uninformed giving—what Passanisi calls "the bleeding hearts"—are the least helpful. For those with a reactionary response, he recommends that instead of sending items that may not be useful in an emergency, they give money to reputable organizations (like those he mentioned). On the ground, he has discovered giving resources to women, especially cash in local currency, is the "best use of it" as women can be relied upon for accountability to take care of families and communities.

"I'm an emotional, impassioned, empathetic person," Passanisi said. "I will cry. I still cry, but I've tried to teach myself how not to do that so I can manage and keep things moving. Sometimes the work I did was not sexy; it was boring. But it's necessary."

Passanisi didn't choose his disaster response management career. It chose him. The year was 1992. He was happily and passionately studying domestic cats living in large groups with his sights on a Ph.D. in zoology at the University of Oxford in England. With a University of Birmingham degree in biological science, zoology and comparative physiology under his belt, he researched evolutionary epidemiology, cooperation and communal care in animals, primarily focused on group-living cats.

"I started out as a white guy with a backpack and passport, but got caught up in a devastating famine and multi-sided war in Somalia," he said.

Passanisi recalled connecting with the international non-governmental organization CARE and being asked if he could "manage a Somali airport in Baidoa, known as the City of Death." He learned that he was good at coordinating and working under pressure with little fear despite being in an area with al-Qaeda-aligned Al-Shabab insurgents and guns everywhere.

Somalia remains the country Passanisi is most connected to with the sad realization that "little has changed with stability" over the years and several of his friends there have died. While admitting his opinion is jaded, he believes, "if you've been bombed once, you'll be bombed again" and "if you've had a storm once, it will happen again."

"Adequately preparing for the next crisis is hugely overlooked," he said. "Focus on predictions and readiness is lacking."

Passanisi is pleased to be back in the "tiny house" that he and an ex-wife built near the island's Methodist Church and to be swimming in the Atlantic Ocean each morning. At the same time, he is acutely aware of the Ocracoke devastation from Hurricane Dorian in 2019 and is concerned for the survival of a village built on sand.

In 2024, Passanisi wonders, too, about the direction of his life. Weary from his international humanitarian labor ("with PTSD most have from the work"), he feels drawn to "exploring my artistic side," mentoring the next generation to serve vulnerable populations and spending time with his 21-year-old son.

He's an adjunct professor in the School of Public Health at the University of North Carolina at Chapel Hill. One course in his wheelhouse is environmental crisis management. He wants to share insights into "how to work alongside a person in need when you're a person of privilege" and reinforce the realization that more often than not someone "local" can do a job as well as an expensive foreigner coming in short term from the outside.

"There are more crises today than 20 years ago," Passanisi said. "It's truly difficult to take it all in but workers who can are needed."

(2024, North Carolina)

Human Rights

Oh, be careful little eyes what you see...ears what you hear...tongue what you say...hands what you do.

This children's song, based on Mark 4:24–25, popular in America today and written in 1956, likely wasn't known in Uganda when Johnson Mayamba was growing up. Nevertheless, the words ring true for the 33-year-old who was abandoned by a father who had eight children by four women, was chased away by relatives unwilling to help a single mom feed a hungry boy and was mocked for his ignorance by teachers and classmates in school.

The most stinging memory was planted by a science teacher at a primary school in Abaita Ababiri Village near Entebbe. She publicly shamed Mayamba for what he didn't know. She mocked him with words and laughter and allowed students to do the same. After one exam he failed with a 50%, the teacher brought out a cane. She planned on issuing 50 strikes to the 12-year-old's buttocks and thighs—one for each missed point—but stopped somewhere after 40 because the boy was flattened out and unable to take more.

"I wasn't stupid," Mayamba said. "I was simply in a new environment, having been transferred from a poorly facilitated village school to the one in the city."

Unbeknownst at the time, Mayamba's "little" eyes, ears, and body encounter that the teacher used to remind him that he wasn't good enough were molding his future as an advocate against mistreatment. Today, he understands it, researches it, writes about it and teaches it.

With a Bachelor of Arts in Mass Communication from Uganda Christian University (UCU) and experience as a journalist, he moved on to get a Master of Philosophy in Human Rights and Democratisation in Africa from the University of Pretoria in South Africa. He's affiliated with the Canadian-based Journalists for Human Rights organization with a role of helping 20 Ugandan members of the press to be voices for unrepresented people. These include print and broadcast human rights stories related to the economically poor, the mentally and physically handicapped and those identifying themselves as non-heterosexual.

While mentoring Ugandan journalists, Mayamba continues his own learning as a Hubert H. Humphrey Fellow at the Walter Cronkite School of Journalism and Mass Communication, Arizona State University, USA. He was among just over 200 from Uganda who applied for the fellowship and was the only one chosen for the 10-month journalism-focused program that ends in June 2022.

"I never thought I would come to the United States," he said, speaking from his dormitory room in Phoenix, Ariz. "All the glory goes to God."

Mayamba had a strong upbringing in the Catholic church, but says his relationship with God strengthened while he studied at UCU. In his studies as well as engagement in the

UCU chapel choir and as a guild and public debate leader, he realized that with God, obstacles and accomplishments have meaning.

"When you give 100% to God and trust Him, you can overcome," he said.

Human rights advocacy and Christianity blend together well, especially guided by the Matthew 7:12 (NIV) "do unto others" scripture, according to Mayamba. As a working journalist, he often prayed with and for those he interviewed for stories. For the journalists he mentors now, he suggests the same along with the urging to be sensitive when writing about people subjected to discrimination. He also cautions reporters about their own safety when covering topics that have opposition from government officials, high-profile opinion leaders and even media houses themselves.

"Have the facts," he said. "That's the best protection to mitigate risk."

Same-sex conduct, which is illegal in Uganda, is one example of a seldom-covered human rights issue in East Africa. Mayamba became more vocal about gender preferences after the January 2011 killing of David Kato, a Ugandan human rights defender and LGBT activist.

"Who has a right to define these life rules as a template we all must follow?" he asked, rhetorically. "Shunning, mocking and being denied services such as treatment at a hospital because of the way you look or are perceived are a violation of basic human rights."

In 2021, 9,000 miles away from his home in Uganda, Mayamba was in Arizona, closely watching another human rights issue—the coronavirus pandemic. He had recently

Johnson Mayamba with Sarah Lagot Odwong during university undergraduate days

published a paper entitled *Low Supply and Public Mistrust Hinder Covid-19 Vaccine Rollout in Africa.* He wrote that in November 2021, only four percent of the world's vaccinated people live in developing countries like Uganda.

"Developed countries who aren't sharing enough of the vaccine are partially to blame," Mayamba said. "Misinformation or lack of information breeding distrust by the media in all countries bears the rest of the responsibility."

Social media and traditional media are accountable for honest story-telling about gender identification and health, Mayamba said. His master's research focuses on media freedom, specifically in Uganda. Reporters without Borders ranks Uganda among the lowest in the world when it comes to press freedom. According to Mayamba's experience and research, while Uganda's constitution guarantees freedom of expression and other human rights, there are radio, TV and print limitations and restrictions related to reporting on certain topics and persons

While the United States press is freer and human rights more respected than in Uganda, "it's not as rosy here as I thought," he said. "In this land of the free, there needs to be more and louder voices for homeless people, immigrants ... and on racial injustice and gun violence."

From his dorm room window in Phoenix, Mayamba daily observes nearly two dozen homeless people living on a square of land. During a visit to New York City and looking past the amazing buildings, he saw men and women living in parks and on the streets. In his brief time in Washington, D.C., he observed first-hand the massive police response and multiple phone video recordings of the arrest of a Black man accused of stealing a small item from a store. He follows the news about arrests, trials and confusion about wrongful deaths on American soil and about Mexican families camped at the USA border who are seeking asylum.

"Telling these stories honestly and fairly is the role of a journalist," he said. "Human rights stories are lacking everywhere."

One such story he hopes to learn more about is that of a middle-aged white man living under the stars outside his residence in Arizona. In the midst of book studies, computer research, and service projects such as preparing food in boxes for people like this man, he wants to "learn his story and tell him mine." So far, the man appears educated but without a home because he lost his job.

Looking ahead to his life a decade from now, Mayamba doesn't see himself reporting the news in a country such as his where the pay is too low to support a family. But he does see himself continuing to train others to "amplify the voices" of those less represented and understood. In three years, he hopes to embark on his PhD studies and be teaching journalism with an emphasis on human rights reporting.

For now, he's navigating the American culture that includes daily conversion of temperatures from Fahrenheit to Celsius and distance from miles to kilometers. He is appreciating a winter in the warmth of Arizona instead of living in a state with cold and snow. He is soaking up knowledge in a school named after Walter Cronkite, a late veteran broadcaster that he never knew. He is learning alongside 13 other journalists from 13 countries, including South Korea, Russia, Hungary, and Palestine.

He thinks about his mother who died of cervical cancer in September 2014, leaving behind her two sons—Johnson Mayamba and the younger Titus Bulega. He also thinks about that childhood teacher who meted out that early punishment and ridicule—illegal but still occurring.

"At the end of the day, I moved ahead of them," he said. "And I learned to stand up for myself and for others."

(2021, Uganda & USA)

Hurricane*

War and weather are two main reasons for resident displacement. One horrific storm devastating homes in the USA reared its head in the autumn of 2022.

On a Tuesday afternoon of one of the final warm, sunny central Ohio days before the winter blast, Carmel Jenkins and I were talking about bad weather—cyclones, tornadoes, typhoons and hurricanes that are all pretty much the same with the name depending on where they geographically occur.

Fortunately, and as a lifelong Ohioan, I haven't personally been impacted by any of these.

Carmel Jenkins has.

Usually, she's asking me questions about Uganda, my work and the dire needs in East Africa. Today, I'm the questioner focused on catastrophic hurricanes, namely the late September 2022 one called Ian, the fourth largest storm in the history of Florida. For 18 years, Carmel lived in this USA peninsula state as one of those people escaping cold winters for a warmer climate, AKA as "snowbirds."

Lived. Past tense. Hurricane Ian destroyed 5,000 homes, including one belonging to Carmel.

Carmel Jenkins

Carmel, who identifies as widow, mother, grandmother, Christian, educator, card player, dance instructor, lover of animals, and now former snowbird, has no plans to go back.

"I cried, more than once," she said, recalling the southwest Florida devastation she watched in the news from her Reynoldsburg, Ohio, home, where she now lives all year.

Carmel, whose name is pronounced like the chewy, toffee candy, lived in Ft. Myers Beach, Fla., for a third of every year. That was before Ian surged in especially hard on Ft. Myers, blowing off roofs, lifting cars, flattening walls and carrying away palm trees, boats, resident belongings and debris in 10-foot-deep water normally contained in the Caloosahatchee River and the Gulf of Mexico.

I sensed what was happening to Carmel's Florida property as the last week of September I read her Facebook posts and, with five housemates, watched Hurricane Ian on TV during a vacation at Ocracoke Island, North Carolina.

"Praying for my neighbors and friends in Ft. Myers who live there year-round," Carmel's Facebook read as Ian touched ground on September 28. "It is such a helpless feeling knowing that there is nothing you can do…" The next day, as she knew many had evacuated to higher ground or further from the coast, she posted a Facebook request for continued "praying for Florida … sad, sad state of affairs. Heartsick but grateful to be safe in Ohio."

I wondered about Carmel as my husband, Mike, and I rode bikes and had food and drinks outside in relatively good weather and saw somewhat nervously how the Ian remnants caused the Atlantic Ocean to move in closer on the tourist-popular Outer Banks where we vacationed. Minus the ferry boat ride from Ocracoke Island to mainland North Carolina, we were about a 17-hour drive to Carmel's place.

I wondered and worried about her along with full-time Florida residents Carolyn, Allen, Barbara and others who I lived alongside for a couple months in a condo complex in the normally unspoiled Punta Gorda area this year and last.

Floridians like Barbara and her husband, Randy, packed bags and moved inland but with hopes of returning to only minor damage to their dream home overlooking the Peace River and Charlotte Harbor. Compared to Ft. Myers 30 minutes away, their area was largely unscathed. Punta Gorda, devastated by Hurricane Charley in 2004, incurred relatively minor damage from Ian.

All the anxiety from hurricanes with knowledge that these coastal areas are continually and increasingly hit with rising sea level caused by climate change makes some wonder if parts of storm-ravaged Florida should be re-built at all. According to the Hurricane Research Division of the National Oceanic and Atmospheric Administration, 40% of all hurricanes hit Florida somewhere. People who gravitate to the "sunshine state" for the warm weather and beaches—either full- or part-time—know this.

But nobody thinks about it happening. Until it does.

In June, I was in Ft. Myers, participating in an anti-gun rally on pristine streets and buying an artist's handmade necklace at a shop—oblivious to what would happen three months later. In early July, I rode a bicycle all over Florida's now Ian-devastated Sanibel Island.

As Carmel and I met on November 8, 2022, another hurricane called Nicole slammed into Florida's central and east sides.

"That part of me is over," Carmel told me.

Over soup, salad and breadsticks—hurried to allow her to pick up a grandson for a dental appointment—the woman who I've known for more a decade, narrated her perspective of the devastation and loss with words like "sense of helplessness," "overwhelming" and "not a darn thing you can do."

At that, and as a Christian, she added, "It's just stuff."

As Ian dissolved from its path along Cuba to Florida and South Carolina, Carmel assembled a plan to assess firsthand the damage to her trailer home at Ft. Myers' Indian

Creek RV Park where, she knew, some full-timers refused to leave and died. Of the 125 mostly elderly men and women who lost their lives to Ian, Carmel "knew of" four in her park.

During our conversation a month after Ian, she recounted three of the four who drowned in 10 feet of surging water. The fourth was a husband who took his own life after watching his wife perish in the storm.

She also knew of two rescued neighbors. As local first responders struggled to do their jobs from a fire station full of water, the nonprofit Cajun Navy arrived. Among those pulled to safety by this cadre of volunteer boat owners were a man and woman struggling in water up to their necks.

With minimal PPE (personal protective equipment)—gloves, boots and borrowed respirators—Carmel and a friend, Mary Kay, drove the 1,150 miles to see what was left. As they approached the RV park, they saw food trucks interspersed with rescue workers and homeless residents sleeping in cars and tents in a Walmart parking lot. After minor security clearance at what was once the RV security gate, Carmel and Mary Kay drove on the road to what had been Carmel's winter escape for 72 months over two decades.

From prior conversations with Ft. Myers Beach neighbors already there and social media posts with photos of streets littered with parts of homes and their contents, Carmel wasn't especially surprised with what she saw. Her normally neat, one-bedroom unit purchased from a flight attendant years ago was in disarray. Walls and the door were broken in with marks showing the depth of water. Pots and pans were scattered. Appliances were destroyed. The stench from septic and rot was intense.

"The borrowed respirators were hot but protected us," she said. "Others were vomiting from the smell."

Carmel found solace in finding years of collected Christmas decorations—Florida seashells, mermaids, stars—nearly all intact in a tote in her shed. She carried the plastic container to her car and sanitized everything from the water leakage when she got back to Ohio. She showed me a photo of her beautiful, seemingly unharmed butterfly bench too bulky to transport. Looters would be sure to take it.

"One man brought everything to his patio to be picked up the next day, but when he came back, it was all gone," she said. "There is supposed to be security, but there isn't. Looters came in right away."

Carmel shared that her park's three recreation buildings and pools were in shambles. There, with other senior men and women, she once exercised, watched movies, played cards and engaged in 50s and 80s theme parties.

Like many Floridians, Carmel had no property insurance. Most living in Florida's coastal "paradise" can't afford it from the few companies who offer it but not for certain damage like "storm surge." Assistance from the government's Federal Emergency Management Agency (FEMA) is only for full-time residents—defined as those living in Florida for six months plus one day a year. Carmel's friends who plan to return to her RV park after water and electricity are restored by the target date of February 2023 will find such coverage even harder to get.

By the time of our Olive Garden lunch 40 days after Ian's strike, Carmel had dried her tears and moved on just as she has done before. A husband who died from Parkinson's in 2008. A close friend now with Alzheimer's. Lots more.

Carmel, age 78, finds strength in being active, pleasure in friendships and "lifelong learning" and peace when "seeing deer in the backyard" of her Reynoldsburg, Ohio, home. With continued prayers for those who lost lives and their only home in Hurricane Ian's path, she hopes for her own legacy in one word—"kindness."

As I drove home listening to the radio music and news, I realized that me and my neighbors in Ohio and probably other states have forgotten about Hurricane Ian. That's what we do. Short memories.

Not so for those directly impacted. Like Carmel.

People, not "stuff" is the biggest loss, she says. Her words: "The lives gone and loss of friendships hurt the most."

(2022, Florida)

After hurricane Ian

Kidney Failure

The kidneys—those two 4.5-inch organs that each of us is born with so we can pee—are taking mom's life. I got the call on Thursday that mom's kidney functionality is 15%, also known as stage 5 (the last stage) failure. Dialysis or transplant are not an option for an already frail, 90-pound, 92-year-old. Last night and as mom sat confused and tired between me and my sister at mom's extended care facility, I put my POA signature on the Hospice paperwork.

Mom's time could be weeks to six months.

The mixed blessing for me and other family members and friends is that while we are more certain of the timing when we will lose our matriarch, now that mom is classified as Hospice "comfort" and "compassionate" care, we can see her more often. And touch her—something forbidden by elder-care facilities concerned with data of deaths due to Covid-19.

Mixed blessing because the tiny woman who lived for human hugs and hand and feet massages, now recoils in pain at even a gentle stroke. Mom's hands are ravaged with arthritis. The toe on her right foot that gave her problems for the past decade is bandaged and joined by a darken and infected one on the left. Skin on her right arm is covered in gauze to protect gashes just above her almost-healed broken wrist. Her left forehead is bruised from a recent fall.

None of these outward scars can compare to the inward ones from the past year's isolation brought on by Covid-19. As our government and facilities rushed to protect our most virus-vulnerable elderly from this disease, and their own statistics and reputations from coronavirus cases and deaths, mom was caught in the cognition crossfire. For nearly 12 months, I watched helplessly outside her window.

Last night, she cried as she told me and my sister how proud she is of her "two girls" about to graduate from high school. While she envisioned us as teenagers, she saw her brother, Bob, seated at the end of the hallway. Uncle Bob, who died in January 2016, is wearing his usual tan pants, she says.

Ironically, and except for mom's few medical appointments and hospital stays, it's almost a year to the day since that

March 2020, glorious outing when mom and I wore St. Patrick's Day hats, had a potato soup and mint chocolate-chip ice cream lunch at Clay's in Hebron and saw old friends. When I returned mom to her assisted living apartment, laughing and carrying bags of snacks from the Dollar store, I was met with a "no entrance" order. That was March 12 last year.

With hospice nurses and case managers at my side this March 17, I hope to bring green fun stuff to mom. I'll do my best to make it glorious. And I'll try not to cry.

(2021, Ohio)

Kite Surfer

The first story I wanted to do on Ocracoke Island, North Carolina, became the last.

"I want to do a story on kites," I said before unloading my stuff and more properly greeting Connie Leinbach, the *Ocracoke Observer* editor-publisher, at her house on March 31, 2023. As patient as any editor who I've ever had, she accommodated my journalistic excitement about kites.

It wasn't just kites that I saw above the Atlantic Ocean and Pamlico Sound, but the people being thrashed around in the sky by them. I'm from Ohio for God's sake. Except for a few crazies by Lake Erie, which is three hours from my house, we fly our kites from and above the ground. They don't fly us over the water.

In the midst of a one-month newspaper internship of interviewing some incredible people on topics of figs, woodcarving, cars, lighthouses, music and more, I met Keith Croghan, 43, the guy you go to for learning to kitesurf on Ocracoke, and Randal Mathews, 64, a Hyde County commissioner who kitesurfs. I met Keith at the post office. I met Randal during a lighthouse history meeting connected to another story.

I didn't want to try kitesurfing. I simply wanted to see it close up, take photos and write about it.

I became obsessed during my volunteer newspaper gig with what I learned is interchangeably called kiting, kitesurfing and kiteboarding. I was frustrated that I couldn't whip out this story on a tight deadline like the others I did.

Alas, kiting (the term I'm going to stick with for the rest of this article) is all about the wind. It's gotta be right.

Randal started sending me text messages of "too high" or "too low" with wind graph visuals.

While people in my yoga class relished in the calm movement of island air on a sunny day, the two kite guys did not.

"It's got to be over 15 miles per hour but not over 60," Keith said.

The answer for people engaged in fishing, boating and kiting is not just blowing in the wind. It IS the wind.

Ocracoke's Captain Rob, who took me and some friends out in his sailboat last September, talks about an ideal 15 to 20 knots, which is a maximum 23 miles per hour.

On Easter Sunday, the Ocracoke United Methodist church was standing-room-only not so much for the love of Jesus but, as Pastor Logan Jackson acknowledged, some less-practiced Christians were trapped by 50 mph winds that suspended their ferry boat transportation to the mainland. Praise God.

Nine days into what Connie and I started calling my "senior internship" and on the afternoon of that April 9 church service, Randal picked me up in his 4WD and drove me to places where kiting would, in better weather, take place. It wasn't the 55-degree temperature or rain pelting his windshield that grounded him that day, he explained. It was the wind. Coming northeast at 30 mph with gusts, there was too much of it.

"I'm thinking tomorrow afternoon for our downwinder," Randal texted that evening. He later told me that's when you rig a kite to a location upwind so you can ride it downwind. Sure enough, it was a go on April 10 but during my yoga "namaste."

Patience is not my virtue, but waiting for another kiting window allowed me more research time. Books from a beginners guide to extreme kiting are available, but with Ocracoke 24 miles from the mainland and Amazon not as accessible, I opted for the only somewhat related book I could find—*A surfing life* by William Finnegan. I skimmed it. What the author said about ocean waves breaking when they reach 80% of the ocean's depth certainly connected to humans flying kites from the water.

"You can catch 10 times more waves with kiting than surfing," said Keith, who has done both.

I looked at the cheaper kite kits in island stores. I was on the internet a lot.

A British guy is credited for the kiting concept as he crossed the English Channel in a kite-driven, canvas boat in 1903. Two brothers from France took it another step in 1984 when they patented an inflatable kite design. Kiting became a mainstream sport with an event in Hawaii in 1998.

Keith shared with me a video of a British guy kiting from a buggy on land. Learning that I'm a snow skier, he sent me a heart-pounding, seven-minute GoPro of a guy tandem (two skis) kiting on a snow-covered mountain. Water kiters use a slalom/single ski, a kite, the wind and themselves. Kitesurf racing, I learned, will be an event at the 2024 Summer Olympics in Paris.

While waiting for the second thumbs up, I also learned more about Keith and Randal.

Kite surfing

Keith was born on Michigan's Mackinac Island, which is about half the size of Ocracoke. He started going to school in Virginia in fourth grade and, like any kid, flew kites—the ones invented in China centuries ago. He learned kiting in his mid-20s. He's done it in the Dominican Republic, Nicaragua, Costa Rica, and throughout the Caribbean since then and has been teaching it for 15 years with 12 of those years on Ocracoke.

"This is the kind of sport you can do all day," he said. "You are using your core, your glutes, your shoulders, but if you do it right the kite does the work. It's like riding a horse but you're bridling the wind."

Kiting, for ages five and up, is less strenuous than e-foiling (electric board with a fin) and surfing and cheaper than buying a foil board. Water skiing—being pulled behind a boat— is more physically demanding, according to Keith.

The kiting learning curve is three lessons of three hours each, he said. Keith teaches on the calm and shallow waters of the Pamlico Sound. He advertises at the Jolly Rodger and the slushy stand (252-928-FLYI). Kiters should expect an investment of several thousand dollars for lessons and equipment. The size, again, is based on wind. Smaller kites (9 square meters/29 square feet) manage better on days of more wind; larger kites (12 square meters/39 square feet) fit best with milder wind.

Randal, an island resident for 40 years and married to a native of Ocracoke, has been a surfer for 50 years. In addition to his political hat, he's known as the "telephone man," based on past work as a network technician. He considers himself a kiter and "waterman," with the latter title related to his love of fishing and boating.

"Kiteboarding makes windsurfing or surfing feel like you are dragging a bucket," he said. "The transition to kiteboarding was natural."

To Randal, kiting is about being with nature, "sharing space with birds" and "cracking open a beer with friends" in the midst of the sport he's been doing for 18 years.

"It's best if the wind blows southwest," he said.

So it was finally on April 22, I watched Keith, Randal and another island resident, Dan Zapoto, age 53, fly over the ocean in 30 mph winds—touching down in choppy water and leaping as high as 50 feet in the air via colorful kites made of Dacron, a strong polyester textile fiber that is wrinkle-resistant and strong.

Keith's 12-square meter aqua-colored kite took him up and fast down the coast. Before exiting with feet planted in his board, he explained that novice kiters often remain in and on the water without aerials, also known as "mowing the lawn." Dan and Randal, strapped in their harnesses and using both hands to steer their smaller, 9-square meter kites, went up and down slower.

At that, Randal later sent me a text that "choppy water conditions made it hard on my legs." It was, he typed, "intense," "manageable," and "exhilarating" before changing out of his wetsuit for a wedding conducted beachside in calmer wind.

(2023, North Carolina)

Michele with one "l"

The inside of my brain is frightening. So is yours.

I've been thinking a lot about the brain, namely the frontal lobe, this past week.

Like yesterday/Thursday…I couldn't stop thinking about several friends who lost their husbands and the holes they can't fill.

Like Wednesday morning… I exited the Groveport Recreation Center as a middle-aged woman laughed louder and longer than "appropriate." I thought that our world would be a more joyful place if we all could express ourselves that way without restraints and judgment. Driving away, I saw the ARC Industries van that brought her and others with disabilities for a visit.

Like Tuesday afternoon …When visiting my dying friend, Nancy, I knew as her body was shrinking with nothing audible from her open mouth and no vision through her glazed eyes, but her brain was there. I knew that she heard me sing her favorite Kermit "Rainbow Connection" song and say a prayer for her peace and appreciation to God for her life and love.

Like Monday…as Mike tapped his leg to Chick Corea and called some North Carolina drivers "dickheads," relieving his road stress while adding to mine.

Perceptions may be the one remaining human cerebral distinction. Devoid of what real or fake media, artificial intelligence or other humans tell us to think, believe or say, humans recall and process immediate actions and memories with matchless discernments.

"There is no identical frame of knowledge," I used to tell students when I used to teach public speaking. Not for husbands and wives. Not even for twins.

On the long drive back to Ohio, after substandard motel eggs and watered-down apple juice in my stomach, I reflected on our recent, seven-day vacation, knowing that the people I lived with and encountered in that time had different thoughts. It was my fourth visit to Ocracoke Island, N.C.

This September week within the North Carolina outer banks, I was aware of auto workers picketing over a bump on their minimum wage that is more than I ever got and asking for a 32 (vs. 40) hour-work week that I never had.

Last week, I was with five housemates for meals, laughter, the Ophelia storm that delayed our island departure by one day and the nail-biter, final seconds of my Ohio State alma mater Buckeyes win over Notre Dame.

My unique reflections this week are many but mostly connected to a new friend named Michele. "It's Michele with one 'l,' " she said when we first met on Ocracoke Island in April.

A thin, almost 70 year-old woman with a long, gray braid down her back, she jumped from her car as she picked me up from the island Variety store lot to watch the sunrise that first full day of our September arrival. She walked, barefooted, alongside me on the beach and let me sing, without discomfort, a childhood song ("Wide, wide as the ocean, high as the heavens above…") and shared that I had recently wanted to end my life.

"Everybody thinks that," she said, without alarm. "If they say they don't, they're lying."

Michele and I took a mid-week, day trip to the nearby, uninhabited Portsmouth Island.

We imagined what it was like when Portsmouth Village began in 1753; the bustle of activity as a shipping port; a time when 500 residents lived among a school, church, tavern and hospital; when two-thirds of North Carolina's exports passed through the inlet; the impact of hurricanes; and before the last two residents left in 1971. We walked through the house where the postmistress lived and learned how she called out names when the mail boat arrived.

Portsmouth Island, well-known for massive, biting mosquitoes, lived up to its reputation as I left with four large red circles around my cheeks. This, despite a black net covering head to waist and repellent sprayed there and elsewhere.

As Michele and I shared a towel on a section of beach that was mostly devoid of the insects, we watched a sand crab grab algae and quickly retreat with it into its tiny holes.

I shared with her about a time in my 30s when during a group trip to Lake Erie found me passed-out drunk and being raped by a popular, older guy. He walked out as I vomited in the toilet. Michele shared how she "dug a hole" and buried her daughter's ashes between the bodies of two grandchildren and how she recently stopped drinking alcohol and smoking cigarettes.

"I sat listening to the birds and heard one sound I didn't recognize," she recalled of that cigarette cold-turkey day. "It wasn't a bird. It was my lungs."

On the Portsmouth trip back to Ocracoke, Michele gave a conch shell to a delighted boy. To a retired music teacher we just met, she put into her hand the words of a song on a worn, typed paper she'd been carrying around.

At week's end, I hunkered down with my husband and two other couples as Ophelia, intermittently called a Category 5 hurricane, a cyclone and a tropical storm, swirled around North Carolina, including near Ocracoke Island. I slept fitfully—more likely because of the Steven King book I had just finished than the 65 mile-per-hour driven swaying of the elevated house we had rented. King's new *Holly* novel is more terrifying than my brain.

That was about the time that Michele put a tiny bag of shells on the hood of our car. A note inside said "little treasures." She is.

North Carolina Highway 12, Virginia's Interstate 95 and I-77 in West Virginia seem endless and only punctuated by gas station stops en-route to Ohio.

From Michele, and at 4 p.m. Monday, there's a text: "I'm swinging on my porch."

In a world of TikTok, X, AI and the ability to "just google it," perceptions like these just may be the one remaining human cerebral distinction.

The red-wormy-looking organ called the brain produces terrifying, joyful and unique thoughts. On a Friday night as I prepare to help celebrate a friend's 59th birthday, these were some of mine.

(2023, North Carolina)

Michele on the beach

Mountain Biker

"If you're going to do it, you must commit 100% to do it right."

My high school friend, Bob Bevard, was talking about bicycling—specifically "mountain" biking, which is one of more than two dozen categories of bicycling and even more sub-categories of those biking types. He deflected concerns that his daring sport could bring him paralysis as happened to a young bicycle-riding neighbor of mine in 1998.

Or worse.

"It's risk versus excitement," he said, pointing proudly to a nine-foot, wooden plank drop with aerial possibilities to the next dip. "If you do it right, you can get 14 feet from that one. Committing less than 100% here can have an undesired outcome."

Two days before the start of 2021 and with his very active rescue dog, Rowan, Bob gave me a tour of some of the 10 trails twisting along the hillsides of Horns Hill Park in Newark, Ohio.

Until the last week of 2020, I knew next to nothing about this sport that Bob has been talking about for 25 years of high school reunions. I only knew the Horns Hill area from my days as a *Newark Advocate* reporter tagging along with cops on drug busts there and more recently, talk about Bob's legacy of creating opportunities for people like him to do jumps and turns among the park's oak, maple and ash trees.

Fully masked and six feet apart in this ever-present COVID environment, we walked up and down some of winter's muddy trails. A single rider whisked by. On better weather days, Bob said, there can be 75 bicyclers with families watching in various spots along 10 miles of trails.

Bob introduced me to the differences between shuttling (rides up a hill in a truck bed trailer) and pedaling (more work). He talked about safety equipment and the $5,000–$10,000 cost of a good bike. He hesitated to say how many bikes he owns, but acknowledged one is an e-bike that he uses for trails with steep inclines.

According to a source on the International Mountain Bicycling Association website, there are more than 33,000 trails over 115,000 miles in the United States, developed since the sport evolved in the late 1970s. According to the Horns Hill website, there are just over 100 trails in Ohio. For mountain biking enthusiasts, the emphasis is on sharing and respecting nature with minimal environmental impact.

"Some birdwatchers might be unhappy with how we disturb the soil," Bob admits.

Over the years, there has been local leader criticism about riders in the park. "But fortunately, most of these people have been supportive and encouraging," Bob says. "And they see how riders coming in help the economy."

Bob, a 69-year-old retired schoolteacher, has notoriety in Ohio not only for his participation and success in the sport but for his financial and sweat equity at the Horn's Hill trails. In addition to meetings, communications and fundraising, he has spent countless hours creating the hills and jumps in the area just past the North Fork of the Licking River. To alleviate costs and facilitate quality of construction, he purchased two excavators specific for trail development at Horns Hill and at his own property in the nearby city of Heath, Ohio.

For Bob, a ride a day at his home, at Horns Hill or at nearby Star Hill is ideal. In non-pandemic times, there are vacation trips to ride in other states, where there are mountains with trails brimming with the beauty of wildlife and clean air.

Admittedly, there are dangers in this sport. But for Bob, a few minor injuries, including a slight concussion, and seeing other riders get hurt is not a deterrent. Exercise outdoors, time alone and with friends, and stress relief are motivators.

For 2021, he's engaged in a 52-week journaling project that he might provide for further sharing.

"Mountain biking is a great analogy for life," Bob said. "You can take the easy path and get meager results. You can take a wrong turn with bad results. Or you can be all in."

For Bob, his passion is all in and (wait for it) all down hill.

(2021, Ohio)

Biker Bob

Musicman

Todd Phillips remembers the spring of 1999 as clear as yesterday.

He was a young middle-and-high-school teacher of vocal music, which, in 2024, continues to be his first performing arts love. Steve Donahue, superintendent for a school district 20 miles from Columbus, Ohio, issued a challenge to Phillips and the band director, Scott Zeuch.

"Be creative," Phillips recalled of the directive in an administrative office of Canal Winchester Schools. "He told us to find something that would make us stand out from Pickerington, Groveport, Teays Valley and Bloom Carroll area schools. I said 'how about a steel drum band'?"

The steel drum, also called steel pan, was an instrument neither the vocal or band teacher had touched. It originated in Trinidad, a Caribbean island neither man had visited, in a time before they were born.

Enslaved West and Central Africans on that island get the credit for the steel pan rhythm started in the 1700s. Before slavery was abolished in the 1930s, they pounded bamboo shoots against the ground, their bodies and onto cans in what later was labeled calypso and chutney styles, both while they worked in Trinidad sugar plantations and during celebrations. Sometimes, they were banned from the reverberation by land-owning aristocrats who believed slaves were passing secret messages through the beats.

Steel drum instruments, made from 55-gallon oil drums, became known in the United States in the 1960s. Performance was primarily confined to adult players both within and outside of universities. A steel drum band comprised of adolescents and teens was an anomaly in 1999. In 2024, the sight and sound of steel drum music is still less common than a marching band.

In late May 2024, seated in the fellowship hall of a small church where the Winchester Steel Company concert of youth and adult players was performed just five days prior, Phillips pulled out his smartphone. Showing a miniature, virtual version of the drum, he demonstrated with his fingers some of the 12-note chromatic scale that players produce with sticks and mallets. He talked about the dozen steel drums, 25–50 pounds each, stored in a nearby room, and the cost of several thousand dollars per drum, plus stands and carrying cases.

He shared the Ellie Mannette story he's told many times. Mannette, known as the father of the modern steel drum, got an oil barrel from a Trinidad shipyard, carried it home on his bicycle and pounded it into an instrument.

The band known as the Winchester Steel Company, founded in 2000, ceased at the school district at the start of summer 2023. But it was easily transferred to the Canal Winchester

Joint Recreation District. Since the fall of 2023, steel drums, vocal music and street performers operate under a newer Performing Arts Collective nonprofit that Phillips directs.

The Collective, a 501(c)(3), was something that Phillips and his wife, Nyla, an accomplished piano performer and teacher, had talked about for at least a year. The Collective includes the Steel Company, a community choir called Winchester Voices and actors who are part of Winchester Street Theatre Troupe. Phillips' daughter, Abbey, who has a background of dance with BalletMet, is one theater director.

An instrumental ensemble is being planned for the fall of 2024. A dance/movement program could be added in the distant future.

The steel drum's uniqueness in the midwestern United States is likely the reason that many inside and outside the music world ask Phillips about it. He started playing the drums when he was 10 years old.

"But I'm a vocalist first and foremost," Phillips said. He started out as a tenor. By grade 10, he was a baritone. He picked up the guitar at age 16 and played at coffee houses in the 1970s James Taylor era.

Countless chorale alum and fellow singers in choirs like Capriccio Columbus attest to his vocal passion, as do his academic credentials. He received his Bachelor of Music Education from Miami University as a voice major and percussion minor. He holds a Master of Music in Music Performance, Choral Conducting, from The Ohio State University.

Steel drum band that Todd directs

"The oldest musical instrument is the voice. Singing is so natural to us. Music is the sound that babies make before they say their first words," he said, mimicking a sound indistinguishable as spoken language. "And babies are always pounding on things."

Some of those babies, like Phillips, grow up and make a career of it. One of four boys to a mom with a music degree and a father practicing law in the farming community of Greenfield, Ohio, he was destined toward music.

"Do what you love, just find a way to make a paycheck," he recalled the words from his father.

Phillips did and does.

"I have a very selective skill set," said Phillips, now in his early 60s. "It's making music and teaching it."

His instructional methodology may seem unorthodox to trained musicians and others who recall growing up with harsh, task-oriented music teachers.

"I certainly have talented performers," he said. "But my emphasis is on providing something that everybody can be part of. We want to perform as well as possible. We set goals and work in every rehearsal to improve skills, but none of us is perfect, and I refused to reject somebody. Music is a field we will never master. There's always something new to learn."

At Canal Winchester High School, many saw perfection in the Women's Chorale and Symphonic Choir and a select Vocals Ensemble; a Shakespeare-inspired Madrigal Dinner Theatre; guitar; music theory; and the Steel Drum Band that Phillips led. All received accolades and performance awards during Phillips' nearly four decades of teaching.

At that, Phillips insisted that while the groups participated in contests, and his daily music lessons were aligned with the Ohio Department of Education standards, he never focused on competition. The program's primary goals were to create a safe space for all students and build a community of lifelong artists.

In his semi-retirement gig, Phillips does the same with an expanded age group.

Working with middle and high school kids and senior citizens up to age 90 and everything in between now, he does not "sit around well," Phillips said.

At the first public performance of the Voices choir in donated space in a local church in late May 2024, he reminded the audience that all people can sing and that singing just might be "your escape from the rest of the world around you."

The non-profit has no official building. Rehearsals and performances are in local churches and in the street. Phillips picks music that is a blend of genres.

"What I am doing is in my DNA," he said, adding that for 99 percent of the Collective's participants, there is "no desire for a paycheck in music."

The semi-retired music man is hard-pressed to provide numbers of those impacted by his skill. When pushed for data, he refers to his early mentors who reminded him that impact is more anecdotal than statistical.

"You can't change the world," he said. "But you can change how students of all ages see themselves in the world, who they can be and what they are capable of becoming. I'm not done doing that yet."

(2024, Ohio)

Native American

Crystal Lake, nestled on two sides of a station where men, women and children board a 20-minute train into the heart of Chicago, could be the setting for a Hallmark movie. On a sunny but chillier-than-normal Saturday morning, people are walking well-behaved dogs, buying locally made knitted hats and scarves, escorting boys and girls to musical instrument and ballet lessons, munching on caramel corn and snapping photos of autumn decorations of straw, ribbons and pumpkins.

"This IS a Hallmark movie," I excitedly told my husband, Mike, as he sipped an oat milk cappuccino inside a toasty-warm coffee shop. A middle-aged woman I had just met suggested a book for me to read—after another elderly woman and her son discussed with me the weather and their plans for the day and after a local shop owner shared a story about her days as a proofreader for the *Cleveland Plain Dealer* as together we wished for the simpler days of 20th century American print journalism

Odd that I would fantasize about life's perfections similar to those in Hallmark movies on the weekend of America's Columbus Day holiday. My country, including the Christopher Columbus fable that continues to be drilled into children's heads, is anything but perfect. As difficult as it is to shake my early learning of the rhythmic "in 1492, Columbus sailed the ocean blue" to bring Europeans to a new land of promise, I must.

With no apology to my elementary school teachers because they were wrong, here are five reality checks:

#1: Italian explorer Christopher Columbus first landed in the Bahamas—not what is known as the United States.

#2: Neither Columbus or, as some believe, Amerigo Vespucci "discovered" North, South or Central America. People, probably coming from Asia, were already there.

#3: Early Europeans like Columbus voyaged across the Atlantic for money and status—not for a better world. Columbus wanted gold for himself and the elite white class, including the king and queen of Spain.

#4: From what are now the Bahamas, Cuba, Haiti and the Dominican Republic, Christopher Columbus took indigenous people (then known as Arawak Indians because Columbus thought he was in India) as slaves that he and his men killed if they didn't produce enough gold and who died from the cold as they were captured and transported to Europe. He was no white savior.

#5: Europeans like Christopher Columbus were all about materialism. They didn't understand or appreciate an indigenous culture of hospitality and sharing that typifies the dwellers (also known as First Nation, native Americans, American Indians) already in the United States.

Like most American schoolchildren and then grownups, I was brainwashed into believing that the Columbus Day holiday in October and the government-designated Thanksgiving

Day to eat turkey and pumpkin pie in November were to be celebrated for the greatness of our civilization. Through research and cultural immersion, I agonize over the dirty truth of what our ancestors did—and what many continue to do—to these First Nation people.

Within a Holiday Inn in the Crystal Lake southwest suburb of Chicago during the evening of October 12 and two days before the 2019 Columbus Day, Mike and I met with more than 100 other USA citizens that share the distress as well as a desire to increase awareness of realities and solutions. We also drank wine; ate chicken, vegetables and chocolate cake; and bought handmade crafts that resemble what I see in Uganda.

The focus last night under a two-decades-old organization called "Re-Member" was on the roughly 19,000 residents of Pine Ridge Reservation in Oglala Lakota County, South Dakota.

As one of more than 550 tribes that represent 2% of the United States' population, here are five Pine Ridge reality checks:

#1: Among more than 3,000 counties in the United States, Lakota County is the poorest. The average annual income is $7,773.

#2: The average life expectancy for men and women in Pine Ridge is 47 and 55 years, respectively.

#3: Just over 42% of the Pine Ridge residents are under age 20 with 70% of them never finishing high school.

#4: Alcohol abuse and diabetes are common disorders with one in four Pine Ridge children diagnosed with fetal alcohol problems. Mental health conditions are common. Suicide rates are high.

#5: Of the more than 500 Native American treaties with the USA government, including those at Pine Ridge, all have been violated or broken by the government.

Among the compassionate, caring, action-driven USA citizens last night, including some indigenous Pine Ridge residents, the word "forgotten" was mixed with "hope" in listening, building relationships and, as more than one person said, "firewood," "construction" and farming for "good food." More than 1,000 volunteers a year come to Pine Ridge to help with those things. Youth from David's United Church of Christ in Canal Winchester (my home place of worship) are among those.

"One third of the Pine Ridge homes don't have electricity," a Grand Rapids, Michigan, volunteer said. "It's like a third world country inside a first world country."

Certainly not a setting for the Hallmark movie channel.

(2019, Illinois)

Nerves

Nancy Beery has got what I've got. One of six of you reading this have it, too. Broadly, at least.

We have neurological disorders. The National Institute of Neurological Disorders and Stroke says there are 400 classifications from the common headache to the Michael Fox-popularized Parkinson's Disease.

Mine is called essential tremors or dystonia.
- Confined primarily to my left hand that shakes slightly.
- Diagnosed 25 years ago.
- Shared by 4,166 people or 24 of 100,000.
- No definite cause.
- No cure. No impact on life expectancy.
- Stabilized through exercise, limited caffeine, drinking wine.

Nancy's is called corticobasal degeneration (CBD).
- Confined (currently) to the left side of her body that she drags along with her still mobile right.
- Diagnosed 18 months ago.
- Shared by one of every 20,000 people or five per 100,000.
- No definite cause.
- No cure. Life expectancy 10 years.
- Curbed by BOTOX and physical therapy and masked with doses of coffee, glasses of wine, cannabis and diverse friends who are both long-time and briefly-known.

As relatively new friends, Nancy and I are making up time. Sandwiched among Elizabeth, Janet, Kathy and other more long-timers, we share stories, intimate thoughts and yes, wine, within what Nancy calls Primrose Cottage. Her clock is ticking.

The timer started in 2014. Nancy was diapering a not-yet-one-year-old baby—a task she had done countless times—when a finger in her left hand started twitching uncontrollably.

"It was my trigger finger, the middle finger," she said, laughing.

She was 64. After 29 years teaching elementary school children in Circleville, a year in England as a Fulbright exchange and some substitute teaching in her birthplace and home in Canal Winchester, she relished her retirement job of watching children and babies. At 6 p.m. those weekdays, she met friends for wine, snacked on her favorite beet hummus appetizer and helped fill a room with laughter.

Weekends had her driving her Mini Cooper to a local park to walk and run.

"I trained for half marathons," she said. "I did three of them."

At 65, Nancy's neurological disorder was diagnosed as spinal stenosis that could be fixed with 40 stitches and back fusions she painfully endured. It couldn't. At 68, one opinion was that she had Parkinson's. She didn't. At age 70 and in the summer of 2020, it was confirmed CBD.

"They really won't know what I have until I die," she says matter of factly. "This disease is only officially diagnosed post-mortem."

On this particular day, January 30, 2022, and munching on one of the heart-shaped sugar cookies that I snatched for each of us from a table after church, my 4'9" barely 100-pound friend joked about her condition label and treatment. She both has CBD and legally takes CBD, a chemical found in marijuana, to combat it.

With more humor than emotion, Nancy candidly shares bits and pieces of her past and present.

She had one true love but never married. One winter of teaching first graders had her bundling them up and marching them single file through a farm field to work off their energy. She lives for sports on TV and for two giggling adolescent girls who stop by after school, call her "Snee" and sometimes spend the night at Primrose.

Her present neurological journey includes waking up when a neighbor starts his car, using her still controllable right hand to type on Facebook, enduring therapy, and entertaining visitors. She has had to humble herself to get help with opening bottles, lifting, showering, dressing.

On this last Sunday in January, my newest best friend talked and sipped coffee while tucked into a chair near a window showing winter's snow. She wears a loose black and white smock with new orange and yellow fuzzy slippers that she ordered from Amazon a size too big so she can better ease a foot inside.

We mostly laugh but sometimes get serious in her tiny house. It's near a school where she moved after her father, a doctor, lost his battle to cancer in 1991. Here, for 15 years, she cared for her mother, who left medical school to marry a doctor. Here, she watched her mother die.

"In this room," she pointed across the room, "there in a hospital bed."

Instead of a hospital bed, Nancy has a newly arrived lift chair in another room next to one with her bed now mostly occupied on weekends by 12-year-old Janna (older sister of the baby she diapered eight years ago). In a closet is a portable toilet so far only used once and emptied by the lady who cleans her house. Her garage that once housed the Cooper is there for a neighbor's car. She's selling some antiques. She is giving away scarves, including one for me, red with black musical notes. .

"I'm the Bermuda Triangle of senior citizens," she says. "I have enough to survive if I don't suffer any catastrophic illness. I'm managing what I don't need to prepare for that."

Nancy hopes her legacy will be that she was welcoming, loving and a good friend.

"I don't want to be a disease," she says.

To stave off that identifier, the 72-year-old needs people. Most of us do.

"Being with people," she says, "keeps me from thinking about my body."

Being a caregiver as she was as a teacher, babysitter and daughter is, Nancy tells me, "the most valuable but challenging experience of your life." She adds that she's not very good at being on the receiving end of that.

Rarely now does she cry herself to sleep. Slumber doesn't come easy in a chair or with the inability to toss and turn.

Her prayer is to retain her ability to think and speak. And for a cure before the clock runs out. While we are here together sharing our thoughts, eating egg rolls and chocolate chip cookies and drinking an occasional hot chocolate with peppermint schnapps, I pray for all that, too.

In the meantime, we are friends, and the "new" label is dimming.

(2022, Ohio)

The late Nancy Beery

Paralysis

Like me, Stacy James drinks smoothies with oat milk and bananas, has irregular sleep patterns and holds a pageant title. Unlike me, her insomnia is sometimes caused by muscle spasms, someone helps her make her smoothie beverages, and one of her contest titles includes the word "wheelchair."

Stacy, 52, broke her neck in a diving mishap when she was 20. In 2023, she is among 291,000 United States residents who have spinal cord injuries.

At first, I wasn't sure I wanted to write about Stacy. For starters, I wasn't sure she was real. In August 2022 and from my apartment in Uganda, I read a private Facebook message that this person I'd never met was reading a two-decades-old book I wrote (*Shattered*) about a paralyzed teenage girl and who wanted to meet that girl.

After returning to the United States, I verified Stacy's existence but failed to connect her with the now 40-something subject of that early book. I wondered if Stacy's story was a good fit for a new book that I had been working on for four years. That book would be a compilation of stories about ordinary people doing extraordinary things. Unlike them, Stacy is an extraordinary person trying to do ordinary things.

Stacy, paralyzed for 32 years, won Ms. Wheelchair Ohio (2002-2003) and Forty under 40 (2010). She is one of the top four central Ohio Remarkable Women (2020). She has over 200 medals in wheelchair track and field events. On-line videos show some of her athletic accomplishments—adaptive kayaking and water- and snow-skiing and 14 painfully completed marathons—as well as her many motivational speaking presentations. Resilience in overcoming obstacles is the major theme of her talks.

Before meeting Stacy in person, I researched enough to know what was amazing about her. I was curious to learn what wasn't. I wanted to discover the raw parts of living with her disability.

On March 10, 2023, from her Powell, Ohio, condominium, Stacy mostly stood next to her wheelchair ("to minimize my leg spasms," she said) and steadied herself at a lectern. I sat cross-legged on her floor, hearing the accident story that she has told countless times. She described how in June 1991, as a University of Cincinnati student, she dove into a pool that was too shallow.

Never again would she twirl a baton or play piano or guitar or easily do ordinary things like running a comb through her hair or brushing her teeth. She was paralyzed, but with her mom and God at her side, she persevered.

Her mother continued to be there for her—taking her to medical appointments, speaking engagements and athletic events and providing companionship. With her mom, Stacy traveled—usually in her role as a chaplain for paralympic games—to places like Greece, England, Italy and Canada. For 20 years, until her mom lost a five-month battle with cancer in 2011, they were inseparable.

"Losing my mom was like losing five people—mother, business partner, cook, cleaner, personal assistant," she said.

That was 12 years ago. Now, it's God and her.

Being a Christian, including her affiliation with Campus Crusade for Christ (CRU) that continued after becoming paralyzed, is Stacy's stabilizer. Philippians 4:13 (NIV) "I can do all things through Christ who gives me strength" is her driver.

At that, Stacy needs people.

"Help is my love language," she said. "If I don't have help, I can't live my life."

Stacy needs assistance to retrieve her mail from a box located a half a block from her door, to change and launder her bed sheets, vacuum the floor, cook, make smoothies, lift her legs in and out of a car, transport her and her wheelchair and stretch her legs. After any spinal cord injury, the normal flow of signals to move body parts is disrupted, causing twitching, jerking or stiffening of muscles, especially in legs.

"I need to have my legs stretched an hour every day," she said. "With effort, I can do my heel cords and arms, but not my legs."

This, then, is one of the rawest of parts. Leg stretching that most of us do without thinking.

Finding someone to stretch Stacy's legs along and provide other assistance and also having the money to pay for it are hurdles even higher to cross since the pandemic that left a diminished health care worker supply. When we talked, Stacy had only one worker who came for a total of eight hours spread over three different days each week.

Stacy James finishing a marathon

"Seemingly normal things I can't do, like lifting a coffee pot," Stacy said. "Other things I can, but they take me three to five times longer than an able-bodied person."

Stacy has an exercise bike that she rides 30 minutes each day. With a reminder from a clock that chimes "Amazing Grace" at five minutes before the hour, she takes pills for her bladder, her bowels, and to curb the leg spasms.

"It takes me 15 minutes to put on pants, socks and shoes," she said. "Sometimes, I'm too tired to get into pajamas, so I take a nap in regular clothes."

Stacy had an adaptive van she drove, but it broke down years ago. On top of regular vehicle costs, replacement carries an additional price tag of $25,000 for such modifications as hand controls, adaptive seat, lowered floor and wheelchair ramp. It's cheaper, easier and less stressful for Stacy to be a passenger. While groceries are delivered to her door, ride-share services and friends take her to hair appointments, concerts and other activities. For 25 years, she has been a regular fan of Elvis Presley tribute artist Mike Albert.

Despite her socialization at events and her many on-line fans, Stacy's in-person connection is a vacuum—a big chasm.

"Not being included gets me down the most," she said. "Being excluded feels like I am not a person. I have to remind myself that I am a whole person in Jesus Christ."

On the night as we talked, Stacy was working on details of a trip to Paris. She had received acceptance as a chaplain for wheelchair track and field para games in France in the summer of 2023, but hadn't worked out the details of travel cost and mobility.

Also, on Stacy's to-do list are cleaning out items from what she acknowledges is a too-cluttered condo, writing her memoir, speaking more through her Walking Victorious ministry, finishing many scrapbooking projects and taking a cruise.

As I drove home in the darkness, much of our roughly four hours together was swirling in my head. Mostly, I was thinking about a text Stacy sent before I arrived, asking me to please come 30 minutes later as she put final touches on an inspirational video for Facebook. She was recording her thoughts about the word "crown" as part of an on-line speech group.

"I wear a crown on the inside because I am the daughter of the King of Kings," Stacy said.

I thought of the cheap silver tiara I had as a Mayfair Queen in sixth grade and the Miss Lakewood pageant sash I wore in high school. Seemingly extraordinary designations back then as were some writing and missionary recognitions in my later years.

But nothing extraordinary like Stacy James. Not even close.

(2023, Ohio)

Parking Lot

Yesterday, at almost precisely the moment that American basketball player Brittney Griner pled guilty to carrying CBD oil in her luggage in Khimki, Moscow, Russia—a "crime" punishable by up to 10 years in prison—Mary Stuckey, a new friend, and I were consuming something similar.

Legally.

Seated on a wooden deck in the Punta Gorda, Florida, 90-degree-Fahrenheit heat, we munched on salads and sipped iced tea drinks with something called elixir and kava originating from somewhere in the Pacific region and, like cannabis, designed to provide relaxation without alcohol.

Russia, where vodka is the national drink, doesn't allow CBD, a chemical extracted from marijuana. Some USA states don't either. Navigating the world's rules isn't easy.

Relationships, delightfully, can be.

In a time when virtual connections seem commonplace and long after ignoring my mother's advice to avoid finding men in bars (where I delightfully bumped into my soulmate 32 years ago), I've taken to meeting women in parking lots.

Next to our cars, friendships have sprouted, spilling over to lunches, glasses of wine and boat rides. In the midst of a primary purpose to travel from Ohio to see a granddaughter growing up too fast and reconnect with an old acquaintance, random women have become my friends.

Women with fascinating stories about their involvement with native Americans, children's literature, the environment, rescue dogs. Mary and Rosemary Lanza, who have shared their dreams and obstacles as I have mine, are new in my phone and on my Facebook.

I bid them in-person farewell.

(2022, Florida)

Mary Stuckey, left, with me and my husband, Mike

Philanthropist

When Americans think of philanthropy, the names of Warren Buffet and Bill and Melinda Gates with their causes of alleviating hunger and healing the sick frequently come to mind.

Believers in Christ might overlook Him until remembering the many Biblical stories (John 4 about the woman at the well, etc.) and scriptures (Jesus's advice to "give freely" per Luke and Matthew and Acts 10 about doing good, among others). Jesus Christ is the son of God, savior of human sin and, yes, a philanthropist.

Then, there is Craig Hammon, who lives with his wife in the small coastal town of Essex, Ma.—just minutes away from their three daughters who have the titles of teacher, therapist and treasurer with five children ages 6 to 19. In addition to his titles of husband, father and grandfather, Hammon has been vice president of CURE, a nonprofit network of children's hospitals; vice president of Christian colleges in Pennsylvania and Massachusetts; and head of development for the World Vision humanitarian aid organization.

Hammon, 78, is a philanthropist. More specifically, he consults about where to give and why. Over the years, he has advised many about responsible giving. Among beneficiaries of those gifts is Uganda Christian University (UCU). Among the givers is the Tennessee-based, Westwood Endowment, where Hammon was affiliated until all funds were expended at the end of 2021. Westwood provided UCU's nursing program with $275,000 over 12 years.

"In 2024, the UCU nursing program marks 20 years," said Mark Bartels, executive director of Uganda Partners. "This seemed an appropriate time to recognize the generous donations of Westwood, where Craig was a trustee."

In addition to Hammon, Thomas H. McCallie III and the late Richard A. West played leadership roles with Westwood since its founding in 1987. Hammon, who has philanthropy consulting affiliations with various health-and-education-related entities, recalled a 2009 meeting at UCU where he was convinced that nursing education was a good investment of Westwood funds. Doug Fountain, formerly involved in UCU health sciences and finance and now executive director of Christian Connections for International Health, was at that meeting in Mukono, Uganda.

"Doug and some folks from Bethel University (Minnesota) said they wanted to develop a transformative nursing school to undergird health care in Uganda," Hammon said. "It felt right."

Fountain recalled that "Westwood showed up ready to help" current and future nurses who had a passion to positively impact Uganda's health care while "struggling to figure out how to pay." He added that Westwood filled that nurse and nurse education gap with finances and "the encouragement and support that lasted years."

A dozen years of grants for UCU equipment, and training nurses from midwifery to bachelor, master and doctoral degrees was aligned with Westwood's Christian focus and other education and health care initiatives. From the start, Hammon observed that UCU had the need and accountability in place to make use of funds during his affiliation with CURE International, a Christian nonprofit organization that owns and operates eight charitable children's hospitals around the world.

"There is a terrible crisis in health care—lack of supplies and equipment and inadequately trained staff," he said. "Things are improving. In 1988 around the world, 35,000 kids a day were dying of preventable diseases; now it's 19,000 a day. Nurses are key."

In his 50 trips to Africa, including 15 times each to Kenya and Uganda, he has observed the worst (malaria, children living in slums, "families cooking food outside for hospital patients inside") and the best, including a neurosurgical hospital in Mbale.

"I'm focused on people and places with solutions to help the least and the lost," Hammon said. "I don't have a medical background, but my 35 years of fundraising provides me the insight into where donations are best used. UCU nursing is one of those areas."

Semi-retired since 2010, Hammon works part-time, consulting various foundations on where their funds can best be placed. His role, sometimes called development, is one of seeing people "caring deeply and passionately about a cause and giving them an opportunity to impact needs."

"Advocating for and helping people less fortunate than yourself is the reason for living," he said. "Philanthropy is not engagement only for the wealthy, but for all who have an altruistic desire to improve human welfare. As believers, we find out what God is doing and become part of it."

The terms charity and philanthropy are often used interchangeably, related to money or talent or both. Differences are associated with length and consistency of giving. Charity tends to be an emotional impulse to an immediate, often short-term, crisis situation. Philanthropy addresses the root cause of social issues and requires a more strategic, long-term engagement. At that, many of the world's 260,000 philanthropic foundations help highly esteemed entities, such as noted universities.

According to Philanthropy Tracker 2023, United States citizens surveyed over 10 years through 2018, 61% reported donating to charity and 42% said they volunteered time to an organization. Education and health are the most supported causes.

"There was a time when I helped support five liberal arts colleges in the USA," Hammon said. "It was a good investment. But faith-based relief for East Africa is a better focus to serve the least and the lost and to enable them to serve themselves."

Regarding the UCU contribution, Hammon said he was "blown away" by the passion, qualifications and leadership. The scholarship funding not only provided nursing credentials for individuals but knowledge and skill to improve communities.

"The key is not sending doctors or medical teams somewhere, but training local people to be as good as they can be to do the work where they live," he said. "With support, they have the ability to help themselves."

The 1,850 small and large contributors to the Uganda Partners organization since its inception 23 years ago have subscribed to this belief, according to Bartels. The current donors of various levels number 1,000.

"They understand the outreach and impact for a developing country like Uganda and the value of a Christ-centered learning environment," he said. "We value all levels of giving."

Hammon said none of the benefactors he has represented has "expressed regret." He said, "Once you've seen the need, you can't turn your back."

"The story isn't about me," Hammon said at the end of the late November interview. "It's about everybody who gives."

(2023, Massachusetts)

Political Sameness*

If you put a Republican and a Democrat in a room together, what would you get?

There is no punch line. Not even a joke. It's simply me, a big D, and Mary, the R, living on a university campus in Mukono, Uganda, in the midst and the aftermath of the 2016 United States Presidential election. It must have bothered her to see me jogging around the track with my "Ohioans for Hilliary" shirt. It disturbed me when her candidate, Donald Trump, won.

But together we are, and often.

As much as we love our Ugandan colleagues and we suspect they like us, this is their permanent home and the place where they raised their kids and have husbands and celebrate holidays with families in their villages. We are Americans. Mary is from Florida and me, Ohio.

We both were born in the 1950s. We know the melodies and words of American songs from that decade and since. We speak in terms of miles and not kilometers, quarts and not liters, pounds and not kilograms. We breathe in red dust and dodge impossible traffic while trying to follow the native Ugandan rhythm on crowded and uneven streets. Sometimes, we'll grab each other's hands to protect one another from a careless boda boda driver.

With Mary Chowenhill towering a good six inches over my 5'2" and with clearly different facial and body features, we laugh that the locals confuse us for each other. We laugh and share a lot as we push ourselves into impossibly crowded and smelly taxis, relish a rare dip in a nearby swimming pool and take an occasional meal outside our university compound. We share a love for Christ, for learning, and for students and a passion to help the less fortunate. We realize that our pasts, including some parts that don't make us proud, aren't all that different.

"Scary," I said recently after finishing one of Mary's sentences as she hesitated over words.

One particularly memorable market trip into Uganda's capital city of Kampala had us trying to select groceries in the dark of a sudden power outage. Our differences were poignant but endearing as the more domesticated Mary squealed in delight over her discovery in the dim illumination of a flashlight, shelves of brown (not white) rice in two varieties and more than one kind of oatmeal, while I danced and sang "This Little Light of Mine" with two clerks and my basket of oranges and dark chocolate.

Squeezed and sweating with other passengers during the nearly one hour route back to Mukono, Mary remarked that she was most disappointed over not finding chutney and pickles. I chuckled. Her bags were overflowing with ingredients for cooking and baking. Mine contained neatly compacted, nearly-made or ready-to-eat items.

Mary has a garden outside her apartment, sharing her tomatoes and cucumbers freely. She provides tasty cookies from her oven. I am frightened each time I light my gas stove top.

Mary prays freely and often, including for me when one of my Ugandan daughters admitted she was pregnant out of wedlock, when I got sick and when I shed tears upon learning Hilliary Clinton lost the Presidential bid.

Sometimes in a faraway place where people buy used clothes from large bales sent by richer countries, where children go to school bare-footed and hungry, where women are imprisoned for disagreeing with a husband's second or third wife, and where clean water requires eight-year-olds to walk a mile to fetch it and carry it back, politics doesn't seem so polarizing. Poverty, inequity and illiteracy unite us.

What you get when you put a USA Republican and a Democrat together here is us.

(2017, USA & Uganda)

Popular Girl Bullying

Somewhere among an unsuccessful trip to buy paper towels from empty shelves, putting down Ta-Nehisi Coates' *The Water Dancer*—a page-turner—and acquiring a green Irish wig to stand outside my mom's window of her Covid-quarantined, assisted-living facility on St. Patrick's day, my mind wandered to a pale pink dress.

Truth is that my thoughts about the dress re-surfaced during a delightful, surprise phone call on March 8—a full week before all hell broke loose with physical-distance restrictions and paper-product shortages related to the coronavirus pandemic. I would have missed the 10:30 a.m. call had it not been for Uganda jet lag, the American Daylight Savings Time change and 3 a.m. insomnia that had me back in bed, oversleeping church.

And I might have forgotten about the pink dress... or whether it was blue.

While my detail about the color may be foggy and not verified by a 1960s black and white photo, the incidents surrounding the dress are clear.

In a Sunday morning phone conversation with a high school English teacher—with words spilling as easy as they always did despite years and miles of distance—we recounted the mysteries, joys and growing pains of teenage years. I remembered the boy with a talent for pushing his shoulders back to look like angel wings, a girl who shared my passion for words, the start of a wrestling team as well as sexual abuse, gender confusion and hushed pregnancies.

I recounted my excitement as a freshman of age 14 or 15 being invited to the prom by a popular, athletic upperclassman. How I picked out that dress with my mother. How it cascaded beautifully and loose to the tops of my new shoes. How I smiled at it and me in the mirror.

And how older girls stole my joy to put me in my place on their turf or to keep me out. They told me that I had to cut the cloth off to my knees as a new "rule" they devised as the only way that younger girls could enter the dance. I said it didn't matter as I watched the cloth fall to the floor of a sewing shop, as I carried the lighter garment home and wore it, moving on the arm of this boy among the older girls who wore long, flowing dresses and—at me—condescending looks.

But the muffled tears in my pillow for many nights reminded me that how I was being treated did matter.

The female intimidation with labeling me what I was not, their demeaning glances and derisive laughter didn't stop with that one event. While I was popular by most definitions—a cheerleader, good student, and former Mayfair queen—I was a victim of bullying for several months.

I attempted to end my life.

The details of how aren't as important as what happened next—how I was put in a hospital for a week of sessions with electrodes, psychiatric interviews and clergy prayers designed to fix me—not the bullies. Clearly, I had to suck up whatever it was I was dealt.

Luckily, I did; I am stronger for it.

Recently, the Ohio Suicide Prevention Foundation noted that for ages 14 to 25, suicide is the second leading cause of death. I have to think this would go down if we let others—especially youth trying to find their way—know how much we value them for who they are. And not try to fit them in a box or push them out of ours.

My former English teacher, Joe Dyser, reminded me that I wasn't the only young person struggling to find her/his way back then. He saw the pain in the journals we kept and that he read and graded.

"I often think," he said in that phone call, "of what the world would have lost."

(2020, Ohio)

Preacher Woman

Desirée Christa Adams writes and sings, strums a guitar, dances and performs in theatrical productions.

The young woman calling Ocracoke Island her home for 12 years has been a performing artist since age 3—mostly under the name Desirée Christa Ricker. She has been on stages in New York, California, Colorado and in North Carolina places like Flat Rock, Asheville, Charlotte, Durham, Washington, her home town of Hendersonville and on Ocracoke.

She is most widely known for music that she relegates third in her "triple threat" assessment. She ranks acting first, dancing second. At that, her voice has been heard at the Ocracoke Folk Festival, in local restaurants and bars, when soloing the "Star-Spangled Banner" National Anthem for Independence Day flag-raising and while directing the choir for the United Methodist Church (UMC) on School Road.

The church is where Desirée's latest and seemingly less connected role—pastor—is evolving. As UMC Pastor Logan Jackson winds up three years in the post and moves to Elizabeth City, N.C., in June, Desirée assumes the clergy position here on July 1. The transition announcements were made before about two dozen parishioners during two separate Sunday services in April.

Speaking in the weeks following the pronouncement, Desirée shared that she knows a reverend role will seem different to some of those around her. But to her, this new leadership function is one that a higher power has been preparing her for since she was a child.

Desiree Christa Adams before becoming a pastor

"What is a call? What does it mean?" she asked rhetorically. "It feels different for different people. At age 10, I felt drawn toward religion. Now, I've got this obsessive passion to do this job. I feel prepared."

That childhood draw toward faith might have a little to do with her near-death episode with viral meningitis at age 9. A bigger enticement is her "love of sacred spaces." Two such spaces as an adolescent and teenager were places of worship—a conservative, evangelical Baptist church that she visited with a friend and the traditional Catholic church she attended with her family. Through these experiences, Desirée saw what she liked (communion) and what she didn't (fake theatrics).

Without regret, Desirée talked about her younger days of living on Ocracoke with other performers on a sailboat and then in a loft filled with sleeping bags and guitar cases. She was immersed in the art of writing and performing music, dancing and teaching movement, and directing theatrical productions. A play about Blackbeard, a pirate who is believed to have died in the Pamlico Sound, is among those she choreographed and directed.

"Some people might view me as lost and wild if they knew me when I first came," said Desirée, one of three children with two older brothers. "I am a free spirit."

When Desirée was in her mid-to-late 20s, her heart, mind and craft were filled with influences of musicians like Jimmy Hendricks, Bob Dylan and Billy Holiday as well as a grandfather at the piano and her mother who was a painter, dancer and dance teacher.

"I still dance at the drop of a hat," said Desirée, who came to the island with bachelor's degrees in philosophy, dance and religion from Appalachian State University (Boone, N.C.).

All three undergraduate diplomas are connected, she contends. Philosophy involves understanding and empathy that she has employed in counseling and disaster ministry. She served as a UMC conference case manager for Hurricanes Dorian (2019, Ocracoke), Delta (2020, Louisiana) and Laura (2020, Louisiana). Religion is service and worship of a superhuman power, including God that is part of her Christian faith. Dance is referenced in the Bible, including Psalm 129:3 and 2 Samuel 6:14–22.

It was dance, in part, that brought former UMC Rev. Laura Stern into Desirée's life. The pastor's daughter was acquiring dance skills in a class Desirée taught in 2012. Rev. Stern learned of Desirée's degree in religion and asked her to teach Sunday School.

"I said 'I'm Catholic and don't teach doctrine or dogma, and I might not be the best person for the job,'" Desirée recalled.

Soon thereafter, however, she was teaching Sunday School, realizing that her performance art teaching was a transferable skill and knowledge of the Bible was compatible in a less familiar denomination.

It was through this experience and association with another former Ocracoke UMC pastor, Richard Bryant, that Desirée nudged closer to the ministry.

In recent years and with the titles of Ocracoke UMC administrative assistant and worship director, she has had a 20-hour-a-week position leading music, handling social media, managing the Web, assembling the printed bulletin and other tasks. At the same time and like most who need full-time employment on Ocracoke, she works two other jobs. She teaches yoga and, with her husband, Will, provides night-time beach experiences with ghost stories and s'mores around a fire. She also occasionally conducts sessions in the Reiki technique for stress reduction and relaxation.

An average day in the past two years includes prayer, Bible reading and on-line classes leading toward a master's in divinity through Duke Divinity School (Durham, N.C.), where she travels once each semester for in-person study and where she hopes to graduate in May 2026. Her volunteerism is vast, including tasks related to her presidency for the Board of the Ocracoke Alive non-profit.

Desirée and Will, a carpenter and realtor, reside on the island with a dog and a cat. The Adams hope to raise a family in Ocracoke, only departing if their children's educational interests can't be supported on the island.

If all goes as planned, Desirée, age 38, will have her Methodist church local ordination in 2025—one year after she assumes the pulpit position at Ocracoke UMC that she officially joined only this past Easter Sunday.

As a pastor's spouse, Will is "getting his potluck recipes together," Desirée joked.

As the gulls squawked and smaller birds chirped near the Silver Lake Harbor where she spoke, Desirée remarked that for the Ocracoke UMC congregation, she will be more a teacher than a preacher.

She spoke about her insatiable curiosity, love of learning and devotion to the Christian faith as well as openness to what the members and visitors seek and teach. She plans to reinforce an atmosphere devoid of judgment about politics, lifestyle and gender preference.

"My job is to love people," Desirée, a Godparent for three children, said. "As Christians, we are told to love. It is not our business to decide who is deserving of love. That's the message of Christ."

She understands that all faith journeys are necessarily different and that adversity may be part of the journey.

"I'm aware that none of us can do anything on our own," she said. "That's what God is for."

(2024, North Carolina)

Public Shaming

I died on January 26, 2016. I, or more precisely someone with my name, was buried in Parma, Ohio. That's according to Google.

I stumbled upon this discovery and more as I spent 45 minutes searching the Net for my name in various forms of "Pat," "Patty," "Patricia," "Huston," and "Huston-Holm." Not that I haven't done this before. I have. But the impetus for this afternoon's search was finishing Jon Ronson's *So You've Been Publicly Shamed* bestseller.

The book, published in 2015, is among 50 pounds of paperbacks and hardcovers residing in a suitcase and slated for delivery to Uganda's Bidibidi refugee camp. I'm on a ridiculously impossible mission to read most of them before making that more-than-10-hour, rugged trip in four weeks.

"Shamed" jumped out at me first because it has a chapter focused on plagiarism and I've been teaching it—rather, I give strategies on how NOT to do it—for quite some time, including to mass communications students this term at Uganda Christian University. I was curious about the back-story of once-noted author Jonah Lehrer who was called out for taking credit for someone else's work.

Lehrer's story recounted in Ronson's book reminded me of Janet Cooke. I was in the beginning stages of my journalism career when Cooke, formerly from Ohio, was caught in a word lie at the *Washington Post*. She made up a story about an eight-year-old heroin addict—an article that garnered her a Pulitzer Prize that she returned after her fake story was discovered. While this occurred in the pre-social media era, it cost an otherwise talented writer her career.

Lying and stealing with words is just plain wrong. But does it deserve being cursed with profanity and self-esteem-battering words?

Ronson, a British writer with homes in London and New York City, gives us a mostly painful glimpse of today's social media attacks on people who might just have a single lapse of poor judgment. Like vultures, Internet trolls lay in wait to pounce an individual's poorly chosen words or misunderstood photos. The profane assaults are ones I can't type with the harshest nouns and adjectives reserved for my gender.

Ordinary and extraordinary people lose jobs and spouses, withdraw and even take their own lives because of comments from strangers judging them on Facebook and Twitter.

Usually, what gets posted on the Internet lasts forever. Not true for the rich. People with enough money can hire a firm like Metal Rabbit to reduce and even erase the negativity that others have created around their lives. In other words, a slick tech team can create another, more positive "fake you" to drive down (and out) defamation.

This afternoon, as I searched myself on the Web, I found mostly positive and humorous content. There is a photo of me with my aging dog, Eddie, in the middle of those of some other women with my name, including one now dead who acted in a horror flick and a soap opera. There are some old articles I wrote. I'm still listed as a contact for the Ohio Department of Education, even though I've been retired for two years now. There is a nice interview of me on a photographer friend's blog.

Then, there it was…Someone I don't know with the name "critic" typed online in 2006 that the writing in the book I wrote in 2002 was "shoddy." Nothing more.

I was publicly shamed.

(2017, Ohio)

Ready to Die

About eight months ago, Carolyn March called me into her assisted living room and told me she was dying. She wasn't going to get dialysis. That, she said emphatically, was no quality of life. I tearfully left and asked Brenda, the activities director, if it was true. It was.

I shook it off. My life went on. So, I thought, did Carolyn's. Oblivious to our obvious 20-year age difference, we grew our friendship over three years. She was messy, like me. She had served in Third World countries like me. She didn't have her own children. Like me.

She had nephews she admired and adored. Once, I met them and took their photo together.

I had a granddaughter who I adored as well as Ugandan children. She met one of my Ugandan daughters, Sarah Lagot Odwong, and Ugandan son, Sailas Oakworwoth, and asked about them when they left the United States.

Together and with my mom, we went to a performance at ShadowboxLive, to fish dinners, on ice cream trips. We gave a presentation together on Martin Luther King Day. Carolyn's late husband had been one of the outspoken Caucasians who transported African Americans when they weren't allowed on public buses.

Carolyn and I talked about religion, politics, the state of the world, acceptance of gender preferences. I brought her coloring books and puzzles. She gave me a blanket with African wildlife images. When I published my first children's book, she was a fan.

In a lonely time in Uganda, a letter arrived from Carolyn—six hand-written pages.

Mostly, however, we gave each other encouragement about lives that were different and that some found hard to accept or understand.

The last time I spoke to Carolyn, it was 10 p.m. in Mukono, Uganda, and 3 p.m. in her Mt. Carmel East Hospital bed in Columbus. She lamented that she would miss a field trip to the Wilds and see all the African animals there at a place in Ohio. That she mostly would "be."

The next thing I heard was mom, telling me by phone that Carolyn was back in her room but not eating her meals with everybody else.

An email from my sister followed. It read, "Carolyn passed."

(2018, Ohio)

Shaking

Some days, I can do a demi-pointe. Many days, I can't. That's how it is in barre fitness, a ballet-like exercise class I take when I'm in the States.

Just like some days I can pour your hot water for tea. Some days I can bring a spoon with hot tomato soup perfectly up to my lips. Some days I can write a legible handwritten thank-you or sympathy note.

I have one of those lesser-known, not-blatantly visible handicaps called familial tremors. It's also known as dystonia, essential or kinetic tremor and is detected in one in five people over age 30. Generally, it's inherited. My hands shake. A neurologist gave me the diagnosis.

I went to see him because of a snow skiing trip.

Workaholic that I am, I was editing a technical content standards document in the dim light of a bus packed with Columbus Ski Club partiers going to the slopes in New York. My seatmate, Claudia Speakman, nudged me to put down the white notebook and get some wine like everybody else. As I reached out my mildly trembling hand to retrieve a filled glass, a man gently grabbed my wrist.

"You've got what I've got," he said. "I'll get you the name of my doctor."

Before that, I thought it was low blood sugar—something everybody understands. It's not. It's also not Parkinson's. But like that disease, there is no cure. The tremor treatment ranges from "drinking wine or grape juice" to "taking prescription medication," both of which make me drowsy. Wellness practices to curb what I have are the typical sleep right, balanced diet and exercise.

Tremors get worse under stress, which is sort of a problem for me because I thrive in a certain amount of that. Not the shouting, negative "get it done" stress, but the positive, "you can do it" type. Mentally and psychologically, I get super pumped with a writing project on a tight deadline.

When it comes to non-visible disabilities, there is also diabetes, irritable bowel syndrome, fibromyalgia, asthma, allergies and even schizophrenia. This is not to elevate sympathy for the less-visible ones above the handicaps of inability to hear, see or walk but to increase awareness so we don't force cake on somebody with Type 2 Diabetes, criticize a coworker for leaving a meeting to resolve an irritable bowel or tell somebody to stop sneezing in high pollen season.

The comments I get include:

"Stop shaking." (Sometimes, I can't.)

"Don't be so nervous." (I'm not.)

"Do you need to exercise so much?" (Yes.)

In a recent faculty women's Bible study on the Uganda Christian University campus, I led a discussion about humility. I shared my tremor story from the perspective that living with it humbles me. I also shared one witness example of how in 2011, a timid teenage boy came over to me and smiled, sharing that he, too, had familial tremors. Unlike mine that are confined to my hands, his is throughout his body. We laughed and discussed our coping strategies—holding a pen tightly in the hand, avoiding stress, not ordering soup from the menu. When you share a vulnerable part of you, others do the same.

In one barre fitness class, a woman called me out for stretching my legs flat-footed and not demi-point on my toes. Her ridiculing laughter and that of others followed me home. They didn't know.

(2018, Ohio)

Skin Color

Skin color confuses me.

We can't change it. Well, we can, I suppose.

You can bleach dark skin to look whiter with everything from lemons to all kinds of creams. The word is still out on whether Michael Jackson had bleached skin or if he simply had a pigmentation loss called vitiligo. You can make white skin darker through ultraviolet radiation in the sun or in a booth and with grease makeup. The former can cause melanoma, the deadliest form of skin cancer. The latter is something American baby boomers like me associate with minstrel shows in which music and dance was performed by white people who blackened their faces to represent what whey felt was a typical Colored person or Negro.

I have now typed the "N" word. In the 1950s and 1960s, it was okay to use this descriptor of a United States person born black or dark brown, native to Africa. Not so today. Yesterday, Bill Maher quickly apologized (and rightfully so) for using it with "er" replacing the "ro" during his talk show. The National Association for the Advancement of Colored People has had the "C" in their acronym since 1909. My mother innocently referred to Colored People when I was growing up.

In the United States in 2017, it is more correct (i.e. less offensive) to say Black with a capital "B" even though most African Americans have variations of brown—not black—skin. However, those of us who are educated and sensitive and living in this country try to avoid using skin color to describe each other. We pretend we look the same.

When I'm in Uganda, people freely say "white" and "Black" when describing muzungus (whites) and Ugandans. Right before I left and to better identify a freelance reporter for a daily newspaper, the vice chancellor at the university where I work referenced the "young man with, you know, the lighter brown skin."

Forty-eight hours after landing back in Ohio and when buying a pair of shoes, I casually told the cashier that the clerk who helped me and should get commission for the sale was "the white girl." The stares I got, as well as the turned down heads, reminded me of the inappropriateness of identifying someone in the United States by the color of their skin.

I was likewise reminded two days prior when I landed in Canada to a sea of white and mostly obese skin. After three months surrounded by thin, Black people in East Africa, I looked eagerly during my three-hour layover in the terminal for my dark skinned neighbors, finding one in a waitress from Nigeria and two from Kenya who were making a trek to a wedding in Oregon. The friendly smiles and enthusiastic conversation with these three women reminded me that the way we regard each other is much more than skin deep.

In a conversation last night, a friend who is—and truly looks—Native American shared her still painful scars of discrimination as a child who didn't look white. Instead of pride about her Cherokee heritage, she was made to feel shame.

Some people can't get beyond color. It pains me to return to the United States and learn that not only do we have the Klu Klux Klan that evolved more than 100 years before I was born, but now we also have Proud Boys touting that white people, particularly white males, reign supreme. All groups claim to be standing up for white supremacy, which seems to be an oxymoron. If a race is already supreme, why is there the need to stand up for it?

A Proud Boys video calls upon Caucasians to "announce yourself as a white, proud Western chauvinist, make sure everyone knows it, and don't be ashamed." The front page of today's *New York Times* reports on a Manhattan fight between a teenage girl protesting Sharia law and the older, much larger male Alt-Right white supremacy leader, who said "The American people are rising up against you." Alt-Right espouses a need to recruit young white men to fight "commies," which is basically defined as anyone disagreeing with established white culture.

To be fair, and in the same June 3, 2017, newspaper edition, there is a photo and article about a trend of college commencements to celebrate Blackness, gayness, etc. But let's be real. White people don't need these ceremonies to commemorate our accomplishments. It doesn't hurt us and shouldn't threaten us to allow somebody else to elevate self esteem.

White privilege exists. As a white woman, I have experienced lack of privilege. My gender has been referred to with the "C" word, and not the one I mentioned earlier. In spite of my hard work and intellect, my paycheck and upward mobility has reflected that I am somehow less than a white male. Yet, and even though I have German and Irish heritage, my skin is white. I can't deny I am privileged.

Underneath the bullying—and that's exactly what it is—is fear. Some privileged people who have never had deep relationships with any culture but their own are frightened when the less privileged start to prove that they are every bit as worthy. This, indeed, is most confusing.

(2017, USA)

Slavery

As Charlie Quinn, great-grandson of Dot Salter Willis, who was one of the last people born on Portsmouth Island, recited more than 60 island descendant last names, people stood up with jubilance and applause for their heritage.

Most of the attendees arose once or twice each at the April 27 Portsmouth homecoming. At every bi-annual Portsmouth Homecoming, under a tent to accommodate the crowd, a tradition is to read all the family names of the various descendants.

For six people, there were seven ascensions and descensions from the metal folding chairs under that tent. The up-and-down movement was more for these three men and three women on that Saturday because the six are descendants of once-enslaved Blacks.

Traveling from Virginia and New York, the six African Americans came to the island to pay respects to the names of Abbott, Bragg, Fulford, Gaskill, Ireland, Piggott and Willis—designations from consensual and non-consensual relationships.

As one of the majority white people among 200 at the event but a minority in that my lineage is not from the South, I was rattled about Portsmouth's lack of recognition for the sacrifice of America's people of color. I kept my composure mostly because my new African American acquaintances were composed.

I was calm until now.

April 27 was my second time on Portsmouth Island. Hailed as the Portsmouth Homecoming, this spring day was designated to celebrate 130 years of the Portsmouth Lifesaving Station, built in 1894 to launch and retrieve boats.

My first trip to Portsmouth Island was Sept. 20, 2023. With an Ocracoke Island friend, Michele, and a dozen others, I paid $25 for the round-trip boat ride to this uninhabited 250 acres—about 3% the size of the inhabited Ocracoke Island across the Silver Lake Harbor. That day, I battled Portsmouth's infamous mosquitos. I imagined what it was like when Portsmouth Village evolved in 1753. I envisioned the bustle of activity of a shipping port—a time when 500 men, women and children lived among a school, church, tavern and hospital and when two-thirds of North Carolina's exports passed through the inlet.

Seven months ago, I was oblivious to the fact that some of those residents were owned by the others.

I read a news story quoting Heather Walker, executive director of the Eastern Carolina Foundation for Equity and Equality. She said 12.5 million Africans came across the Atlantic Ocean as slaves. Around 300 disembarked at Portsmouth Island. A June 2023 event on Harkers Island, roughly 38 miles from Portsmouth, accentuated the slave contribution to American history with a dedication of two markers acknowledging the North Carolina ports for slave arrival from Western Africa from 1619 to 1865.

Thereafter, one of those markers was erected on Portsmouth Island.

As I got off the boat for the homecoming "celebration" held every two years, I read the tan-colored sign. It states that after nearly 260 captive Africans disembarked at Portsmouth, "at least 343 more passed through the inlet and were sold into slavery in nearby towns such as Bath, Edenton and New Bern."

I am white, born and raised in Ohio, the North, and not a Portsmouth descendent. My main purpose for the second trip this April was to add to my knowledge about this particular enslavement and meet some descendants of Portsmouth's enslaved Blacks. I deepened my understanding by hanging out with the homecoming's six African Americans who have that slave ancestry.

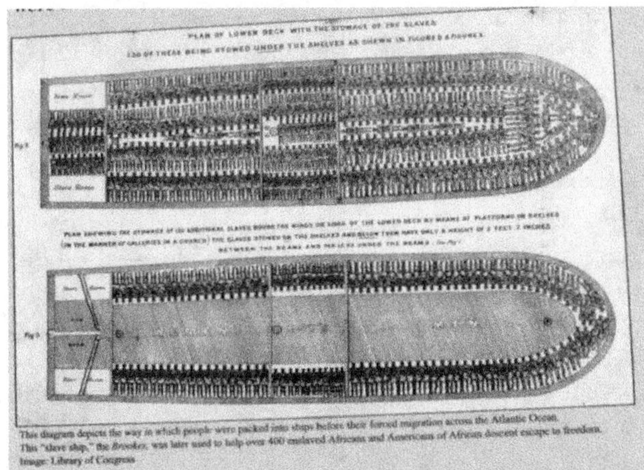

This diagram depicts the way in which people were packed into ships before their forced migration across the Atlantic Ocean. This "slave ship," the *Brookes*, was later used to help over 400 enslaved Africans and Americans of African descent escape to freedom. Image: Library of Congress

Captive Africans were forced into the holds of ships, where they would remain until they reached their intended ports. Without space to sit up or move around, the captive people were forced to lie in their own waste, and the waste of others, for the duration of the roughly 80-day journey to the Americas.

Snapshot of new marker on Portsmouth Island

Recording comments into my phone but later asking that their names not be used, they shared how the economy of the island was driven by African slaves. They told the story of midwives who went to other people's homes to deliver children and returned pregnant. They said that some of the wealthiest people associated with the island were the most embedded in the slave trade, both trans-Atlantic and breeding. They told me what many on-line sources concurred—that enslaved persons did the work to enable white people to live.

One of these six descendants of Portsmouth's enslaved Blacks expressed her strong belief that Thomas Jefferson's words in the *Declaration of Independence* that "all men are created equal" were originally and intentionally written to refer to only "rich white men" and not about women and not Blacks.

Under that tent and in rows three and four from the front stage where Caucasians spoke and led music, the six descendants of enslaved people joined everybody else to sing "America," listen to a bagpipes song related to Scottish ancestry, to pray, to hear the church bells and to joke about mosquitoes. They posed for the traditional group photo but skirted the fried chicken lunch to walk some more around abandoned buildings and grave sites.

Like others at the April homecoming, they paid tribute to African American Henry Pigott, the last man living on the island and who had resided in a house once belonging to Rose Pigott (sometimes with the Ireland surname). Born an enslaved person but eventually a free property owner, Rose named her children after their white fathers.

The six African descendants were among eight Black Americans, including two with no Portsmouth roots, at the Friends of Portsmouth Island event. In addition to specific connections to Portsmouth, the six shared broader thoughts about United States segregation (against it) and affirmative action (for it but wanting my thoughts).

David Quinn, father of Charlie and a history professor at Carteret Community College (Morehead City, N.C.), said in his event remarks that "home is where you go to find solace from ever-changing chaos, to find love within the confines of the heartless world." Portsmouth Island, he noted on this sun-filled day and before a crowd seated under the tent, "is where our people are buried...our people's home."

Portsmouth Island is their "people's home" too, the six descendants of former enslaved people said.

"I come here to recognize them and stand up for them," one said.

They were proud as they jumped to their feet seven times to honor their ancestors.

They told me that they have mostly shifted their frustration to acceptance and even "privilege" to honor the role their descendents played in America's history. While appreciating the heritage celebration by white Americans, the Black Americans are privileged to be part of a conversation, to know where they originate and hear that their descendants "endured one of the darkest periods in our ancestors' lineage."

As the homecoming event concluded under sunny skies, I walked to a boat for the return trip to Ocracoke Island, which, as I later learned, wasn't a slave boat depository but had white residents owning a smaller number of enslaved persons in those earlier days.

I stopped to photograph and re-read the relatively new sign.

The plaque mentions that African people were trafficked. It speaks about the "unpaid labor that made this place a once-thriving maritime trace center" and points out their contributions to USA agricultural and commercial development. It also proclaims the tragedy that 2.5 million children, women and men died on the journey across the Atlantic due to "lack of sufficient food and water, and acts of physical, emotional and psychological torture."

I searched the six panels of the homecoming's printed program, remembering the words of one Portsmouth slave descendant.

"The story isn't fully told," he said.

I was shaken as I climbed into the boat that took me and a dozen other white, laughing men and women and one white, fussy baby back to Ocracoke Island. I envisioned how years ago Africans arrived, partially clothed, malnourished and frightened as cash changed hands from one white person to another, as Black families were separated, as someone with beige skin owned someone colored black or brown.

A week later, I was still rattled, wondering why a person of color wasn't on the speaker's podium that homecoming day and wondering when and if that story will be fully told at Portsmouth and elsewhere.

This, then, is why I am sharing this story, albeit not fully told, here and now.

(2024, North Carolina)

Stink Bug

The only visitors we had this Christmas were stink bugs.

Normally, I find this tiny, brown insect more repulsive than the worst ill-mannered human. But with our Covid-isolated holiday, I welcomed each one so much that when my husband tossed one out into the Ohio rain on December 25, I flinched.

I didn't even have time to get that bug's photo.

In these past several weeks, I've taken to photographing the visiting bugs (formally called Halyomorpha halys in the Pentatomidae family) wherever they roam. In our house, they pop up in the bathroom sink, on a checkered table cloth in the kitchen, on a magazine I read in bed.

My husband—the only other occupant that I know about inside our house—is used to my photographic obsession with what most consider bizarre. For years, I have zealously taken photos of ticks, rats and cockroaches. Dead and alive.

As I record the lives and demise of the perceptive hideous, I wonder about how we define beauty. Except for the rare nature lover and an occasional child not yet stigmatized about beauty, most of the civilized world, myself included, find creatures you can't cuddle with revolting.

In this pandemic, my mind harkens to how on a deserted island (*Cast Away*), Tom Hanks built a relationship with a volleyball he named Wilson. And to the movie, *Unbroken*, where a WWII prisoner took to liking an ant and mouse that were his cellmates and much kinder than his captors.

Like the last example based on the true story of an American mistreated in a Japanese POW camp and the 2020–21 coronavirus accusation, the stink bug blame has been rightly or wrongly placed on Asians, namely somebody in Japan, China or Korea who came to Pennsylvania with it in 1998.

Stink bugs don't hurt humans. In their six–nine-month life span, they might lay eggs and damage crops and other insects, including the more-cuddly caterpillar. The centipede in my bathtub that I photographed and then was likely consumed by a stink bug is carnivorous with fangs.

I haven't noticed any stink bug poop—a real thing—decking our halls this holiday. Possibly because our guest infestation is low. We don't smash them which, supposedly, releases pheromones that attract an army of bugs out of revenge or sympathy or both. We don't even try to repel them with dryer sheets or oils that the internet says they hate.

Stink bugs provide a lesson in what attracts and repels. Like, why do we condition little girls to adore a princess with blonde hair and blue eyes and abhor a woman with a crooked nose and pimples? And why are boys directed to grow up to be tall and handsome men and to view shortness as inferior?

This morning on CBS news, Peter Dinklage, a famous dwarf actor, spoke about struggles with people looking at him beyond his size.

This afternoon, when seeing a Vincent Van Gogh exhibit at the Columbus Museum of Art, I was captivated by a quote from the famous but troubled and suicidal artist. He asks: "For what does a beautiful body really matter? Hasn't life been given to us to be rich in our hearts even if our appearance suffers from it?"

If this is not enough to stretch your acceptance of who you want around you in this unprecedented time, remember that (so far) rats, cockroaches and, yes, stink bugs won't bring SARS variants with them as they edge through the cracks of your home. Living creatures who we are conditioned to have outside just might be the most welcome of guests in 2022.

(2021, Ohio)

Termites

Barefooted in the early morning of Cinco de Mayo, I had my first physical termite encounter. Like a horror flick, some of the 1,000 or so of the tiny insects appeared in the floor space between our front porch and house and fluttered their wings between my toes. I scooped three still fluttering creatures into a plastic sandwich bag for a slow death and quickly killed the rest.

Or so I thought.

"You've always had them—always will," a Terminix guy named Joshua told me after I proudly stated that in 25 years as homeowners, we had been termite free. "Everybody does."

He pointed to the grass and proceeded to explain how thousands of termites, also known as the Isoptera insect order, are living around every American home except in Alaska. He figured there was a colony of a million living among us. Maybe more than one colony.

Most of the bugs are male—the workers—just hanging around waiting for a female, namely the queen, to tell them what to do.

"She orders them to swarm," he said. "And they do. That's when they eat your home."

Swarming, for sure, is what was taking place within the entryway of the house. While I had killed some, other mostly brown insects were climbing in through a floor register.

The good news is that a termite is small with a life span of two years; I would be long gone before a single termite could eat his way past the front porch. The bad news is that females can lay a million eggs in her lifetime, and no termite works alone.

The Terminix guy looked at my three now-dead termites in the baggy I pulled from the freezer. I also snapped I-phone pictures of the living climbers. They are termites and not, as one of my margarita-consuming friends said on May 5, "flying ants." Like the Biblical Joshua in Jericho, the terminator said he would help me fight the battle of varmints. For $1,600.

Jacob, a Terminix technician, arrived the next day to assist. He spent three hours planting 15 pesticide tubes into the ground around our property, spraying the house gutters and foundation and placing black plastic mouse traps in the kitchen and attic crawl space.

I couldn't help but wonder, as my manicurist from Vietnam and I have often discussed, why living creatures are valued differently around the world. In her country, people eat mice and rats. Mexicans eat crickets. In Uganda, fried grasshoppers are a tasty snack.

For sure, termites have value. Of the more than 2,000 species, only 20 are considered pests in the United States. When those species stay in the soil, they make things better for other insects. Elsewhere around the world, termites are valued for their calcium and iron. In April of 2017, I was shocked when a Uganda Christian University student named Shawn told me that Africans eat termites.

"They are fried, like the grasshoppers," he said. "You should write about them."

Now, I have.

(2018, Ohio)

Termites in our house

Un-Mother's Day

On USA Mother's Day weekend 2021, I am writing about two seemingly conflicting topics: A mother (mine) who is dying and a daughter (me) who is living with no biological children. Both scenarios make many people uncomfortable in diverse ways.

First, the awkward subject that I've dealt with for much of my 60-plus years. Female and no childbirths. I married late and had no child from my womb.

As I type this, an article, *Women Who Said No to Motherhood,* appears in the *New York Times* with a stereotypical assumption, including an open statement by Pope Francis in 2015, that childless women are "selfish." In contradiction to that label is a 2017 environmental research study (S. Wynes, K. Nicholas) that notes having one fewer child per family can clean up the earth by saving an average of 65 tons of carbon dioxide emissions each year.

Another stereotype placed on childless women is that we must certainly be "sad" or "unfulfilled." The most piercing misperception, perhaps, is that women without children don't like children. Spoiler alert. Women who have children don't always like them.

I love my granddaughter. I love the seven young adults in Uganda who respectfully call me "mom" for my financial, spiritual and academic support.

"Without children, who will take care of you when you are old?" So ask well-meaning, misunderstanding people.

Thus, the topic of my mother. She took care of me when I was young.

I adore my mom, who suffers from dementia and stage 5 kidney failure. She's the same size as the tiny woman seen in national news clips this week—a Loveland, Colorado, mother and grandmother who had her shoulder dislocated during a June 2020 rough up by police because she forgot to pay for a Pepsi and candy bar at Walmart. As my husband and I listened to the 73-year-old's voice cry "I want to go home" and "you hurt me" on the video, we exchanged knowing glances. People with Alzheimer's, like the injured woman and like my mom who is almost 93, say those two phrases frequently.

Twenty years ago, mom was riding her bicycle, changing the spark plugs in her lawn mower, taking care of elderly neighbors and walking to the post office every day. At 92, mom is a frail 87 pounds. From her wheelchair, she sees my Uncle Bob (her brother) who died in 2016, hears an imaginary band outside her window and frets about picking up her car that we sold five years ago. Sometimes, she cries that her wrinkled hands hurt and that she wants to go home.

I try to cheer her up with songs and with talk about the adventures of seeing her friends, how my high school classmates love to stop and chat with her on the porch and how incredibly blue her eyes are. We talk in the moment however mom defines that moment.

I don't show mom current photos of herself—especially ones that show her sagging skin and facial bumps common for people with end-stage kidney disease. Most days, mom sees herself—and me—as young and vibrant. I relish the moments even if those moments are re-lived over and over again within minutes.

So far, even with her drastically failed hearing and diminished mental comprehension, mom hears me say I love her, and she says it back.

On May 9, 2021, Mom won't know it's Mother's Day.

But, for today, mom knows I'm her daughter. I'll take that.

(2021, Ohio)

Un-Ocracoke Vacation*

On Palm Sunday morning and after a restful night in our apartment overlooking Silver Lake Harbor, we were intermittently seated and standing to propel our paint-chipped bikes—the old-fashioned kind with one gear and foot brakes—around the island I'd grown to love in four previous trips over five years.

My husband, Mike, and granddaughter, Ava, a feline fan, kept our eyes peeled for the Ocracats feral felines as we headed for a lighthouse that is the oldest operating light station in North Carolina. After that, we got ice cream named after the infamous Blackbeard who died here on Ocracoke Island in 1718. Then, some yoga on a dock, a stop at the place with crab-stuffed pretzels, and a look at some handmade jewelry.

At least, I smiled, 12-year-old Ava was off her media for a bit.

Then, I woke up.

The three-day Ocracoke Island excursion we had planned for months didn't happen. I dubbed it the un-Ocracoke vacation.

The reason, as Hyde County Commissioner Randal Mathews stated in his March 29 Facebook post, was a "crisis." Before that, Randal, an island resident who I most associate with his skill and passion for kitesurfing, described the frustration of Atlantic Ocean and Pamlico Sound high tide overwash on NC Highway 12 and how North Carolina Department of Transportation employees "worked tirelessly" to clear the road and add sandbags to keep the water from drifting in.

At the same time, the island's newspaper, *Ocracoke Observer*, was reporting about the "dire situation" that, while going on a long time, most recently kicked up again on the Outer Banks in December 2023.

For Ocracoke residents, lawns are flooded, anxiety about medical service access is heightened, and everyday services—food and mail delivery and garbage collection—are impacted. Businesses suffer. And one local law enforcement official worried about ocean water buckling the road.

I scanned the NC Ferry System Facebook, seeing 200 comments with some condolences for Ocracoke residents and others cruelly saying it's time for the island to go. People getting into the business of where other people live always irritates me.

"We have it better than the people there who can't get off," I said out loud more than once as each day our traveling trio tried to figure out if we might get two, then one and even perhaps scrape a few hours of our planned three nights/four days on Ocracoke.

Phone calls and Internet searches with glimmers of Ocracoke hope eventually extinguished, became part of our thrice-daily routine to salvage the March 23 to 26 vacation.

"We're vagabonds," I joked half-heartedly as we packed and unpacked at four locations. "And it's not normally this cold."

Ava, who we retrieved from her cozy warm Florida home, walked around the Outer Banks in a blanket. Even as Ohioans, the 30–40 degree chill for me and Mike wasn't pleasant or expected.

I did my best to create positivity. This, I said, was an opportunity for our trio to learn about the power of wind and water, what sand can and cannot do, and, mostly, flexibility and adaptability.

Most of the time we were on islands—just not ones accessible via ferry boat.

From our ocean side room at Lighthouse View (recommended by Ocracoke's Harbor Inn that graciously refunded my deposit there), we watched the largest waves we'd ever seen bounce upon huge sandbags. As the sky darkened and we were tucked inside this Buxton Beach area of Cape Hatteras, we listened to an indescribable roar and learned that the impact could be more than shoreline and roadways -- that the Atlantic's storm surge might be causing petroleum contamination from Cold War era Navy infrastructure.

After one Buxton night and the realization the Hatteras ferry would not be running in time for us to board it, we drove back up the coast, first through a storm of sea foam reminiscent of snow from Ohio, and then slowly and carefully through brown puddles in Rodanthe (nothing like how Nicholas Sparks described it in his 2002 novel).

We salvaged fun along the way. We consumed smoothies and acai bowls as Ava painted a ceramic cat at Avon's Studio 12, where a photo of owner Dawn Eskins's relatives from Ohio is on one wall.

We met a delightful artist over coffee at the nearby Ugly Mug. I bought a fascinating 150-page guide (seven pages mention Ocracoke) about North Carolina sand in a downtown Manteo bookstore.

We returned to Virginia Beach, where a friend, Sue, graciously housed us, and Norfolk, Va., where Ava was flying home, and had amazing experiences in an art museum, glass making workshop, aquarium and exploring the now retired 1940s, Wisconsin Navy ship.

My granddaughter lives near Miami, Fla., and is familiar with beaches. Without realizing it, those sections of sand she's experienced are polluted with people, houses, businesses.

I wanted her to experience the many charms of Ocracoke, such as its unspoiled beach. It is pristine—except when nature spoils it.

(2024, North Carolina)

Us, too

Me, too. Not me. Us, too.

(First of three parts)

Me, too.

The exact years are foggy. I think I was four. I think he was 12. He was a neighborhood boy who watched my sister and me while mom cared for her sick mother-in-law in our tiny house with no indoor bathroom. He called the shed our "secret place." Anything that happened there was likewise. How often or how long, I don't know because it stopped the day I came home holding myself and lied to mom and dad that I got hurt on a swing set. I don't recall seeing that boy again but later learned he died in the Vietnam War.

When I was in my late 50s, my sister and I talked about it for the first time and even participated in a support group. But nobody has discussed it since or wants to.

Me, too, or two.

He was a high-ranking official—the highest, actually. He was the boss of my bosses' boss. I was in my early 30s. He was in his late 50s. We both worked hard and late and weekends. There was no touching. But there was uncomfortable closeness and heavy breathing and questions about my sex life. His glasses steamed up a lot. At the same time, I was receiving late-night phone calls from an elected board member—also a much older and more powerful man. He wanted to go out. I repeatedly said no.

I mentioned these incidents to two different supervisors. One cautioned me to be careful because these were highly regarded, powerful men. The second advised, "Don't get in the car with either of them" and "Try to get your work done somewhere else…but make sure you get the work done." This was before laptop computers and Wi-Fi.

Me, too, or three

I had been working 80-90 hour weeks. I needed a fun break. Signing up for a weekend at Lake Erie with some people I didn't know seemed perfect. I drank too much. He overpowered me in size and strength. I said "no." My roommate, who I didn't know, was not invested in rescuing me. Both left the room as I had my head in the toilet.

Legos girls at Easton Mall, Columbus

Hours later, I softly uttered the phrase "date rape" to a seemingly friendly and nice woman. She told me the accused was a "good guy—a catch actually." She quickly distanced herself and spread the word among the group. Nobody, including the "catch," wanted to talk or even sit with me over the next 24 hours. No group wanted me in their cars for the three-hour trip back to Columbus. One couple agreed to transport me, but gave me a short timeline to gather my stuff and accompany them. If I wasn't in their car on time, it was no fault of theirs.

As I settled breathlessly into the back seat, the woman turned around and said, "Just so you know, we don't want to talk about that."

I saw the guy once after that weekend. I was married and with my husband, who wanted to "say something to him." I begged him not to. So he didn't.

The number of boys and men who have treated me badly at work and elsewhere number to about a dozen, including two stalkers, one who threatened to tell my frail father lies and cause him to have a heart attack and another who tried to kill my dog—all because I didn't do exactly what they wanted.

Not now.

I'm 66 years old. I grew up at a time when little girls were taught to be people pleasers and to smile—a lot. Unfortunately, I still see that with little and big girls in advertisements and real life. I'm part of the problem. I can't stop myself from complimenting girls on their hair and outfits while admiring boys for their physical strength. Only as a college professor do I separate the looks and athletic prowess from the intellect. There, I dish out academic compliments and criticism equally.

Alas, it's not enough.

For those angry that you're reading this and angry that I wrote it, know that I'm angry doing it. I'm angry that women are bringing up sexual harassment and abuse from their past in that it causes me to dredge up mine. I hate the "Me Too" *TIME* magazine person of the year cover. I wish I didn't see it on TV every day. It's not that I don't think it's important. I simply don't like these triggers to remember dark things in my past. And I don't like acknowledging that some of my bad behavior in my 20s and 30s just might have been precipitated by that first violation.

I'm angry that I woke up thinking about this.

Not me

(Second of three parts)

Not me.

Just as it's important to bring the injustice of sexual abuse and power (because power is what it really is) to light, it's important to discuss men who behave properly. As women like me emerge from the "Me Too," shadows with stories of guys behaving badly, let's accentuate good male role models. There are many and not necessarily in categories you might think.

Not me.

At a recent high school class reunion, I missed an "after" party. But I heard about it. I got all the details, including how a male classmate tried to take advantage of an inebriated and flirting female classmate until another guy intervened. The guy who stopped it didn't surprise me. Jim was a former basketball jock—once tall, thin and handsome. By appearance alone, he could have been typecast as the jerk obsessed with himself and disrespecting girls. Except he didn't fit that stereotype. I can still hear his voice as he urged his hormonally-charged teen peers to "Take it down a notch." He wasn't a choirboy. He didn't go to church. He was just a nice guy.

Jim's career since high school and his military service involved positions of power. In the small town where we grew up, he was a frequently invited speaker, including for veterans events. That night, the former athlete and now not-so-thin and older but still nice, respectful guy saved two marriages.

Not me, two.

My first newsroom managing editor was a short guy with bushy eyebrows and a greyish-brown beard. Bruce's main passion was photography, but he was a decent writer and even more decent boss.

I was right out of high school, working a part-time dream job while helping to pay my way through college. Mostly, I paid my dues while writing obituaries, but the "M.E." as we called him, encouraged me to stretch into covering sports and didn't laugh at my interest in crime stories in a time when only men covered both of those. He lamented that my byline had to be shortened from "Patty" to the gender-neutral name of "Pat" to better appease reader expectations for someone on the police beat. In staff meetings, he listened to everybody. For those more timid, including females, he encouraged feedback and ideas. A picture of his wife and daughter were always on his desk. He smiled as he said great things about them.

I naively thought that all bosses were like Bruce and dreamed that I someday would have a husband just like him.

Not me, three.

It took a while, but I did. In my late 30s, and ready for a lifetime of being single, I met a kind, respectful guy who adored his eight-year-old son living over 1,000 miles away. As agonizing as it was to have his only child at such a distance, Mike said he never would put his son through the painful process of choosing one parent over another. If that character test didn't clinch the deal for a lifetime partner, Mike's respect of my freedom, my career and my passions did. He didn't care if I changed my last name when we got married. He was okay with my "girlfriend" nights and weekends out. He encouraged my writing and ideas. He was okay with my imperfections. He believed in God.

Mike liked doing new and different things and being different. When I started helping girls in Uganda, he supported me. Together, we dug deep into the issues of injustice for women, including for those in poorer countries. Hidden in the latest "Me Too" awareness from a beautiful actress' social media post is that this phrase actually started in 2006 to raise consciousness of empowerment for sexually abused women of color, particularly those living in poverty and especially in societies where polygamy is commonplace.

Our African daughters adore my husband. He's a male role model the likes of which they have never seen. Someday, the young ladies tell me, they hope to find husbands just like "Dad."

I recently saw a Facebook post where a father said all this talk about harassment against women made him wonder how to advise his sons about relationships with girls.

The number of boys and men who have treated me well as a friend, as family members and at work are many more than the dozen who behaved badly towards me.

The good guys are out there. Look around. And be that guy.

Us, too

(Third/last of three parts)

Us, too

When speaking in late November to some Ohio elementary school students about my new children's book, a staff member pointed out, with anguish, that she just learned one little girl in the room was being sexually abused. I cried about it during the drive home. I diverted my thoughts with radio distractions. I had myself together by the time I pulled into the garage. As adults, that's what we do.

Until now. Perhaps. Hopefully.

An October 2017 ABC-*Washington Post* poll found that more than half of all American women have encountered "unwanted and inappropriate sexual advances." A 2017 United Nation's report notes that 35% of women around the world have experienced physical or sexual violence. According to the 2016 Equal Employment Opportunity Commission Task Force Report on Sexual Harassment, roughly 70% of women, and some men, who experience harassment at work never file a complaint. Of those that do, 75% experienced retaliation.

Kiss and don't tell.

Reasons for silence are fear, shame, and personal blame. It hinders our ability to gain traction at work and be accepted in society. In less developed countries like Uganda, women are shunned even more. As I get to know my female students, their stories of violation, lack of self esteem and being ostracized by family and friends unfold. The rape and ill treatment start as they are young girls, and define them as women if they let it.

Regardless of where we live, our culture has conditioned us to easily dismiss a child's account as fantasy. We are more likely to believe a sexual violation has happened to a beautiful woman than to one that society labels "plain."

As a teenager, I was aware of employer advances on a shy, overweight and slightly older co-worker. She came up the basement steps disheveled after doing inventory with our married boss. Her outward appearance started to improve. She ditched the glasses for contact lenses and appeared at work with dark red lipstick and eyeshadow. As far as I know, nobody, including me, intervened to guard against what was disappearing inwardly. Nobody was there to help this young woman say "no." And nobody did anything before to make this unpopular high school girl feel confident enough to say it on her own.

Likewise, nobody seems to be talking about the backlash on the people who surround abused girls, women and yes, even men. Parents feel they weren't good parents. Workers feel devalued and don't work as hard.

I was in an office in which a male supervisor and one female subordinate ate from the same Chinese food container during meetings while the rest of us tried to do business around the table. This instance appeared consensual but was still fueled by male power. In addition to our discomfort and work inefficiency, a highly qualified female co-worker was denied her expected promotion as the boss elevated his fried rice companion to the top.

Us, too.

Equal, respectful treatment is a shared responsibility.

I had this conversation with a friend, Lisa, after church a couple weeks ago. We talked about how women dress, act and talk and how adults treat little boys and girls differently. We admitted our own roles. We steer girls to princess movies and get boys latched to action animations. We get sucked into the perfect look of ads, TV glam and traditional expectations. Girls can cry and sit on laps much longer than boys.

Lisa and I agreed that both men and women have a shared responsibility to better drive us to gender equality.

I never liked high heels and heavy make up. But I do succumb to other fashion. I remember wearing mini-skirts in college for fashion and in the name of women's right to free expression. I was honestly oblivious to how male students and professors might have reacted to that or to the bikini I wore when mowing the lawn at home. Naiveté is no excuse for my own personal responsibility.

Today and no longer innocent, I wear my tight but comfortable workout pants everywhere. I like form-fitting skirts as well as sloppy, big sweatshirts. I'm still not responsibly perfect, but Jesus is a bigger part of my decision making.

I struggle with 21st century female responsibility related to cleavage-revealing tops, high-heeled pumps, short dresses and photos accentuating "booty" and "pouty" lips. Are we saying "yes" when we mean "no," or are these women simply expressing themselves as the younger version of me did? Do women have a shared responsibility for focusing attention on intellect over bodies and teaching children to do the same? Do men have a shared responsibility to learn to focus their attention on female mental abilities instead of physical attributes and to serve as role models for boys to do the same? Is a certain amount of flirting okay?

On December 10, 2017, I watched a news segment featuring Michelangelo nude art. A female critic of the noted Italian artist admiringly noted that the "beauty of the human body reflects divine creation." How do we balance recognition of male and female human beauty with a sense of decency and realization of natural human sexual desire?

In mid-December, and during a visit with a neighbor, I complimented her on her Christmas gifts for her granddaughter—a camping vest and other outside gear for a not-yet-three-year-old. As I left, I pondered the weightiness of providing multiple choices for girls and boys as part of this responsibility.

Twenty-six years ago—after the "me, too" incidents that I wrote about in segment one and 20 years before the original, national "Me Too" campaign evolved—I was watching the news with my father. The segment was about Anita Hill and now Supreme Court Justice Clarence Thomas. Hill, who is five years younger than me, recounted sexual harassment when working as an assistant to Thomas.

"That never happens," my father asserted. Sitting on the couch next to him, I flinched.

That was 1991. This is now.

"Me Too," unfortunately, is centuries old. The questions remain with no easy answers. But at least in 2017, we're talking and listening. In 2018, let's keep growing respectfully together.

Us, too.

(2017, Ohio)

Veteran*

In 1968, my childhood friend, Jimmy, staged an innocent teenage rebellion against our high school basketball coach.

"We didn't like the way he was treating us or some stupid shit," Jimmy Layton recalled more than 50 years later. "Some of us started our own team, the Buckeye Lake Bay Area Bombers."

Buckeye Lake was a central Ohio village containing a lake polluted with uncontrolled resident sewage. Bombers is and was then a name attributed to all kinds of sports teams.

The "bombers" part had nothing to do with the explosives that the U.S. was dropping on Vietnam, Laos and Cambodia while Jimmy and I were in high school.

At the time, men not much older than me and Jimmy were 8,600 miles away releasing bombs from airplanes and shooting guns with the initial "M" followed by numbers. While lanky, 17-year-old Jimmy was shooting hoops and thinking about a job at a local car dealership and I was a cheerleader preparing for college, men were dying in a section of Southeast Asia in a war that more than half of Americans said they didn't want. Men started dying there when Jimmy and I were learning the letters of the alphabet.

In 1968, as Jimmy played basketball on his made-up team, he had one eye on the evening news that reported U.S. and South Vietnamese losses of limbs and life.

Barely able to sing in the Sunday morning church choir after weekend cheering for the better-recognized Lakewood High School Lancers basketball boys, I was vaguely aware of Jimmy's outside team with opponents such as guys training to be Catholic priests at a local seminary. I was even less informed about a war that was never mentioned in our history class.

I don't remember the January 31, 1968, Tet Offensive, when 246 American soldiers died in what was the United States' deadliest day of the Vietnam War. Jimmy, who is called Jim or James by nearly everybody but me and his family, does.

In Hebron, Ohio, Jimmy's dad was in bed at night, hoping that his only son of three children would not have to be part of that war. But Jimmy was.

Jimmy—the boy in the house with the tree that I jumped from and broke my arm at age 11—was number 56 of 366 (days in the year, including Feb. 29) in the USA December 1, 1969, draft drawing. Jimmy, the twin brother of my childhood girlfriend, Joanie, is the only high school classmate I know who went to Vietnam.

Like roughly one-fourth of American Vietnam veterans, he didn't want to go.

Jimmy's number 56, based on his 1951 birthday, was drawn in a lottery as I was wrapping up my final exams in my first quarter of journalism studies at The Ohio State University and Jimmy worked in a job that he enjoyed at Hebron Chevrolet.

In 1969 Woodstock happened, Ohioan Neil Armstrong walked on the moon, Jimmy and I earned high school diplomas and Jimmy was drafted.

"I thought of myself as a flower child. I didn't want to fight in a war," he said. "But I didn't want to run to Canada and never see my family again and I didn't want to go to jail."

His dad tried to convince him to choose the Coast Guard that seldom sent anybody to Vietnam. Jimmy chose the Army because the service term was two fewer years. He'd do his time, get out and come home.

"The war was winding down," Jimmy said.

That's what he thought during his 10 weeks of basic training that wrapped up in January 1970 and again in the aircraft parts school after that.

A woman organizing recruits going to AIT (advanced individual training) like Jimmy's assignment to learn about aircraft echoed his thoughts. As the young soldiers assembled in a Newark, Ohio, office building, she consoled them.

 "Chances of being sent over there are slim," the organizing woman said.

Never during his time at Ft. Lee, Va., or Ft. Knox, Ky., or in California did Jimmy think he would go to Vietnam.

Eating grilled cheese and noodle soup on a blustery October 2022 day on a break from his job as mayor of Hebron, Jimmy reflected on his time in Vietnam, that "nobody asks me about." He said he thought at age 18, at 160 pounds and 6'3", he would be too young, too skinny and too tall to be of much use in a war, especially after watching other recruits assigned to Germany, Japan and bases around the United States.

The U.S. military looked at the midwestern boy whose father taught him how to shoot rabbits with a

Jimmy Layton in Vietnam

shotgun at age 12 and with recognized skills in car mechanics in the half year since he left high school and thought otherwise.

"Layton," they said, "you're going to Nam."

In 1972 and after basic training and about a year of drills on American soil, Jimmy had a quick USA wedding with a girl he had been dating, got on a plane "scared shitless," looked down at "miles of pristine coastlines" and got off in tropical Vietnam "hit with heat that I'll never forget."

"If anybody tells you they weren't worried there, don't believe it," he said. "A regular Army enlisted soldier was not the same as the drafted like we were."

At Bien Hoa Air Base near Saigon, Jimmy was ordered to type without typing skills. He fixed helicopters, relying on how he would repair cars. He rode in choppers and airplanes to check security towers—sometimes five hours at a time for a week at a time without time off.

"There was no day off," he said. And with shots from the North Vietnamese and Viet Cong rebels fighting in the south against their government, "It wasn't clear who we were fighting for. Even the 'John Wayne' types were shaking."

He ate rice cakes, bread and barely edible meat of some sort. He slept on a mattress in a hooch. An Army recruit from Oregon rigged a parachute outside for shade. He carried an M-16 rifle.

The servicemen got music and news when signals were available. They snickered at war reports, especially official statements from President Nixon. They listened to Nancy Sinatra's songs recorded before they left home and to Jimmy Hendrix, who, like them, had served in the military and, like them, didn't like it.

"Most of us didn't know what the hell we were doing and wanted out," Jimmy said." "Keep your head down and your mouth shut. We knew that was the best way to survive."

Jimmy has a scrapbook with black and white photos, including one of a stray puppy named "Slow." Not pictured are the few women around—a cleaning woman known as Manna Sun and "doughnut dollies" at the USO club. The men posed with Jimmy are nameless except for one who was among the last Vietnam veterans to die.

According to a document in Jimmy's scrapbook, Spec. 4/c, U.S. Army Vietnam War-Spec. Frakes was killed in action near Phan Thiet, Vietnam, on January 26, 1973—seven days before Jimmy flew back to the States.

"Frakes and I sat up all night and talked about what we would do when we got back," Jimmy recalled. "He loved to bake. He was going to open a bakery. He told me he would make me the best cake I've ever tasted."

In that scrapbook, Jimmy has more than a dozen badges with not much meaning and that "locals churned out." A favorite, however, is black with red letters proclaiming "If you haven't been there, shut the fuck up."

That's what he would have said if he had heard the "How many babies did he kill?" question that his sister Joanie got from a man at the Columbus, Ohio, airport as she alone waited to pick up her returning veteran brother on a cold late January day in 1973.

"Children in war are not the same as innocent children here," Jimmy said. "They can kill you."

According to U.S. Defense Casualty Analysis System, there were 58,220 American military fatalities during the two decades of involvement in the Vietnam conflict. Other estimates indicate two million civilians and one million fighters of all countries involved lost their lives there.

"We were supposed to be fighting against the Communist Chinese takeover," Jimmy said. "The truth is that if somebody is holding a gun at your face, you pull your trigger first. That's what it came down to."

War, he says, should only happen to protect your homeland. Vietnam wasn't the right reason for the United States, for France, and other countries waging war there.

Like most Americans alive during the war, I remember the images are of the naked napalm-burned girl running from her village, piles of bodies from the My Lai massacre and the young woman screaming over the dead body of her war-protesting friend at Kent State University. More recently but less visible is John Stewart's awareness campaign about the impact of spraying millions of gallons of toxic herbicides to protect soldiers from bugs and starve local enemies by killing their crops. Called Agent Orange, it causes cancer and birth defects.

Jimmy suffers from prostate cancer, likely, he shrugs, from that year in Vietnam.

Seldom does anyone ask about his Vietnam story, Jimmy told me as we met over lunch. And except for an honor flight to Washington, D.C., 50 years after he got home, "nobody thanks me for being over there," Jimmy said.

Out of guilt, ignorance, curiosity and compassion in 2022—too many years later, I asked. And I expressed appreciation.

Thank you, Jimmy, or in Vietnamese, "cam o'n."

(2022, Ohio & Vietnam)

What Matters

For three days now, I have been waking up thinking about Ronnie Zwink.

One summer when we both were 16 years old, Ronnie and I connected as his fingers danced on a steel guitar while I belted out country tunes. We practiced "Mansion over the Hilltop," "Cincinnati Ohio," "Lonesome Me" and "Send Me the Pillow that You Dream On" at Keller Music Store in Hebron, Ohio. With a couple other guitar players, we performed at local fairs and the American Legion Hall.

Except during those connections, we were an odd coupling of quiet seriousness (him) and bubbly cheerleader (me), passing each other with only nods in the halls of Lakewood High School.

Ronnie died at age 26. I was on a newspaper deadline when I found out. I don't remember feeling sad. I don't remember feeling at all or even later reaching out to his widow, Beth, who was the smartest girl in our class.

I just kept working. That's what I do. Or did.

Keeping busy is a way to deal with forgetting about pain, including that these lives on earth are not forever. Even when my teenage church friend, Beth Ann Braig, died when flipping her car in the Buckeye Lake Canal. Even when Uncle George was found hanged in a Muskingum County jail cell…When Dad lost his battle with cancer…When the many dogs and cats that took residence with me moved on.

I've been pretty good at compartmentalizing tears and filling discomfort with busyness.

My husband and I used to joke that surely he would outlive me as he is two years younger, and I'm never sleeping, always working, trotting across the ocean to Africa all the time. I was simply too busy to die.

The Oct. 27 news of Mike's need for open-heart surgery shifted that mentality. Nobody knows, of course, but it does bring forth the often-posed question: If you could know when you would die, would you want to know?

Ronnie Zwink's high school yearbook photo

And the trickle-down questions include:

To make the most of my time on earth, how much energy do I give to people who don't like me and/or treat me badly? Who and what should I care about? Finally, what should I be doing about those things and those people, including the love of my life (my husband), who I care so deeply about?

I find solace in that the United States just elected its oldest president and joy with all the people in their 80s still making a difference. Yet, there is an end to this earthly life. For believers like me, that end is with Jesus. At that, we want to do a good job for Him while we are here.

Today, as we are waking up on a Sunday, Mike and I began a discussion about what really matters... and what doesn't.

At 3 a.m. Saturday, I discussed my current obsession with morbidity with my insomniac friend and high school classmate, Bob, whose father suffers from pneumonia as well as memory issues, like my mom.

"My dad is slipping," Bob typed on Facebook private messaging. "He left the water running in the sink, and it overflowed on the floor."

Two days ago, I reached out to Ronnie's widow, Beth, the Lakewood Class of 1969 valedictorian who has since remarried and has had a career in nursing. She reminded me that Ronnie died as a result of malignant melanoma. He had a stroke on July 15, 1977, was in a coma after brain surgery, dying on Thanksgiving Day 1977. His daughter was 3-1/2 years old. His son who he never met was just three weeks old.

"I guess we all should live and love and be kind," Beth typed in a Facebook Message.

While the sadness of the coronavirus doesn't escape me, the COVID-19 travel restrictions and rules about social gatherings, coupled with my husband's current vulnerability to the corona virus, might just have some silver linings.

It is giving me time to "be" and not just "do."

It has given me time to think about Ronnie and to reach out to Beth.

Better late than never—I told her I am sorry.

(2020, Ohio)

Elsewhere

Broken

The most physically painful experience I recall involved a careless motorcyclist, a slightly elevated sidewalk lip, cement pavement, a brick wall and my left wrist. It was a rainy December 6, 2023, in the British territory of Gibraltar.

As a motor bike narrowly sped between a large, red bus and me, I spiraled backwards several feet before the wrist of my nondominant hand slammed into the wet pavement, shortly followed by my backpack and my head into a wall. In what my husband, Mike, would later describe as "like a choreographed play," he held a plastic bag for possible vomit (my request) and helped a second motorcyclist get me to an upright position while a 30-something woman dialed and waited with us for an emergency squad. Two EMTs joined the ensemble in my first-ever ambulance ride.

A "tragedy" is how I would label it, but not of the caliber of Shakespeare's Hamlet or Romeo and Juliet. Nobody died. But the pain of what I later learned was multiple bones splitting apart reverberated to agony and nausea.

The drama of that day and the ache I feel on Christmas Eve aside, I suffered what the Gibraltar Health Authority called a "left-sided intra-articular distal radial fracture." On December 7, I had "emergency open-reduction and internal fixation." In short, Dr. Nicholas Van Der Hauwaert and his team at St. Bernard's Hospital, the only non-naval infirmary in Gibraltar, sliced open my wrist and re-connected things with a titanium plate.

"You are like a bionic woman," Mike said.

Hardly. For 14 days as we returned to our holiday apartment in Nerja, Spain, I typed with one hand, slept a lot and couldn't tie my shoes or independently take a shower. I opened jars and bottles securing them between my knees with more than one messy mishap. I learned that the smallest finger is responsible for 50% of hand strength and the ring finger is the weakest.

Except for a Canadian woman who put my earrings in, Mike has been my patient caregiver—a godsend. Together, we managed my disability and medical

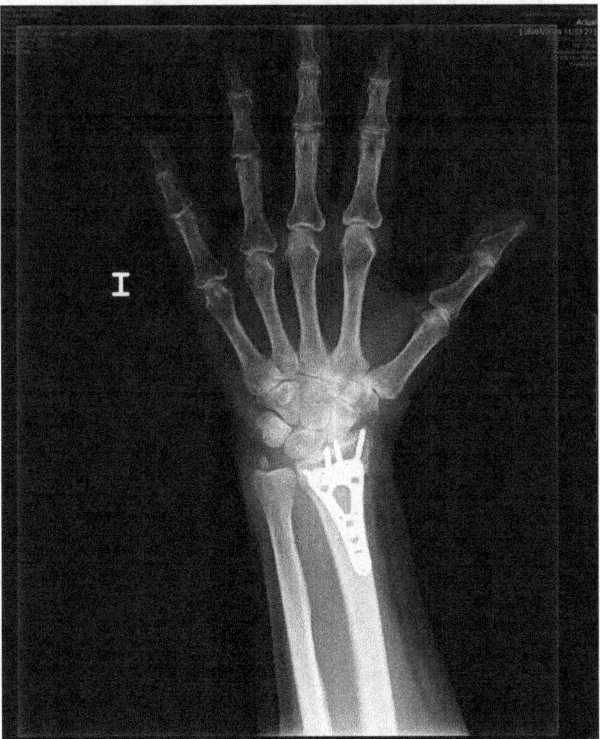

X-ray showing plate in wrist

finance needs. We rejoiced with the realization that Aetna Medicare would cover nearly everything of a bill that when converted from pounds to dollars was significantly cheaper than such a procedure and care in the USA.

"Welcome to socialized medicine," Dr. Nicholas said smiling. "The added cost in your country is mostly because of litigation."

Americans are a litigious people.

Two weeks after surgery and following a two-bus, five-hour trip from Nerja, Mike and I returned to what the Brits call "the Gib" for a checkup that appears to be a thumbs up with a couple months minimum of self-disciplined, physical therapy. While it is painful, deliberate movement of my left wrist and fingers increases blood supply that keeps the bone alive and enables the plate to settle into its job.

Outside the hospital before the bus trip back to Nerja on December 21, we walked around Gibraltar, remembering the good time we had in that day before the accident. Seeing the Barbary macaques, the Gibraltar monkeys believed to be originally from Morocco. Learning how the British captured Gibraltar from Spain in 1704. Exploring a cave and seeing some military-established tunnels in the large rock we had previously known only from Prudential insurance commercials. Eating fish and chips.

We finally found and tasted an advertised Gibraltar-famous food—calentita, a simple unleavened bread made from chickpea flour and olive oil. Calentita is said to have been brought to Gibraltar by Genoese immigrants in the early 18th century.

We talked about how we are grateful to have each other and how my accident could have been worse if the bump to my head had been more severe, if the break was to a femur bone and our belief that my backpack and God protected my neck and spine.

It was a bit magical as we walked to Spain across part of a 6,000-foot airport runway strip between the Mediterranean and the Bay of Gibraltar.

We thanked God for each other and this opportunity to heal. Uganda, where I planned to be for three weeks in January, would need to wait.

Today, at the service of the New Life church, the pastor privately and gently suggested that "this is maybe a time for you to slow down."

With single-hand engagement and energy diverted to pain healing, I have cut my Uganda virtual work week from 20 hours to five. So far, the world hasn't ended because of it.

On December 23, as Mike played with a group of musicians at an Irish bar in Nerja, I discussed my left-hand frustrations with a new friend named Jean. In the midst of my discourse on how humans don't appreciate our non-dominant appendages until they are absent, she shared that her 42-year-old son recently took his own life.

"He was very talented," she said. "He shot himself."

While an abundance of social media posts would have us believe many lives are perfect, they aren't. We aren't. Two of my Facebook friends are battling cancer with one in hospice. Some church friends back home have COVID. Three high school friends recently lost their spouses.

Once physical healing occurs, our bodies are generally designed to forget pain. Not so with our minds that may convince us we aren't worthy and loved. Most adults shed more tears from psychological than bodily harm.

For Christ believers, love is the theme of this fourth Christmas advent week. Previous weeks were hope, peace and joy. I'm saddened that in the midst of gift giving and overindulgence of food and drink, many do not celebrate the true meaning of Christmas and Christ's love.

This year, I desperately seek glimmers of hope, peace, joy and love as He intended.

For me, I am thinking about the young boy and girl among Spanish adult drummers during last night's "Feliz Navidad" parade in Nerja. During the two hours of marching, the tiny percussionists' arms joyfully drummed on. I'm picturing the father who danced in the inflatable Santa carnival atmosphere of the Christmas plaza as his loving family looked on. And I am remembering one little girl hoping to master the fake ice among fake snow in that plaza. No matter how many falls, she smiled, laughed and got back up.

I will, too.

(2023, Gibraltar)

Conversation with Santa*

'Twas the week before Christmas 2023 that I caught up with St. Nicholas—AKA Santa Claus.

I tried to reach him for a year after we first met on the dance floor of a place called Sevillano on Calle Huertos (Huertos Street) in Nerja, Spain. That was December 2022. As I gyrated with people I didn't know, he placed a striped candy cane in my hand and, through his white beard, a smile in my heart.

I hadn't believed for 60 years. I wanted to believe or, for once and all, expose this jolly guy with the sparkling eyes for who he truly is. This could be the interview of a lifetime, defining me in the best or worst of ways.

He immediately agreed to talk. It was simply a matter of scheduling.

Santa is one busy guy. In the next 12 months, he jetted to California, USA; Australia; European places, including England, Budapest, Prague and Spain. I was on the move, too, on Ocracoke Island, N.C.; and in Ohio; Florida; Uganda; Spain. As Facebook friends, we knew about our travels and more—like our shared progressive politics and passion to help others.

While Santa cares about us all, he is especially focused on helping men in the fight against cancer, particularly prostate cancer. The American Cancer Society says one in eight men will get it, and 1 in 41 will die from it. Via social media, I saw Santa was relentless in November to raise awareness and money during a Movember annual event that involves growing mustaches to focus on men's health issues such as prostate cancer.

I know that thousands, even millions, don the red hat and suit around the world at Christmas time since a Turkish monk named St. Nicholas started the Santa movement in 300 A.D. We tell these Santas what we want under our trees, assuming they already know if we've been good or bad. Yet, for goodness sake, we don't reciprocate and ask Santa his wishes.

Finally, the week (give or take some days) before Christmas 2023, our schedules aligned as we both were back in southern Spain's Costa del Sol city of Nerja. The morning of December 14, 2023—12 months from that first, dance-floor encounter—we spoke.

Unless you are on a tight deadline or fighting for space in a press conference, journalists are taught to build the subject relationship, saving the tough questions for last. On this day, I broke that rule.

"Are you Santa Claus?" I blurted.

Looking at the blinking lights of his tree in the corner of his Mediterranean Sea apartment, he answered softly, "I believe I am."

"Santa" Robert Morgan

For the next 90 minutes, Robert Morgan who informally goes by "Bob" and also has a Santa alias, patiently answered my questions. He shared his story—both extraordinary and ordinary—that I summarize now in this time when statistics say 80% of those under age 10 believe that a man delivers gifts worldwide on December 24 and 25, and nearly 100% of us over 12 don't. Bob is a decade-long, unpaid working Santa who applies a lifetime of learning into the job.

"As a young boy, I looked into the mirror and asked 'what is this life, what will I be?' and now, I am still figuring it out but with more certainty," said Bob, who recently turned 65.

He was seven when two older sisters tried unsuccessfully to shake his Santa imagination loose by showing the closet of gifts that wouldn't be coming down a chimney that the family didn't have.

While Santa Claus was never his career aspiration, Bob believes his life packed with taking chances and devoid of a solid plan, prepared him for this past 10 years of gifting candy canes and posing for photos with "ages 5 to 85" through impromptu gigs on streets, in bars, on the beach.

"We are all a product of everything we see and hear," he said. "You and I are writing our own story."

Santa Bob shared some of his childhood. He recalled being part of a Texas working family on a tight budget, helping his mom handcraft Christmas gifts for a slew of cousins and in-laws with only $20 on one financially challenging holiday. Later, they were materialistically rich "so ridiculous that someone made our beds for us."

He was poor again as an adult, selling shoes and working in retail to pay the rent and put himself through college. At one point, he was $60,000 in debt as his once-booming business of clothing design fell victim to a fashion industry crash. He worked in the film and TV industry alongside the famous and became noticed himself with a nomination for an Academy Award in the category Best Costume Design for the 2021 film *Dune*.

Bob and his friend and colleague, Jacqueline West, imagined a world set 20,000 years in the future as they collaborated and co-designed costumes in the successful *Dune* 1 film about a noble family embroiled in a war for control over the galaxy. The winning costuming nominee at the Oscars that year was Jenny Beavan for *Cruella*.

"I've always said science fiction will never win," he said with laughter delivered as only Santa could.

Bob waves off his resume that shows he studied fine art at the University of Nevada, Las Vegas, and at the University of California, Los Angeles. His mom gets the early credit for his creativity, followed by many who gave him chances and his own toil—"sometimes 90 hours a week."

He skirted the question of what he wished to have for Christmas, preferring to talk about his favorite story (Charles Dickens' *Christmas Carol*), movie (*White Christmas*) and song ("Jesu Joy of Man's Desiring"). That he walked on the red carpet two years ago wasn't a pinnacle as much as where he walks daily, especially during the Christmas season.

"Being in the film business and an artist has taken me to palaces, mountains and amazing places with wonderful people—people who tell me that everybody knows them but they know nobody," he said. "All that is second to my hope and dream of being a good person."

As Santa, he feels he is that. Or tries to be.

Bob explained to me that Santa Claus is the "why of magic." The belief may not align perfectly with science or every religious faith or culture, he said. It's a role that chose him as his beard turned snow white, and one that he hopes does not expire.

"If I can bring a smile, it's pure joy," he said. "If you can be Santa, be Santa."

Belief that doesn't come in a neat package under a tree seems to be this Santa's unspoken Christmas wish.

Last year, the NORAD (North American Aerospace Defense Command) Santa Tracker website received nearly nine million unique visits from more than 200 countries and territories around the world. That's a lot of believers.

In this time of wars in Israel, Ukraine, Sudan, the Congo and many backyards, I desperately, unapologetically wish to be among them.

(2023, Spain)

Graduate*

Gabriel Kuereng Mareet and I are different in a lot of ways.

He's tall. I'm short. His skin is black. Mine is white. His country of South Sudan is the poorest in the world. Mine, the United States, ranks among the wealthiest. He's Dinka, which includes 25 of South Sudan's 64 tribal groups. My heritage is mostly Irish.

We laugh about mermaids—fictional women living half-human and half-fish in the sea. As he shares that African mythology describes mermaids as mystic and dangerous women, I tell him about the newly released movie featuring a mermaid who saves the life of a prince.

At 41, Gabriel is the same age as my step-son. Generationally, we're three decades apart.

I suspect we might disagree on a lot of things. Polygamy comes to mind. It's legal in 58 countries, including his, and illegal in mine, except maybe in the state of Utah where a violation there might be a fine similar to getting a parking ticket.

One thing we agree upon is education—his.

Together, and 7,000 miles (11,265 kilometers) apart from his work place in Bor, South Sudan, and my computer in Canal Winchester, Ohio, USA, we worked virtually for nearly four years with a singular goal of quality research toward his master's degree at Uganda Christian University (UCU). Through Uganda's nearly two-year COVID lockdown and for the time after until mid-July 2023, we did Zoom conversations and email exchanges.

Under the research topic of *Exclusive Breast Feeding Among Mothers in Bor County, Jonglei State, South Sudan*, we learned from each other. As I have done with roughly 150 other university post-graduate students, I guided his focus, organization, grammar, spelling, punctuation, writing flow. He taught me about the types of breast milk and the health benefits to new mothers and their babies. As I bought bread, fruit and soda, Gabriel's research reminded me of people who can't. South Sudan's poverty rate is 82%.

Gabriel Kuereng Mareet at his graduation

In our on-line communications, we shared our frustrations with university politics. I encouraged Gabriel not to give up, sharing as a Christian a Romans 5:5 scripture about hope.

We asked each other about our families. His mother, age 81, and sister, 45, live with him in Bor while his wife and children ages 12, 8 and 2 are in Kampala. Separation of spouses is common as one lives in another country and sends money for the rest.

From 2019 to now, Gabriel and I stayed in touch and worked through revisions that different university supervisors wanted. We prayed. We persevered.

"I'm not a patient person," I laughingly told him. "But I don't like giving up."

We didn't.

So on July 28, 2023, I rejoiced with about 20 of Gabriel's South Sudanese family as Gabriel was awarded a Master of Public Health Leadership at UCU. His was #63 of #122 names read for post-graduate awards and number 63 of just over 1,000 master's and bachelor's awardees. He walked the red carpet between the university white tents occupying the area where students normally play soccer. He gave me a subtle thumbs up as I snapped his photo.

The day before, on July 27, we embraced under the noon-time, hot sun outside the Mukono campus library and walked to a canteen to share a meal of juice, rice and g-nut sauce. It was our first in-person meeting.

Gabriel has a $1,500-a-month job with the World Food Program in South Sudan. Roughly ¾ of what he makes goes to his wife and kids in Uganda. It's a five-year job that may be ending, he says, because the United States has diverted USAID funding to help Ukraine.

He's not sure of next steps, but mentioned an older brother living in Kentucky since 2001. The brother is one of the "Lost Boys," a name given to the six-and-seven-year-olds who fled during a 1987 civil war in southern Sudan, which became South Sudan in 2011. Those that survived were in Kenyan refugee camps where countries like the USA picked them up and relocated them.

The older brother is "doing well and may have a job for me there," Gabriel said.

Employment is important, but this day—getting the degree—is for shouts, laughter and eating homemade cookies from a large plastic bin. I don't know how to say congratulations in the Dinka Western Nilotic language, so in English, I'll simply say, "Well done."

(2023, Uganda/South Sudan)

Homelessness*

David Fabre has a house roughly 50 feet above Playa Carabeillo (Carabeillo Beach, a slice of Spain's Mediterranean coast, and 20 steps below a white balcony). His outer room that is constructed of bamboo and a few timber pieces has a couch, table, chairs and a mismatch of artwork both hung and leaning on the ground near a crock pot, toaster oven and microwave. A room with a bed and cold-water shower is behind the cooking appliances wall, protected by a large plastic sheet ceiling held in place by rocks.

"Homeless?" he asked rhetorically while rolling a cigarette. "I don't have an address, so one way or another, I guess I am."

David is one of 40,000 homeless people within Spain's 48 million population.

The place where David lives is a house if not a home in Nerja, Spain. It was once a saloon—away from the more heavily populated and commercial shops and restaurants surrounding the Balcon de Europa section of the Costa del Sol. Today, and after securing a metal gate to deter wandering drunks and deliberate thieves, David, 43, sleeps and eats here with his two mixed-breed dogs, one-year old Rocky, and 10-year-old Roxy.

Next door lives a slightly older neighbor—"my friend," David says. The friend, who works "cleaning the city," has had a place several feet from David's for 20 years. He allows David, the dogs and six cats who David jokes "run the place" to reside free of rent, water and electricity bills.

Most days, David, Roxy and Rocky leave the sound of lapping ocean waves, ascending up balcony steps to work 10 a.m. to 2:30 p.m. two blocks away on Calle Carabeo (Carabeo Street). There, near one of Nerja's high-end restaurants called Bakus, David sits cross-legged with his back against a wall, Rocky on his lap and a place for coins in front, while Roxy mostly sleeps in a carriage hooked to a nearby, very-used bicycle.

"I don't fly," David said. "I ride a bike everywhere—one country to the next."

Bicycles have taken David through and to places like Portugal "that I love" and the "freezing cold" Camino de Santiago. Theft has taught him to keep his transport, his backpack, clothing and tent a bit shabby—the latter always ready if more stationery housing falls through.

Mostly, "people say hello" and are kind, dropping coins and petting the dogs that wear festive red and green tinsel around their necks in the holiday season. David takes in an average of 50 euros ($55) a day or 300 euros ($332) a week. He makes just under the average annual Nerja wage of 18,000 euros ($19,870).

After spending most of what he gets on food at the French-owned Carrefour or Spanish Mercadona supermarkets, David has about 2,000 euros ($2,207) "in the ground in four places if I can remember them," he said. He plans to send some of his extra earnings to a former Nerja "street guy" now back with family in West Africa's country of Gambia.

"We all have stories," David said. "His involves marrying a German girl who left him with their baby. The guy got on drugs and never got over that."

David has held traditional jobs—cook, bar bouncer—that paid five euros an hour. His current work that he says is "sort of like public relations" suits him best "because I am loose and don't report to nobody." He believes he is more successful than most because of the two dogs, because he's friendly and because he speaks seven languages (Dutch, German, Italian, English, French, Portuguese, Spanish).

"Some call me a street beggar," David said of those who look down, away or avoid his station altogether. "They think I'm shit. I've done shit. Most people have."

Interspersed with coughs, and while watching the beach below, David recounted some of his non-sugar-coated journey from a childhood of estrangement from parents and "fat bullying" by peers to drug abuse, prison and multiple failed female relationships. His growing up years with a mother from Belgium and French father contain memories of hostility with him as the victim until age 17 when he was big enough to fight back—and did.

One vivid memory in the second year of his only marriage was "coming home and my best friend was f***ing my wife."

Now at 130 kilos (287 pounds), David said his size tends to ward off unwanted approaches, including during his seven years in a French prison, where he learned "to keep my mouth shut" among mostly Muslim inmates and their guards.

"Loose" is how he describes himself walking out of the prison 11 years ago with culinary arts certificates and nobody meeting him at the gate. Loose defines life after his divorce, his relationships with four children (ages 26, 25, 24, 17) from four different women, other romantic hookups and his employment.

"I did drugs and shit," he said about his incarceration. "Now, it's just weed while I see others do cocaine and hash."

"I'm not their father; I'm a biological donor," he says of the children. "I was never there for them."

"I don't believe in love anymore," he says of women finding him and his lifestyle intriguing. "All the people in my life who said they loved me, betrayed me. Women say they like you as you are, but they want to change you."

Of his job, he says: "I work for myself. If I change, I do it for myself."

A few fortunate friends in Nerja may get invited to David's dinner table with culinary delights involving fish, potatoes and more learned in prison classes and from YouTube recipes called up on his phone.

David's strongest love and allegiance these days are to Roxy, a 30-pound long-haired canine who has cheated death twice; and Rocky, the smaller, short-haired newcomer who replaced a Dalmatian-mix that David left with a girlfriend in Portugal last year.

"She's my baby," David said, pointing to Roxy sleeping on his couch. He wasn't looking for a dog 10 years ago when three-week-old Roxy emerged "shitting worms" that a veterinarian said would claim her life but didn't. More recently, she survived cancer.

Even more recently, David survived two heart attacks.

"We are all born for dying one day," he said, extinguishing a cigarette in a nearly full ash tray. "I do see things a bit differently since my clogged arteries and know I won't live to 82. I could die next month."

David values his freedom with "karma" understanding the shortness of life with no belief in God. He is more aware of the need for kindness and helping others. Among those he looks out for is a new friend from Sweden, a woman financially taken advantage of in Nerja.

"She had some shit," he said. "I helped her find another, better apartment."

David is aware of "people in all the f***ing fighting in Russia, Israel, the world." While his life has been fractured, his is not the only one.

"I don't gonna cry about anything," David said. "People may think I am a piece of shit, criticize me, look at me from up high while I sit in the wind and rain, stumble past me drunk and full of a meal, judge me, but I'm still gonna smile and be nice to them."

(2023, Spain)

Roxy with David and Rocky in background

Lost Boys

When Deng, Lual and Alier got together in late August 2023 and after brief, welcoming exchanges in their native Dinka tongue, the first topic was the height of Alier's 16-year-old son, Kuereng. He towers at six feet, three inches.

"Basketball tall," Lual said as the teenager left the room with his mom, Yar, and four siblings ages 5 to 12.

Kuereng was born in Kenya and emigrated to the USA with his mom at age three. He's never been to his parents' native country, Sudan (now called South Sudan), where most everybody is tall, second worldwide only to the Dutch in the Netherlands.

Kuereng is too young to be a "Lost Boy." But his father, Alier Mareet Kuereng, and the two visiting friends, Lual Aker Deng and Deng Magot Riem—all Louisville, Ky., residents in their 40s—have that designation.

While the term "lost boy" originated from the fictitious Peter Pan story of boys flying away from their beds into a land where children never grow up, the label for Sudanese boys refers to displacement from their homes because of a war.

Sudan has had on and off conflicts and government and religious-related discord since its independence from British rule in 1956, but the escalation in 1987 was huge. There were 20,000 children who started a 1,000-mile escape walk that year. Deng, Lual and Alier were among them, falling into the 50% survival group who were able to stave off hungry lions, starvation and death from poisonous berries to end up in Ethiopian refugee camps.

They credit their independence and their work ethic—both learned early in life—for their perseverance.

Three "Lost Boys" in Kentucky, USA

"We worked in the fields with cows and away from our parents," Deng said of the area now known as Bor, South Sudan. "Cattle camp made us stronger and helped us not miss our mothers and fathers so much."

In the Ethiopian camp, the three grew from boys to young men until a 1990s Eritrean–Ethiopian civil war forced them to run again. They fled this time to Kenya's Kakuma Refugee site, 59 miles from the Kenya–Sudan border.

There, in that northwestern Kenya camp, they were plucked from among more than 3,000 young Sudanese refugees for American emigration. In the summer of 2001, cameras flashed and headlines blared as the first dark-skinned, lanky young men, holding stomachs sick from aircraft food, descended from their first plane rides to various states, including Kentucky. Alier and Lual were among them. Deng came in 2006.

"We are grateful to the United States," Alier said.

"Any Lost Boy appreciates what the USA did for South Sudan, where it was so bad," Lual said. He applauded former President George W. Bush and former Secretary of State Hillary Clinton, who made ending Sudanese fighting top USA foreign policy priorities.

United States aid to the area has been instrumental in mitigating problems with genocidal rape, torture and killing in Darfur, western Sudan; war conflict; and all gross human rights abuses.

In 2023, the three men are not naïve that their "rescue" was all about reducing suffering and improving lives. Both South Sudan, which became a country in 2011, and Sudan are rich in oil and gold.

"We understand that the humanitarian effort had an economic side," Alier said. "If the United States hadn't given us this opportunity that Sudan and later South Sudan appreciated, China might have stepped in."

Alier, Lual and Deng were sponsored by the World Council of Churches with local assistance from St. Paul United Methodist Church in Louisville, Ky. The congregation helped the three young men who had previously lived in Sudanese mud-and-wattle huts and white refugee tents. Kentuckians expanded the orientation the three men got in Africa to help them learn about refrigerators, flush toilets, electricity and running water in apartments and acquire better English skills.

Mostly, nobody today asks Alier, Lual and Deng about that difficult period of their lives— about those who suffered and died or about their own psychological and physical pain. But when someone does, they open up.

"We're grownups now," Deng said about the "Lost Boys" label and its baggage slapped upon him nearly four decades ago. "Some people may use it negatively, but overall, we're proud of it."

In 2023, with near-perfect English, USA citizenship status, college education and employment in technology, health care and logistics, the three men are among 600 Sudanese-Americans in Kentucky with 75 in Louisville.

On August 26, 2023, while sipping bottled water and sodas and seated on soft couches in Alier's home, they confirmed that accounts of the displaced boys in news stories, documentaries and books are largely true.

"I walked two weeks, barefooted, no pants, wearing just my Daddy's shirt," Deng recalled of his childhood trek across Sudan. "There were thousands of us going toward Ethiopia with no sure direction of where it was or how to get there."

While children in what is now known as the Bor region of South Sudan were accustomed to walking without shoes, the trek took a foot-blistering toll, Lual recalled. To alleviate pain, children used "savannah grass intertwined among the toes," he said.

Alier remembered crossing the Gilo River in southwestern Ethiopia. Those who couldn't swim, drowned. Some were eaten by crocodiles.

"If you had been coddled, you were more vulnerable," he said. "It was a hard life that cattle watcher kids like us could better adapt to."

While eating porridge with flour and beans and engaged in some schooling in rugged camps, all three wrote letters to their parents, never knowing if they were received. Deng has since learned that two brothers and both parents were killed in the war. The Dinka tribe was the hardest hit.

According to the United Nations High Commissioner for Refugees (UNHCR), there are 35.3 million refugees in settlements around the world. In 2020, the camp where Deng, Lual and Alier once resided in Kenya had nearly 200,000 refugees and asylum seekers from Sudan, Ethiopia and Somalia.

Today, the states of Virginia, Washington, Maryland, California, Idaho, Minnesota, and North Carolina have the largest Sudanese populations in the United States. Many are Lost Boys and their families. One study shows about 20% of the Lost Boys remain lost—suicidal, mentally ill, homeless.

For Alier, Lual and Deng, they feel strong. For them, they are the first in their families to complete high school. Not resting on their laurels, they are helping family members back home.

"There are a lot of opportunities here in America," Alier said. "Not so much in South Sudan. I am grateful."

(2023, Kentucky)

Rabbits

Not everybody likes the Easter bunny.

"We kill them," the retired motor oil salesman, a New Zealander now living in Australia, told me. "It's an Easter weekend massacre."

Halfway through my second margarita at Amigos in the Central Otago/Wanaka area of New Zealand, I gasped.

"They do it with their children," his wife nodded. Sipping her Chardonnay, she shared that she was born in England and was never a Kiwi, as they call New Zealanders, and thus totally wipes her hands of the rabbit slaughter. She added, "They even call it the Easter Bunny Hunt."

This casual conversation during a 25th anniversary trip my husband and I took from the United States to the South Island of New Zealand pushed me into a research mode. From more than a half dozen news sources with headlines like "massacre" and "nightmare" and photos to match, I learned that the statements from the Aussie couple we met in a Mexican restaurant were true.

In Wanaka, New Zealand, they kill bunnies in a celebratory event that starts at 9 a.m. on Good Friday and ends by Noon the day before Easter Sunday. Fathers and sons (and maybe a few mothers and daughters) form teams called "anti-pestos" and "happy hoppers" and the like. For nearly three decades, they have been killing anywhere from 10,000 to 20,000 rabbits a year in the designated 27-hour period. Some are eaten, some become dog food and fertilizer, and some carcasses are buried.

This event attacks my traditional core. In the United States, Christians and non-Christians alike revere the Easter bunny as a symbol of new birth. Sadly and by some, this cuddly animal either alive or reproduced in chocolate is up there above the real meaning of Easter, which is the resurrection of Jesus Christ. In the States, a chocolate or marshmallow bunny is a staple in everybody's Easter basket.

In New Zealand, where around half the population is Christian, rational minds seem to have prevailed around the annual rabbit event. From the onset, the practicing Jesus believers seem to have kept a distance on the Easter bunny shooting. SPCA, PETA and other animal-rights groups who first protested with the specific concern that baby rabbits without parents would starve or be eaten by predators have pretty much backed off, as have gun control advocates.

In short, they all get it. Bunny rabbits are messing up the New Zealand ecosystem, which is a big word for meaning that there is an imbalance in how things living in the ground and things living on top of the ground get along together.

Before bunnies, New Zealand only had plants and birds.

People brought mammals like rabbits mostly because they wanted creatures that reminded them of home, but also to fight off other mammals. Eastern Polynesians, who evolved into the Maori native tribe in New Zealand, brought rats and dogs. Settlers from England, Germany and France brought deer, cattle, sheep, pigs, goats, possums and, yes, rabbits. Australians carted in wallabies, who are a bit smaller than kangaroos.

Somebody got the idea to bring in weasels and ferrets to control the rabbits, but it turned out that all three ruined gardens. In time, these many mammals carried diseases like salmonella and others I never heard of and became predators of each other and of the birds and plants.

Bunnies, introduced to New Zealand in the 1800s, seem to be taking the biggest rap for environmental damage, primarily because it is true that they "breed like rabbits" and secondarily because of their massive demise during an Easter weekend event. Because New Zealand's seasons are flipped from those in the United States and the time zone is more than half a day ahead of where I live in Ohio, the New Zealand Easter is autumn—not the re-birthing time of spring—and not exactly on the same day as when most Americans celebrate the day of our Lord or our bunny. But it's still Easter.

Two days before meeting the two Aussies over Mexican food and drinks, I had a one-on-one encounter with a New Zealand hedgehog. As I approached a pool for an early morning dip, the spiny creature was there, close to drowning it seemed. I beseeched an employee to rescue him or her, only to later learn that the hedgehog, too, is among the ecosystem violators and carries some disease.

"But hedgehogs aren't as bad as rabbits," a clerk in a clothing store said. "Rabbits are horrible."

Given the environmental threat posed by animals, the New Zealand government has vowed to wipe out a list of mammals, including the bad bunnies, by 2050—a goal most believe impossible. The highly domesticated dog isn't on the list despite the canine role in the disappearing status of the Kiwi bird. And thankfully there is no mention of annihilation of humans, who are the mammals most messing up our world.

More often than not, perceptions are more emotional than factual. Like many aspects of our lives, traditions, culture and long-held opinions like those that surround the endearing, cuddly Easter Bunny are hard to shake.

Thanks to the Kiwis, I am better informed about Peter Rabbit's darkest side.

Bambi could be next...

(2018, New Zealand)

Ricky Ricardo

"Me gusta 'scarf.' Es muy bonita."

In my rudimentary Spanish-English combination and while making my way down the narrow airplane aisle, I smiled at the elderly Cuban–American passenger and pointed to her purple scarf. The elderly woman understood that I liked (gusta) the garment and thought it was pretty (bonita). She pulled the silken fabric—indeed beautiful with its floral pattern and silver sequins and obviously handmade—from around her neck and handed it to me with a smile.

Bienvenida (welcome) to Cuba, which is the latest "hot spot" for travelers.

For the record, I planned, booked and paid for my eight-day trip before the Obamas, the Kardashians and even the Rolling Stones drew attention to the Caribbean island south of Florida.

It's a place where 1950s Chevys and Fords line the streets. Drinking glasses coated with sugar on the rim and a sprint of mint leaves are assembled, waiting for the ice, club soda, lime and rum to become a mojito. Men sit on concrete steps, smoking and avoiding the eyes of foreign passersby. Dogs and cats with protruding ribs roam the streets or lay listlessly in the dirt in 80-degree-Fahrenheit heat. School children wear red or blue kerchiefs signifying Communist party support. And nobody openly says anything bad about the government.

Like most Americans, I had an innate curiosity about Cuba—that country I associated with Castro, Communism and old cars. Being born in the 1950s, my Cuban frame of reference was seeing Ricky Ricardo (Desi Arnaz in *I love Lucy*) on our tiny black and white TV set and hiding under a school desk, ridiculously shielding my head during May Day drills that supposedly prepared children for being hit by nuclear missiles. Except for these rather-incomplete pieces of education and the controversy over custody and immigration of a six-year-old Cuban, Elián González, in 2000, I was fairly ignorant about much of Cuba until my research prior to and experiences during my trip in April of 2016.

Among the dozen countries I have visited, none was Communist. I wanted to go to Cuba before it became spoiled with modern civilization and spilled over with tourists. The tiny Havana airport already is packed with foreigners, amusingly perplexed about the lack of signs telling them where to retrieve their luggage from one of only two conveyor belts. The lines where you pay the equivalent of 25 cents to go to the bathroom at a rest stop are long. And not all the cars are from the 1950s.

Through a government-approved organization called Road Scholar, my friend, Sue Rieger and I, were among those foreign visitors, assigned to a study leader approved by the Cuban government. People from other countries call themselves "tourists" in Cuba, but U.S. citizens are "visitors with a purpose" because of still-strained relations. I stayed in nice hotels with plenty of hot running water, toilet paper, chicken dishes and mojitos. I listened and danced to Afro-Cuban music. I got the news not just from government-approved TV channels, but from CNN and BBC. I walked along a pristine beach.

Realizing that what I experienced was tainted through a Cuban propaganda lens (i.e. our guide was the daughter of a leader with the Communist Party), I synthesized the music, dancing, art, food, tobacco farms, Cuban obsession with baseball and ice cream and the more abstractness of religion, words, body language and survival on $22 a month. I jokingly told several members of my education travel group that I was "looking for Ricky Ricardo." I longed for Ricky's "babalu"—that fun, mystical word he often used, to wipe away my Communist corruption feelings associated with Cuba.

While searching, I found stories of human survival. Cubans can't use ration coupons for healthy food like the fruit and vegetables I ate. Those selling that food at the market have to give the government 51% of their profit.

One "work around" I stumbled upon was a man who walks around a neighborhood street, shouting

Desi Arnez, Wikimedia Commons/Public Domain

"tomatoes." As long as he gets pesos for his tomatoes without stopping, he keeps all the profit.

Another story involves a talented artist. He expands his living wage by selling to foreign visitors who pay him after leaving the country—sending a check to a Cuban relative living in Florida as an American citizen, who then forwards the money to the seller in Cuba.

A third story emerged when sitting next to a young Cuban woman at dinner. Living with her parents, she gets a monthly check from her husband who works for a company in Spain and may not see her and their son for three years.

When taking the microphone at the front of our bus as we approached the Havana airport for departure back to Miami, I admitted to everyone that I had questions I might never get answered. I made a list of what never got shared—political prisoners, free speech, technology, access to unbiased information and treatment of Afro-Cubans.

Alas, I never found Ricky Ricardo.

Back in Ohio, the smell of oldness—a nearly indescribable mixture of moldiness and mustiness from the aging hotel in Havana—permeated the clothes I unpacked from my suitcase. Sandwiched within were Cuban souvenirs of cigars, rum, music CDs, coconut bracelets and the purple scarf. On a Sunday morning and from the Hallmark channel not in Cuba but in the United States, emerged big and little Ricky, playing the drums and shouting "babalu."

I continue to search for Ricky Ricardo and the babalu of life.

(2016, Cuba)

Starvation

The most hungry I've been was in 2011 when climbing up into the Impenetrable Forest behind a woman with a banana hanging from her backpack. I watched the yellow fruit for two hours before boldly asking if I might have half of it while admitting my stupidity for not carrying a lick of food. She gave me the whole thing. The ecstasy from that moment is a feeling I still remember—not just the banana but also the gracious gift of a stranger from Norway to a stranger from the USA.

I was hungry.

I've been sort of hungry more than once. And I've met truly hungry people, watching their delight as I share food. One of my Uganda Christian University students took half of my granola bar, tearfully telling me how her uncle's wife denied her food out of resentment about caring for a child she didn't birth, how she was forced to sleep outside and spat upon.

She grew up malnourished.

I've suffered malnutrition, mostly for not eating the right foods and sometimes not enough food, but it was self-imposed. I've seen malnourished children and animals. Any level of malnutrition I've experienced or seen pales to what is happening right now in Yemen, which is northeast of where I sit in Uganda, by about 1,500 miles. There, by most news reports, 50% of the people are suffering malnourishment to the point of starvation.

I read about the Yemen starvation a week ago. The face of the story was a seven-year-old girl. On October 28, *The New York Times* published the photo of Amal Hussein with her deep-set, blank-stare eyes and protruding ribs. A single fly sat undisturbed on her right thumb. Like other social justice Facebook users, I tried to post her story, but ignorant Facebook screeners blocked it as "child pornography." Several times this week, I shared the photo with campus colleagues and students, along with my frustration that I couldn't play my part in bringing attention to a humanitarian crisis.

Malnourished wildlife in Uganda

Last year, I used the Yemen cholera epidemic for discussion in classes. Now, sadly, it's starvation.

This morning, a young Ugandan journalist, Olum Douglas, sent me a personal message: "That malnourished Yemen girl you told me about has died."

Lest you think that this has nothing to do with the United States, take note that we are backing the Saudi coalition there. Between the Saudis and the Iranian-aligned Houthis, we've bombed the hell out of Yemen, killing thousands, wrecking the economy and starving millions of men, women and children. According to CNN, Amal and her family were four miles from a hospital and food they couldn't afford.

So, yes, geographically, America is 8,000 miles away from this crisis as we generally are from many of these conflicts to which we contribute. And yes, most of us have known hunger and some malnutrition.

But we've never known dehydration and food deprivation to the point of starvation. Like Amal.

(2018, Uganda)

War

At 9:30 a.m. on Monday, Oct. 9, I teared up during a Love/Soul Train melody.

Sweating and pedaling on a stationary bike, my joy during a Groveport, Ohio, recreation center spinning class was momentarily diminished with the 1970s O'Jays' song urging "all the folks in Israel to come on board." I pictured more than 260 young people who died, and more of them screaming while being whisked away from an Israeli music festival celebrating the end of Sukkot, an annual event commemorating the Jews journey from Egypt. That happened on Oct. 7, 2023.

I knew very little about Israel. Still don't. But I knew that on Oct. 10, Mike and I had been scheduled to start our nine-day "bucket list" trip to the Holy Land—aka Israel.

That was before all Hell broke loose for 3,500 men and women at a techno music event in a southern Israel field near the Gaza Border. When all was said and done—which it still isn't as I type this on Oct. 15—a terrorist group called Hamas had kidnapped 150 and killed over 1,300 Israeli men, women and children at the festival, in nearby streets and inside homes.

Subsequently, the anti-Hamas Israelis laid claim for even more Hamas and Palestinian lives.

Eight days from the start of the massacre and before leaving for church today (Oct. 15), I was getting emails from the U.S. Embassy in Jerusalem. In my pajamas in Canal Winchester, Ohio, I read the embassy advice about how to get out of Israel—how individuals who could verify American citizenship would board a boat that would cross the Mediterranean Sea to Cyprus.

No need to get on board. Our Holy Land trip was smartly rescheduled for November 2024 but later canceled.

But my distress isn't over.

After that Oct. 9 exercise class, I struggled with guilt of that initial worry about my trip and losing money instead of anguish for Israeli, Palestinian and some American lives lost and for lives still in balance. My conscience was somewhat redeemed as I crammed through Eric Alterman's 400-page book, *We Are Not One*, Internet coverage and multiple media sources to attempt to fill the gaps of my ignorance of Middle-East history, especially Israel.

What I read and saw in my Fodor's Travel book and viewed in videos from our travel company before Oct. 7 is a sharp contrast to the images and information coming from multiple news sources this past week. Photos of smiling people in Bethlehem and Jerusalem are in juxtaposition to the carnage of bodies and bombed houses and cars in these past eight days.

An Oct. 15, 2023, NBC newscaster said inflated publicity has pitched Israel as "a land of faith, grace and reconciliation."

On a rainy Oct. 14 and during a break of a Richland County, Ohio, creation care environmental conference that I wouldn't have attended if our Middle Eastern trip wasn't disrupted, I asked a pastor friend what he thought of the Israeli–Palestinian mess.

"It's not religious; it's political," he said. "The Israelis promised the Palestinians something they never delivered." The promise was homes and more. The pastor agreed with the terrorist label on Hamas. Brutal murder of non-fighting, unarmed men, women and children makes the killer a terrorist.

But Palestinians should not be punished for Hamas actions, he said, adding, "Hamas to Palestine is like saying all Americans think like the Ku Klux Klan."

Mike and I are not feeble travelers. We have been in dangerous and compromised areas in Haiti, Uganda and France over the past 15 years. As Christians, travel and actions are about discerning God's will and purpose. We were excited about visiting the land where Jesus walked, talked, healed and lived. We understood Israel as a place of discord, but also knew it was a place where Christ gave lessons to love enemies. People who don't practice a religious faith of any kind scratch their heads and wonder why anyone would want to go to such places.

It saddens me to watch as people shelter from rockets in Jerusalem, a city considered holy for Christianity, Judaism and Islam. While understanding the need for Israeli forces to look for terrorists and for Hamas-held hostages, I'm likewise unhappy to see Palestinians forced from their homes.

In the midst of it all and while unpacking my Israel-bound suitcase, 2,000 dying from an earthquake in Afghanistan hardly makes the news.

Why does Israel, a country the size of New Jersey, matter so much to Americans?

"Jesus was a Jew," one of my Bible study friends said.

"Israelis are God's chosen people," another friend texted.

Perhaps, Alterman alludes in his 2022 book, it's because we feel guilty that we didn't do more during the Holocaust.

In 1948, Israel was established as a safe haven for Jews persecuted in Europe. Forty years later, Palestine became a state, with lesser status than a country. Sort of like the Puerto Rican territory is to the USA.

Arabs, which are often referred to as Palestinians, didn't like it. Some were forced into refugee camps. In 1967, there was a six-day war that cost lives but paled in comparison to the carnage of the past eight days since Hamas opened its brutal terror attack from the Gaza Strip, a small, densely-packed Palestinian territory it has controlled since 2007.

I would like to narrow the events of the past eight days to an elementary explanation of who started this fight. But defining "start" isn't easy. Like parental favoritism, Palestine is supported by Iran, while Israel has the United States at its back.

Not to trivialize lives lost and in balance within the grasp of terrorists on this eighth day, maybe Dave Mason was marginally right in 1977 when he sang "there ain't no good guys; there ain't no bad guys; there is just you and me, and we just disagree…"

(2023, Ohio & Israel)

Appendix

Nonfiction Storytelling Strategies

Writing has been my trade and passion for so long that I sometimes make false assumptions about what others know within my area of expertise. It's akin to a nurse who assumes the vaccination administrator knows when the needle goes in straight or diagonally or a guitarist who presumes a new student knows how to string an instrument.

My best storytelling strategies come from within and from Stephen King (*On Writing*) and William Zinsser, the latter thanks to a journalist friend, Connie Leinbach, who gave me my first copy of *On Writing Well: The Classic Guide to Writing Nonfiction*.

I once aspired to be as good as Tracy Kidder (*Old Friends*, among others) and William Leist Heat-Moon (*Blue Highways*, etc.). Sadly, when I met both of them, they were not interested in encouraging me. If being that good means I don't inspire other writers, I'll settle for less.

Writing creative nonfiction is my gift. It is one thing I do well.

While I could fill an entire book with strategies, here are my top 12:

1. Begin with a compelling lead—You must pull the reader in at the onset.
2. Use colorful descriptions—Show vs. tell.
3. Be truthful with respect to the subject—While honest depiction is important, it shouldn't be at the expense of embarrassing the subject except in rare instances, such as when featuring public figures.
4. Eliminate extraneous words (very, many, etc.)—Rarely do these add anything.
5. Develop a synonym expertise—Avoid repeating words or terms in the same paragraph.
6. Cut what doesn't fit—As much as you might be in love with a phrase or sentence, take it out if it interferes with the flow.
7. Understand topic sentences—Each paragraph needs to fit with the main sentence.
8. Intersperse quotes, full and partial, with descriptors—If featuring a person, let them speak.
9. Focus on organization—Doing an outline and/or reading out loud or using software AI to hear words will help with the flow.
10. Fact check the source—Protect yourself with assurance that what you are told is true.
11. Edit and, if necessary, revise—Double check grammar, punctuation and spelling.
12. Have a strong ending—Tie back to start or have the reader wanting more.

Epilogue

An epilogue is supposed to be to tie up loose ends.

In *Dolls in Trees*, one loose end is information on how my writing style evolved. Another is a reader's question about what happened for some people and things in these stories.

In my days as a news reporter in the 1970s and 1980s, a story was restricted by column inches and objectivity. In public relations in the 1990s, writing was confined to the 5 W's and the H (who, what, when, where, why, how) for a media release, number of pages in a newsletter, and within the time-frame for a ghost-written speech. At the turn of the 21st century, writing became multi-strategic with message and length dictated by Web content and social media as well as other traditional placements. In 2024, it's okay to be both objective and subjective in non-fiction—also called literary journalism.

When true stories are in creative style for a book, length and voice are freeing. Stories in this manuscript range from 400 to over 1,000 words each. They are objectively third person, opinionated in first person or a blend of first and third person.

For this book, it was easy to determine a working title, *Dolls in Trees*. One of my delightful engagements was with a woman who has dolls and doll body parts hanging from trees in front of her Ocracoke Island, North Carolina, home. Like most interviews for this book, I learned that she was much more than this visual novelty that I saw when riding past her place on my bicycle. The working title stuck.

For me, I started thinking I would include 50 true stories. I ended up with more than 100. While not all people mentioned have seen a story with their names, all the men and women featured had prior review and approved the final text. While emancipating to write, it's hard to know when to stop. I wanted to keep going. Still do.

Apologies to the few that I didn't include. It wasn't because your story wasn't good. It was simply that I didn't "feel" it. Another day, another year, perhaps, I might.

Follow Up to Story Topics

So what happened to the people, places and things I wrote about? Instead of providing you 100-plus boring updates, I'll provide 12 in no particular order of importance. As of press time in August 2024:

Bob Bevard—The septuagenarian mountain biker is still racing and establishing a legacy with a mountain bike park in Horn's Hill, Newark, Ohio.

Nancy Beery—She died in the fall of 2023. Accompanied by my husband on guitar, I led funeral attendees in her favorite song, *Rainbow Connection.*

Susan Dodd—She is still accepting dolls and doll body parts to place onto the limbs of her trees on Ocracoke Island, N.C., and our friendship continues.

Robert Morgan (AKA Santa Claus)—He calls Spain "home" and works to raise awareness about male cancer, the evils of Donald Trump and other causes.

"Julie" (one of only two stories with anonymous comments)—She settled a lawsuit regarding her disability.

Todd Phillips—His non-profit in performing arts continues to grow; I joined his community choir.

Akongo Ruth Rose—She still lives in the USA, supporting herself with part-time jobs and is uncertain if her dream of a university master's degree here will happen.

Mary Chowenhill, Steve Winegardner—We remain friends despite USA presidential preferences.

My broken wrist—While the Gibraltar surgery was good, the lack of overseas follow up means that my left wrist will never fully heal.

My tremors—I'm officially diagnosed with dystonia, but it doesn't keep me from being active.

Parking Lot Ladies—I no longer see the women I befriended in parking lots in Punta Gorda, Fla., because the condo I rented there was sold.

Rat in my toilet—It was a one-off. Since that incident, only my body waste has been in my commode in Uganda, Ohio and other places.

Who Is in This Book?

While strangers and friends inspiring these stories are many, special mention is noted. These are my stories and yours.

A:

Akena Luck
Akongo Ruth Rose
Alex Taremwa
Alicia Swisher
Alier Mareet Kuereng
Amy Henricksen
Andrea Walker Carson
Angella Napakol
Anne Darling Cyphert
Anonymous
Arif Husain
Audrey Holm Wittman
Ava Holm

B:

Barbara Cotner
Bea Garrelts
Beatrice Masinde
Becky Hoffman
Beth Meacham
Best Nyapendi
Betty Milligan
Bob Bevard
Bonnie Finneran

C:

Carmel Jenkins
Carolyn Kvam
Carolyn March
Catherine Ranger
Claudia Speakman
Connie Leinbach
Craig Hammon

D:

Daphine Oitamong
Dave Cleaver

Dave Cyphert
David Fabre
David Hodge
Deb Holm
Debby Eveland
Dennis Wandera
Deng Magot Riem
Desirée Christa Adams
Diane Ross
Dottie Galliher
Douglas Olum

E:

Ed Asner
Ed Hoffman
Eleanor Maxine Ankrah
Elizabeth Bacwayo
Emily Buck
Eriah Lule
Evelyn DiSalvo

F:

Fran Ryan
Frank Huston
Frank Obonyo

G:

Gabriel Kuereng Mareet
Greg Farra

H:

Heather Baugess
Helen Artz
Hugh Nichols

I:

Irene Best Nyapendi

J:

Jacqueline West
Jacki Mann
Jack Speakman

Jean Huston
Jerry Griffin
James Taabu Busimba
Jim Kreimer
Jimmy Layton
Joan Layton
Jack Klenk
Joe Dyser
John Griffin
John Senyonyi
Johnson Mayamba
Joshua Kabitanya
Joy Wambuzi

K:

Kasule Kibirige
Kathryn King
Keith Croghan
Kevin Eveland

L:

Libby Kinsel
Logan Jackson
Linda Hanby
Liz Kizito
Lori Bias
Lotyanga Maxben
Lual Aker Deng

M:

Maggie Gainer
Manyimanyi Gilbert
Mark Bartels
Marna Lombardi
Mary Chowenhill
Mary Stuckey
Mhtyang Betty
Michael Ford
Michele White
Mike Holm
Mike Nadolson
Miriam Mutabazi
Molly Nantongo
Nahush Mokadam
Nancy Beery

Nancy Ongom
Nannyanga Restetuta
Nicholas Van Der Hauwaert

P:

Paul Mukhana
Paul Newman
Paul Swisher
Pam Jarvis
Pauline Atwine
Pegi Lobb
Penny Loeffler

R:

Randal Mathews
Richard Mulindwa
Richard Ranger
Robert Morgan
Robyn Petras
Ron Ishoy
Rosemary Lanza

S:

Sandy and Shell Scott
Sailas Oakworth
Sarah Lagot Odwong
Sarah Walamaku
Sheila Hosner
Stacy James
Steve Winegardner
Stevie Wilson
Sue Rieger

T:

Timothy Wangusa
Todd Phillips
Tonny Kato
Trisha Eyler

W:

Warner Passanisi
William Kayumba

www.ingramcontent.com/pod-product-compliance
Lightning Source LLC
Chambersburg PA
CBHW071306140726
47996CB00005B/1651